# Workplace Psychological Health

# NEW HORIZONS IN MANAGEMENT

**Series Editor: Cary L. Cooper, CBE**, *Distinguished Professor of Organizational Psychology and Health, Lancaster University, UK.*

This important series makes a significant contribution to the development of management thought. This field has expanded dramatically in recent years and the series provides an invaluable forum for the publication of high quality work in management science, human resource management, organizational behaviour, marketing, management information systems, operations management, business ethics, strategic management and international management.

The main emphasis of the series is on the development and application of new original ideas. International in its approach, it will include some of the best theoretical and empirical work from both well-established researchers and the new generation of scholars.

Titles in the series include:

# Workplace Psychological Health

## Current Research and Practice

Paula Brough

*Associate Professor of Psychology and Director of the Social and Organizational Psychology Research Unit, Griffith University, Australia*

Michael O'Driscoll

*Professor of Psychology, University of Waikato, Hamilton, New Zealand*

Thomas Kalliath

*Associate Professor in Management, Australian National University, Canberra, Australia*

Cary L. Cooper, CBE

*Distinguished Professor of Organizational Psychology and Health, Lancaster University, UK*

Steven A.Y. Poelmans

*Assistant Professor and Academic Director of the International Centre of Work and Family, IESE Business School, Barcelona, Spain*

NEW HORIZONS IN MANAGEMENT

**Edward Elgar**

Cheltenham, UK • Northampton, MA, USA

Published by
Edward Elgar Publishing Limited
The Lypiatts
15 Lansdown Road
Cheltenham
Glos GL50 2JA
UK

Edward Elgar Publishing, Inc.
William Pratt House
9 Dewey Court
Northampton
Massachusetts 01060
USA

A catalogue record for this book
is available from the British Library

Library of Congress Control Number: 2009922760

ISBN 978 1 84720 765 4

Printed and bound by MPG Books Group, UK

# Contents

# Figures and tables

## FIGURES

## TABLES

# Authors

**Associate Professor Paula Brough**
Associate Professor Paula Brough is an Organizational Psychologist at the School of Psychology at Griffith University, Brisbane, Australia. Associate Professor Brough's research focuses on the evaluation and enhancement of occupational psychological health, with specific interests in occupational stress, coping and work–life balance. Her research has focused on two main categories: reducing experiences of occupational stress within the high-stress industries; and enhancing individual health and organizational performance. Associate Professor Brough has published over 40 academic works based on her research, is the Chief Investigator on several local, national and international research grants, and supervises both post-graduate and post-doctoral organizational psychology researchers. Associate Professor Brough holds memberships in journal editorial boards, serves as an academic reviewer for competitive research grants, psychology journals and conferences, and regularly presents her work to both academic and industry audiences.

**Professor Michael O'Driscoll**
Michael P. O'Driscoll is a Professor in Organizational Psychology at the University of Waikato, Hamilton, New Zealand, where he both teaches courses and convenes the post-graduate programme in organizational psychology. He has a Ph.D. in psychology from the Flinders University of South Australia. His primary research interests are in the fields of job-related stress and coping, and the interface between job experiences and people's lives off the job (especially family commitments and responsibilities), including conflict between these domains. More generally, Professor O'Driscoll is interested in work attitudes and behaviours, and the relationship between work and health. He has published empirical and conceptual articles on these and other topics in organizational psychology. He has served on the editorial boards of several academic journals, and was editor of the *New Zealand Journal of Psychology* (2001–2006).

**Associate Professor Thomas Kalliath**
Associate Professor Thomas Kalliath has a Ph.D. in organizational psychology from the Washington University in Saint Louis, USA. Prior

to joining the Australian National University, Canberra, as a Senior Lecturer in Management, he taught organizational psychology, organizational development and change, and personnel training and development in the University of Waikato, New Zealand from 1995–2004. Since 1996, Associate Professor Kalliath has produced more than 100 research outputs either independently or in collaboration with research colleagues in the occupational and organizational psychology domain. A significant amount of this work has focused on furthering our understanding of the work–family interface, as well as the nature of job stress and burnout in organizations. These contributions have helped the field of organizational psychology to advance through the availability of more refined research instruments and improved theorizing. Associate Professor Kalliath is the recipient of a number of excellence awards in teaching and research, including the University of Waikato Vice-Chancellor's Medal for Excellence in Teaching (2003).

**Professor Cary L. Cooper, CBE**
Cary L. Cooper is Distinguished Professor of Organizational Psychology and Health, and Pro Vice Chancellor at Lancaster University, England. He is the author/editor of over 100 books (on occupational stress, women at work, and industrial and organizational psychology), has written over 400 scholarly articles for academic journals, and is a frequent contributor to national newspapers, TV and radio. He is currently founding editor of the *Journal of Organizational Behaviour* and co-editor of *Stress & Health*. He is a Fellow of the British Psychological Society, The Royal Society of Arts, The Royal Society of Medicine, The Royal Society of Health, British Academy of Management, and an Academician of the Academy for the Social Sciences. Professor Cooper is past President of the British Academy of Management, is a Companion of the Chartered Management Institute, and one of the first UK-based Fellows of the (American) Academy of Management (having also won the 1998 Distinguished Service Award for his contribution to management science from the Academy of Management). In 2001, Professor Cooper was awarded a CBE in the Queen's Birthday Honours List for his contribution to occupational safety and health.

He holds Honorary Doctorates from Aston University (D.Sc.), Heriot-Watt University (D.Litt.), Middlesex University (Doc. Univ) and Wolverhampton University (DBA); an Honorary Fellowship of the Faculty of Occupational Medicine in 2005, was awarded an Honorary Fellowship of the Royal College of Physicians (Hon FRCP) in 2006, and in 2007 a Life Time Achievement Award from the Division of Occupational Psychology of the British Psychological Society. Professor Cooper is the editor-in-chief of the international scholarly *Blackwell Encyclopedia of Management* and the editor of *Who's Who in the Management Sciences*. He has been an adviser to two UN agencies; the World Health Organization (WHO) and International Labour Organization (ILO), published a major report for the EU's European Foundation for the improvement of living and work conditions on 'Stress prevention in the workplace', produced a scientific review for the WHO/ILO on workplace violence in the health sector internationally, and was a special adviser to the Defence Committee of the House of Commons on their Duty of Care Inquiry (2004–05). Professor Cooper is Chair of The Sunningdale Institute, and a think tank on management/organizational issues in the National School of Government. He is also a scientific adviser to Government Office of Science on their Foresight Programme on mental capital and well-being in the UK. Professor Cooper is also the President of the Institute of Welfare, President of the British Association of Counselling and Psychotherapy, a National Ambassador of The Samaritans, and a Patron of the National Phobic Society and National Bullying Helpline.

**Associate Professor Steven A.Y. Poelmans**
Associate Professor Steven Poelmans holds a Master's in organizational psychology (Catholic University of Leuven, Belgium), a Master's in marketing management (Vlerick Management School/University of Ghent, Belgium) and a Ph.D. in management/organizational behaviour (IESE Business School/University of Navarra, Spain). Associate Professor Poelmans is Assistant Professor at the Managing People in Organizations Department of IESE Business School, Barcelona. He currently teaches organizational behaviour, managerial communication, and self-management to MBA students and executives. He is co-founder and Academic Director of the International Centre of Work and Family (ICWF) at the IESE Business School. His research, teaching and consulting mainly focuses on work–family conflict, managerial stress, work–life policies, and cultural intelligence and coaching (mostly with a cross-cultural perspective). This has resulted in publications in such journals as *Human Resource Management Review*, *Academy of Management Journal*, *Journal of Organizational Behaviour*, *Applied Psychology: An International Review*, the *International Journal of Cross-Cultural Management*, and *Personnel Psychology*. He is currently the external consultant of Roche Diagnostics and Nike Iberia in Spain for coaching development and work–life balance, respectively. He is co-author and editor of the academic volumes *Work and Family: An International Research Perspective* (Lawrence Erlbaum Associates) and *Harmonizing Work, Family, and Personal Life: From Policy to Practice* (Cambridge University Press). He has published over

a dozen peer-reviewed journal articles and chapters in academic volumes. He experiences daily cross-cultural transitions between his Catalan-born daughter, his family in Belgium, his Spanish colleagues, and his international students at IESE from more than 40 countries around the globe, and practises four languages on a daily basis.

# Acknowledgments

My sincere appreciation goes to my partner Roger Snow, for all his support and encouragement throughout the production of this book.

Paula Brough

To Parveen, for her support and care.

Thomas Kalliath

I would like to acknowledge the ongoing support and encouragement of Elizabeth O'Driscoll, whose understanding and love has contributed very substantially to my personal well-being.

Michael O'Driscoll

In addition, the authors and publishers wish to thank the authors and the following publishers who have kindly given permission for the use of copyright material: Professor Cary Cooper, Professor Tom Cox, Professor Eva Demerouti, Professor Ed Diener, Professor Susan Folkman, Professor Esther Greenglass, Professor Ricky Griffin, Professor Bryan Robinson, Professor Janet Spence, Professor Peter Warr, Blackwell Publishing, Edward Elgar Publishing, American Psychological Association, HSE Books, New York University Press, Sage Publications, Taylor & Francis. Finally, we acknowledge the assistance of Dr Jackie Holt in preparing preliminary material for Chapters 2 and 8.

# Introduction

The psychological influence that employment can produce upon work performance and safety, and employee health and relationships was increasingly acknowledged throughout the twentieth century. Industrial and organizational psychology began in earnest investigating the work hours and work organization among factory workers, incorporating ability and personality tests into the selection process for military personnel, and treating the 'shell-shocked' survivors of the World Wars. The period of approximately 1920 to 1950 was marked by the creation of various kinds of Psychology Boards (for example, Defence and Public Service) and Applied Psychology Units established within some universities in Europe and the US. Thus formal recognition was finally applied to the profession of Organizational Psychologist. Since this period of course, the field has further diversified to include 'hard' industrial topics such as ergonomics, job analysis and recruitment testing, as well as the 'softer' organizational topics such as occupational stress, job control and work–family balance.

Most recently the sub-discipline of *occupational health psychology* has emerged within the organizational psychology domain, and the interest in this field has generated dedicated journals, academic texts and university courses. The growth of interest in occupational health psychology has occurred in response to employment changes within the last few decades. Thus Western countries have experienced a substantial shift of employment from manufacturing industries to service and knowledge industries, labour markets have changed to include more female and educated workers, while work design has incorporated technology allowing work to be conducted not only in the workplace, but also at home and whilst travelling. The traditional constraints of employment within the early twentieth century have therefore largely disappeared.

In a response to these changes, this book discusses eleven topics pertinent to contemporary workers and to occupational health psychology researchers in particular. Some of these topics such as organizational coaching and work addiction are relatively new additions to this field, while other topics such as occupational stress and job satisfaction have a longer research history. All eleven topics, however, form the core of occupational health psychology and each is expected to be of interest for researchers throughout the coming years. The book begins by reviewing the impact of work on employees' psychological and physical health. Chapter 1 defines psychological well-being and discusses its common antecedents such as biological predispositions, gender, marriage, personality characteristics, employment and finances. The consequences of well-being are also reviewed, such as job satisfaction, organizational citizenship behaviours, absenteeism and turnover. Chapter 2 discusses how work influences the physical health of employees, with a specific focus on the influence of psychosocial work characteristics such as job demands, job control and working hours. The negative health and behavioural outcomes caused by employment such as cardiovascular disease, reproductive health, obesity, suicide, alcohol and drug use are also discussed.

In Chapter 3 we focus on job satisfaction, one of the common criterion variables within organizational psychology research. The recent developments in job satisfaction research are reviewed, including its measurement and theoretical basis, and its relationship with job performance, absenteeism and turnover. Common individual antecedents of job satisfaction such as gender and personality characteristics are also discussed. Chapter 4 reviews two psychosocial work characteristics in detail: job support and job control, and assesses the impact each has on the development and maintenance of psychological well-being. The chapter discusses both the direct relationships and the moderating influence of these constructs in their respective relationships with well-being. Chapter 5 describes recent advances in occupational stress, coping and psychological burnout research. The chapter specifically reviews the Job Demands–Resources model, proactive coping strategies that can be adopted to manage occupational stress and the measurement of burnout. The chapter also discusses the effectiveness of stress management interventions and identifies the common problems associated with these programmes. Chapter 6 reviews the growing research literature on work–family balance. The chapter discusses the definition of work–family balance, reviews its common causes and consequences, and assesses the influence of organizational policies such as parental leave, supervisor support and flexible working arrangements.

Chapter 7 examines work addiction (also referred to as workaholism) research, which is a relatively new field of enquiry. The chapter describes the different types of workaholics and explores the impact of organizational and national culture as antecedents of work addiction. The chapter discusses the consequences of working long hours in relation to individual outcomes (such as personal relationships) and organizational outcomes (such as job performance). Chapter 8 reviews research on workplace violence and aggression, which is another area of increasing interest for organizational researchers. The chapter explores the theoretical models which underpin this research, and identifies how employment changes, such as the growth of the service industries, are associated with increasing incidents of workplace violence and aggression. The chapter also discusses the common forms of workplace aggression such as harassment, as well as newly identified aggressive behaviours such as upwards bullying. The chapter also assesses common organizational policies employed to manage workplace violence and aggression.

The final three chapters focus on the advances in three relatively new fields of research. Chapter 9 reviews the impact of new technology on the health and well-being of workers, specifically focusing on information and communications technology such as electronic mail and the Internet. The chapter discusses the adverse outcomes associated with these technologies such as technostress, technological anxiety and frustration, and the impact of these outcomes on individual perceptions of control and mastery. Chapter 10 explores the new field of executive coaching, and describes the coaching process. The chapter also reviews both the antecedents and consequences of coaching and explains how coaching research methods could be improved to further advance this field of enquiry. Finally Chapter 11 provides a review of the current organizational fitness and counselling research. The chapter defines what is meant by a psychologically healthy workplace and describes the work characteristics which create an unhealthy workplace, including high job demands, excessive workloads, and a lack of work support. The chapter also reviews the methods by which workplace health can be improved including the issues of employee growth, development and involvement. The chapter concludes with a discussion of the common organizational fitness programmes including employee assistance programmes, exercise programmes, and anti-bullying programmes.

The book therefore provides reviews of the principal theories and considerations in each of these eleven contemporary topics and serves as a reference source to the current issues concerning organizational researchers. This book celebrates the emergence of occupational health psychology as a research field and we anticipate that the topics described within these chapters will increase in relevance for both workers and researchers over the coming years.

# 1. Work and psychological well-being

## OVERVIEW

The fact that work can directly influence the psychological health and well-being of workers has become a point of increasing interest over the last few decades. Associations between work and psychological well-being are firmly established. The occupational stress literature in particular has demonstrated a variety of causal relationships between working environments and well-being, with some of this evidence now entrenched in specific legislation (Chapter 5 focuses specifically on occupational stress). The various ways in which paid employment influences the well-being of workers are also generally discussed in each chapter throughout this book. This first chapter focuses on the specific perspectives that best describe psychological well-being, the common antecedents of well-being and the associations between well-being and job performance.

## DEFINITIONS OF PSYCHOLOGICAL WELL-BEING

Psychological well-being can be defined by physical, emotional and psychological perspectives. Numerous antecedents of work-related well-being have been identified such as job characteristics, work design, ergonomics and psychosocial behaviours (communications and relationships between co-workers, harassment and bullying). Both individual and organizational consequences of poor well-being have also been identified and include adverse performance, attendance, decision-making, accidents and both physical and psychological employee ill health. Danna and Griffin (1999) provided a useful framework summarizing the common antecedents and consequences of occupational health and well-being (see Figure 1.1). Figure 1.1 depicts the core constructs of well-being as being *satisfaction* (life and job) and *health* (physical and psychological). The common workplace hazards and their impact on a worker's physical health will be discussed in detail in the following chapter (Chapter 2). Figure 1.1 also illustrates that interventions to improve occupational health and well-being may be targeted at well-being directly and/or may focus on the antecedents or consequences of well-being. The specific organizational

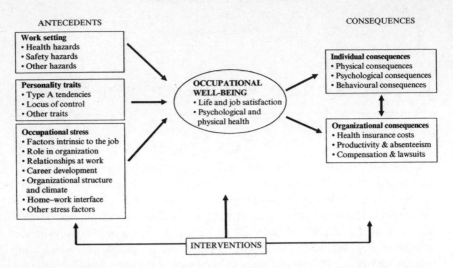

ANTECEDENTS                                                    CONSEQUENCES

**Work setting**
• Health hazards
• Safety hazards
• Other hazards

**Individual consequences**
• Physical consequences
• Psychological consequences
• Behavioural consequences

**OCCUPATIONAL WELL-BEING**
• Life and job satisfaction
• Psychological and physical health

**Personality traits**
• Type A tendencies
• Locus of control
• Other traits

**Occupational stress**
• Factors intrinsic to the job
• Role in organization
• Relationships at work
• Career development
• Organizational structure and climate
• Home–work interface
• Other stress factors

**Organizational consequences**
• Health insurance costs
• Productivity & absenteeism
• Compensation & lawsuits

INTERVENTIONS

*Source:*   From Danna and Griffin (1999). Reproduced with permission from the publisher.

*Figure 1.1   Framework of occupational health and well-being*

interventions relating to workers' physical and psychological health will be reviewed in Chapter 11.

Definitions of what exactly constitutes health and well-being are broad. The World Health Organization (WHO, 1948) has not changed its core definition of health since 1948: 'a state of complete physical, mental and social well-being and not merely the absence of disease or infirmity'. Diener and Seligman (2004) defined well-being as 'peoples' positive evaluation of their lives, [that] includes positive emotion, engagement, satisfaction, and meaning' (p. 1), while Warr (1987, 2005) suggested that mental health is best described by six principal dimensions: *subjective well-being, positive self-regard, competence, aspiration, autonomy,* and *integrated functioning.* Warr suggested that subjective well-being is the principal indication of mental health and is defined by two independent axes of *arousal* and *pleasure* (see Figure 1.2). Warr suggested that subjective well-being can be mapped on to the arousal and pleasure axes, with locations furthest from the centre representing the most intense feelings. Subjective well-being, in turn, is specifically defined by three intercorrelated axes of affect (Figure 1.3): *displeasure to pleasure, anxiety to comfort* and *depression to enthusiasm.* More recently Warr (2007) included an additional axis of experience or *self-validation* to the model depicted in Figure 1.2. Warr described how self-validation is a broad theme encompassing constructs such as self-determination, intrinsic motivation, personal meaning, growth and goals.

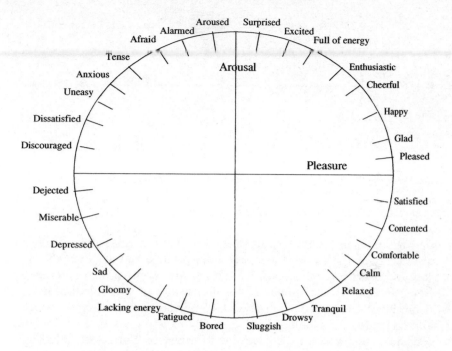

*Source:*    From Warr (2005). Reproduced by permission of the author and the publisher.

*Figure 1.2    Psychological well-being*

It is these constructs that focus on the actual meaning of work for individuals and explain some individuals' complete absorption in their work (such as work flow).

The model of affective well-being explains individual perceptions of job control, occupational stress, job-related anxiety and other work-related affective states. Senior job positions for example are often characterized by high arousal levels (high levels of anxiety and low levels of depression) as compared to lower job positions (Warr, 1990). It is also important to note that Warr's model of psychological health can be specifically applied to the occupational setting (job-related well-being) as well as broader life experiences (context-free well-being). Research has generally provided support for this multi-dimensional aspect of subjective well-being (Daniels et al., 1997; Mäkikangas et al., 2007; van Horn et al., 2004).

Warr (2005) also discussed how well-being can be measured. Job satisfaction for example evaluates the pleasure axis of well-being (axis 1 in Figure 1.3) but ignores arousal. Similarly, psychological burnout assesses negative well-being by focusing on anxiety (2a in Figure 1.3) and

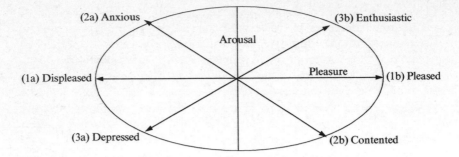

*Source:*   From Warr (2005). Reproduced with permission from the publisher.

*Figure 1.3   Warr's model of affective well-being*

depression (3a in Figure 1.3). It is pertinent that more recent research has also identified the value of assessing both positive and negative affective states such as the focus on positive and negative occupational experiences (Brough, 2005a). The remaining five dimensions of psychological health defined by Warr (positive self-regard, competence, aspiration, autonomy and integrated functioning) have generally received less specific research attention as compared to subjective well-being (see Warr, 2005), although we discuss autonomy (job control) in more detail in Chapter 4.

Diener (1984) and colleagues have conducted a substantial quantity of research exploring the subjective nature of well-being. They suggest that individual perceptions of happiness, relationships, life circumstances, goals and achievements combine to provide a sense of well-being: 'The term subjective well-being refers to people's evaluations of their lives. These evaluations include both cognitive judgements of life satisfaction and affective evaluations of moods and emotions' (Diener and Lucas, 1999, p. 213). This view of well-being includes both positive and negative evaluations across all life domains (work, family, leisure, health). Diener et al. (1999) suggested that subjective well-being is a multi-dimensional construct consisting of seven pleasant components (joy, elation, pride, contentment, affection, happiness and ecstasy) and seven unpleasant components (guilt/shame, sadness, anxiety/worry, anger, stress, depression and envy). The two core factors (pleasant and unpleasant) are related but independent from each other and the 14 specific individual components are intercorrelated. Diener et al. emphasized that researchers should include both the positive and negative factors in research investigations in order to provide an accurate estimation of well-being.

Diener et al. (1999) explained that cognitive evaluations of life satisfaction are an essential but *separate* component of subjective well-being.

For example while demographic variables are important for identifying population differences in well-being (such as health, marriage, money, age and education), they typically explain only a small proportion of variance. Instead internal individual factors such as personality, cognitions, goals and adaptation strongly influence an individual's life experiences and therefore provide a more thorough assessment of subjective well-being levels. Individual perceptions of physical health, for example, have a greater influence on subjective well-being than objective measures of health. Diener et al. suggested that this explains why individuals with a severe illness (such as cancer or AIDS) may only differ slightly from healthy individuals in their scores of life satisfaction and well-being. The use of adaptation coping responses (such as the positive appraisal of one's health/illness in comparison to others) can therefore override any objective health assessment.

# ANTECEDENTS OF WELL-BEING

We review here the primary antecedents of psychological well-being. These antecedents include both demographic characteristics such as income, marriage and gender as well as individual variables including personality and employment. While not discussed in detail we also acknowledge that constructs such as age, culture, nationality and adaptation are also recognized as significant antecedents of psychological well-being.

**Biological Antecedents**

William James (1884) queried whether we run from a bear because we are afraid or whether we are afraid because we run. James's query generated discussions concerning the extent to which emotional states such as fear and well-being are influenced by physiological activities, and these discussions continue today. Researchers have discussed the formation of emotions from a purely subjective perspective by focusing on feelings and consciousness, and from a more objective perspective by assessing cognitive activity. LeDoux and Armony (1999) provided a review of these perspectives and of the knowledge gained when examining the *interaction* between the subjective and objective explanations of human feelings. These authors described the key components of human feelings and related constructs (such as well-being) as consisting of *consciousness* and *working memory*: 'an emotional feeling results when the working memory is occupied with the fact that an emotion system of the brain is active' (p. 496). LeDoux and Armony proposed therefore that psychological well-being (and other emotions) can be understood by identifying which cognitive brain systems are feeding working memory when individuals confess to be in a state of well-being.

Other research has delved deeper into the biological status of well-being with explanations focused upon hormonal secretions, neural responses, and reinforcement and conditioning perspectives (for example Kahneman et al., 1999). Research has identified a biological basis of emotion in young infants that demonstrates stability until middle childhood, although this predictive pathway rarely proceeds into adulthood. In a review of this research Diener and Lucas (1999) suggested that the emotion displayed by infants as young as two days old illustrates some genetic explanation for emotions and well-being. Twin studies have offered further evidence of a genetic basis of well-being. In their investigation with both monozygotic and dizygotic twins, Tellegen et al. (1988) concluded that approximately 48 per cent of the variability in well-being can be attributed to genetic composition, and approximately 13 per cent of variance is explained by a shared family environment. Diener and Lucas concluded that biological research does provide evidence of the inheritability of some individual differences in subjective well-being. Thus an adult's level of subjective well-being is partly influenced by inherited characteristics.

## Gender

The investigation of gender differences in subjective well-being has produced mixed results, providing limited evidence that men and women significantly differ in their perceptions of well-being. In a review of this research, Diener et al. (1999) identified that women experience more extreme high and extreme low emotional affect than men. Women on average report more depression and more positive affect than men, resulting in overall well-being levels which are comparable to male scores. Diener et al. suggested that gender social norms were one explanation for these extreme emotional affect scores: a woman's caregiving role encourages more social connections and emotional responsiveness which are positively associated with well-being. This emotional responsiveness also explains why women are more susceptible to depression than men.

In his review of the research Warr (2007) noted that women employed in either work or family roles generally have similar levels of well-being. The pertinent factor here is *personal preference*. Thus for men or women who wish to work and are unemployed whether this is due to family circumstances or not, their levels of well-being will be lower, in comparison to their peers who prefer *not* to work. Warr also noted that across investigations conducted within a number of countries, average job satisfaction scores were comparable for male and female employees. However, investigations have also reported small but significant differences indicating that female workers have *higher* levels of overall job satisfaction as compared to their male colleagues. For example Clark (2005) in an investigation involving 19 countries reported that female workers produced significantly higher ratings of their work, pay, work hours, workplace relationships and support as compared to male workers. These findings are especially surprising considering many female workers typically still experience less favourable working conditions (such as lower pay, less job security and fewer benefits) compared to male workers. Social norms are suggested to be one explanation for the gender differences in job satisfaction. That is, some women are satisfied with their job conditions due to lower expectations based on the traditionally more tenuous level of female employment. If this explanation is valid, then it would be expected that these gender differences in job satisfaction would diminish over time as female employment becomes more firmly established within these social norms.

**Personality**

Associations between personality and well-being are generally strong and consistent. Extraversion has repeatedly been found to be associated with positive affect while neuroticism is associated with negative affect. Reported correlation coefficients are as large as .74 (Diener et al., 1999; Warr, 2007). Thus the social-behavioural component of well-being appeals to an extravert, which is in turn reinforced by the pleasant reward of positive affect. Larsen and Ketelaar (1991) explained the association between extraversion and well-being by the fact that extraverts rate stressors and daily events significantly more positively as compared to introverts. Both optimism and expectancy for control have also produced significant associations with well-being. Optimistic individuals for example generally consider events and goals in a positive light. Thus goals are generally considered to be obtainable and the subsequent reinforcement of this perception positively influences levels of well-being. Similarly repeated rumination on negative events adversely influences well-being: 'the happy individual is one who is extraverted, optimistic, and worry-free' (Diener et al., 1999, p. 282). Less evidence exists for any direct associations between psychological well-being and other personality factors such as conscientiousness and openness. Theoretical approaches such as person–environment fit and effort–reward imbalance have also been employed as frameworks to further explore the associations between personality and well-being (Warr, 2007).

**Marriage and Personal Relationships**

Research has consistently produced a positive association between marriage and well-being. Married individuals report greater levels of happiness than do single, divorced, widowed or never married individuals, and
these results are consistent across countries. In a review of this literature
Diener et al. (1999) identified that the association between marriage and
well-being occurred regardless of gender, that is both married women and
men reported higher levels of well-being as compared to unmarried women
and men respectively. Brough and Kelling (2002) replicated these results
by demonstrating that New Zealand women who were married or cohabit-
ing had significantly lower levels of psychological distress when compared
to single women. Explanations for the positive association between marriage and well-being include the *selection effect* (happy, well-adjusted
individuals are more likely to marry and remain married) and the *buffer
effect* (marriage provides emotional support against life stress). Diener et
al. suggested that an interaction between selection and social support is
the most likely explanation: 'Happy people may have a better chance of
getting married, and, once they commit themselves to the marital relationship, the psychological benefits of companionship can further boost subjective well-being' (1999, p. 290). Naturally a happy marriage/relationship
increases levels of well-being even more.

It is also pertinent to note that recent social changes appear to be weak-
ening this robust association between marriage and well-being. The social
importance of being married (especially for women) has significantly
declined; not marrying, cohabitation and divorce have each become more
socially acceptable, at least within Western societies. With changes in the
social status of marriage, the emphasis is instead being placed upon the
experience of *meaningful personal relationships* in the prediction of well-
being. In an investigation of the characteristics of happy people, Diener
and Seligman (2002) concluded that 'very happy people have rich and satisfying social relationships and spend little time alone relative to average
people. In contrast, unhappy people have social relationships that are
significantly worse than average' (p. 83). It is anticipated that the declining strength of association between marriage per se and well-being caused
by social changes, will be an interesting association to track for current
researchers in this field.

**Financial Income**

Despite the popular saying that money buys happiness, the associations
between income and subjective well-being tend to be small and statistically

insignificant. Diener et al. (1993) for example obtained a correlation of .12 between income and well-being in a large US sample, although stronger correlations (of approximately .45) were produced more recently within a sample of low-income Indian respondents (Diener and Seligman, 2004). Research therefore generally indicates that wealth is positively associated with happiness but that the effects are small in wealthy societies; stronger associations are produced among poorer societies where material wealth ensures that basic needs (food, shelter and clothing) can be met. Surprisingly, changes in income levels tend to have little impact on the association between income and well-being: rises and falls in income tend to produce only temporary changes in well-being levels. Diener et al. (1999) explained this lack of change by indicating that individuals quickly adapt to specific levels of wealth. In his vitamin model of well-being Warr (1990) suggested that income exhibits a curvilinear association with well-being such that both low and high extremes of income are associated with lower levels of well-being. This curvilinear association could explain why some individuals who win substantial sums of money on lotteries and other financial competitions subsequently experience a *decline* in well-being. It has been suggested that new stressors associated with a large financial win (such as conflict with family and friends) combined with the loss of social relationships if employment is given up, can produce a decline in well-being.

The relationship between finances and well-being was described in further detail by Diener and Seligman (2004) in their graphical illustration of US gross national product (GNP) and reported levels of life satisfaction (Figure 1.4). Figure 1.4 illustrates that despite a significant growth in GNP since 1940, levels of life satisfaction remain relatively unchanged. Diener and Seligman also observed that if increases in mental ill health rates were acknowledged in Figure 1.4, then levels of satisfaction/well-being would actually *decline* as GNP increased. The authors reported that after accounting for inflation, a 1973 income produced a higher level of reported happiness compared to the equivalent level of income in 1995. This finding implies that income levels are required to rise over time simply in order to maintain a base-line level of well-being.

The direction of causality between income and well-being is difficult to ascertain due to the dominance of cross-sectional research in this area. In a rare longitudinal investigation spanning 19 years, Diener et al. (2002) demonstrated that levels of well-being predicted *subsequent* income levels. These (and other) results imply that happy people are subsequently successful at earning money. Interestingly the specific pursuit of money and materialistic goals is often *negatively* associated with well-being. Diener et al. (1999) suggested that once basic needs are met (such as food, shelter and health

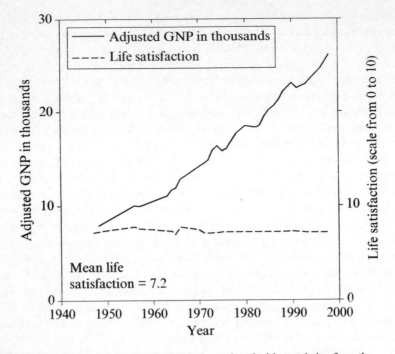

*Source:* From Diener and Seligman (2004). Reproduced with permission from the publisher.

*Figure 1.4    The relationship between GNP and well-being*

care), the pursuit of materialistic goals conflicts with other well-being goals such as social relationships and self-actualization, therefore resulting in a *decline* in well-being. Similarly Diener and Seligman (2004) reported that materialistic individuals tend to have lower levels of well-being due to the sizeable gap between their income and material aspirations. Indeed these authors argued that while money is a means to an end, the actual *end* itself is well-being. They suggested therefore that national ratings of well-being should replace economic indices and financial reports in order to provide a more accurate measure of growth and prosperity: 'Media attention should spotlight how a society is progressing in terms of well-being, and politicians should base their campaigns on their plans for reducing distress, increasing life satisfaction and meaning, enhancing marital and leisure satisfaction, and optimising engagement at work' (p. 2).

Finally the influence of income on well-being is also significantly affected by the social context. A specific level of income is generally not sufficient to be associated with well-being alone; rather it is the *comparative* income level

*Table 1.1   Life satisfaction across different groups*

| Group | Rating |
| --- | --- |
| *Forbes* magazine's 'richest Americans' | 5.8 |
| Pennsylvania Amish | 5.8 |
| Inughuit (Inuit people in northern Greenland) | 5.8 |
| African Maasai | 5.7 |
| Swedish probability sample | 5.6 |
| International college-student sample | 4.9 |
| Illinois Amish | 4.9 |
| Calcutta slum dwellers | 4.6 |
| California homeless | 2.9 |
| Calcutta homeless | 2.9 |

*Note:*   Respondents rated their level of life satisfaction from 1 (low satisfaction) to 7 (high satisfaction).

*Source:*   From Diener and Seligman (2004). Reproduced with permission from the publisher.

that is significant. Thus it is the individual's income in comparison with the incomes of colleagues/friends/ family that is important. Both Warr (1987) and Clark and Oswald (1994) demonstrated this point by finding that well-being is influenced by social comparisons (social worth). Warr for example noted that an income that is deemed by the individual to be inadequate and/or unequal to comparative colleagues' incomes is associated with low levels of health and well-being. Diener and Seligman (2004) considered the level of well-being among various social groups to determine the extent of any comparability. Table 1.1 depicts these results and demonstrates that while wealth does influence well-being, it is not in fact a direct association. The richest Americans and individuals with far less material wealth such as those living in Amish or Inughuit societies, each reported a similar high level of well-being, whilst the African Maasai who live without electricity, running water or solid houses also reported levels of well-being comparable to the levels of the richest Americans. Table 1.1 also indicates that the consequences of being homeless are also comparable across societies and homelessness is responsible for the lowest levels of well-being regardless of whether individuals reside in California or Calcutta.

### Employment

The maxim that happy workers are productive workers has been debated for the past century. Initial evidence was produced by improving the working conditions of factory workers in the early twentieth century; shorter working hours (reduced to about eight hours a day) and breaks during work were found to improve employee satisfaction and to increase productivity levels. Contemporary research generally reaches the same conclusion; Diener and Seligman (2004) for example concluded that 'When the workplace is properly structured to increase well-being, profits will likely rise. Thus, well-being at work not only is desirable as an end in itself, but also can help to promote greater economic productivity' (p. 11). Some job satisfaction research even suggests that work produces higher levels of satisfaction than non-work (family or leisure) activities. Kahneman et al. (2004) suggested this can be explained by the fact that work produces a defined daily structure, social contact, challenge, meaning and respect. Indeed Warr (1987, 2005) in his vitamin model described ten specific work characteristics that directly influence work-related well-being: *valued social position, opportunities for control, variety, opportunities for skill use, appropriate goal and task demands, environmental clarity, opportunities for interpersonal contact, availability of money, physical security*, and *supportive supervision*. Warr (2007) also included two additional work characteristics in the vitamin model: *career outlook* and *equity*. Key job characteristics such as the appropriate opportunities for control and support and an appropriate level of job demands (occupational stress) are also widely recognized as influencing levels of both job satisfaction and well-being (discussed in more detail in Chapters 4 and 5).

Sparks et al. (2001) noted that the perception of job insecurity is negatively associated with employee well-being. Major organizational restructures such as downsizing and mergers are associated with increased levels of employee sick leave, occupational stress and low levels of morale, motivation, performance and well-being. An important caveat here is one of individual choice; workers who choose to engage in jobs with high levels of job insecurity, such as contractors, generally have better outcomes than full-time employees (Sparks et al., 2001). Employment ranking or level is also associated with well-being, with a number of investigations indicating that middle managers and supervisors are especially susceptible to occupational stress and consequential low well-being. This can have a domino effect in that stressed managers are more likely to adopt inconsiderate management styles (for example ineffective communications and feedback) which in turn can adversely impact their workers' well-being (Hoel et al., 1999).

The unemployment literature also provides further evidence for the direct relationship between meaningful employment and well-being. Unemployed individuals who wish to work typically experience more distress, less life satisfaction and well-being, and have higher suicide levels than employed individuals (Diener et al., 1999). The structure and purpose that employment can provide is obviously absent in the unemployed and contributes significantly to these low levels of well-being. Furthermore these adverse health consequences tend to increase over the length of time of unemployment. Again the direction of causality is important here; Lucas et al. (2004) reported a longitudinal investigation of whether unhappy people are more likely to be unemployed. Lucas et al.'s research refuted this proposition and instead demonstrated the critical impact of being unemployed: even individuals with high levels of pre-unemployment well-being experienced low life satisfaction when unemployed and in some cases did not regain their initial high levels of well-being when subsequently employed.

In a review of this literature Warr (2007) concluded that unemployment has a detrimental impact on the health and well-being of both the individual and their family. These relationships are enhanced when contextual factors such as the local level of unemployment are also considered. Thus being unemployed when most around you are employed is more problematic. Finally Warr also provided a pertinent review of the associations between well-being and retirement, which can be considered as socially sanctioned unemployment. Similar to unemployment, retirement circumstances such as financial resources, individual health, social relationships and the local context significantly influence levels of well-being.

## WELL-BEING, WORK ATTITUDES AND JOB PERFORMANCE

Finally in this section we review the consequences of poor health and well-being upon job performance. Specifically we discuss job satisfaction, work withdrawal and turnover, organizational citizenship behaviour, depression and the impact of time away from work. Other work-related consequences of poor well-being such as accidents, physical violence, stress and work–family imbalance are also pertinent and are specifically discussed in the subsequent chapters.

### Job Satisfaction

A number of reviews have described the positive relationships between job satisfaction and job performance. Warr (1999) for example discussed the stronger relationship between *intrinsic* job satisfaction and job performance, as compared to *extrinsic* satisfaction. Thus workers who are able to use their skills adequately and perceive their job to provide opportunities

for growth and development generally perform better, compared to
workers who are primarily motivated to work by their salary or their job
security (Chapter 3 specifically discusses job satisfaction). Employee rank
is also a contributing factor in these relationships; management, professionals and white-collar workers generally report the strongest associations between work performance and well-being (Warr, 1999). Petty et al.
(1984) investigated whether an organization with high levels of worker
well-being also has high performance levels. The authors found that
schools with highly satisfied teachers generally performed better (in terms
of students' academic performance and behaviour, and school administrative efficiency) compared to schools with less satisfied teachers. Similarly
in a comparison of hospital wards, performance was higher on the wards
where nurses reported high levels of job satisfaction (Robertson et al.,
1995). Employees reporting low levels of well-being (high anxiety, high
job stress) generally have lower levels of job performance as compared to
their colleagues (Warr, 1999). This relationship is also described by French
et al.'s (1982) Person–Environment fit (P–E fit) model. The P–E fit model
acknowledges the curvilinear relationship between work characteristics
and employee strain (and performance), such that both low and high job
demands cause strain and reduce performance. Moderate job demands
slightly increase occupational stress levels which in turn raises performance levels.

Recent research, however, has reported no significant association
between job satisfaction and job performance. Parker (2007), for example,
discussed how the relationship between job satisfaction and job performance is generally stronger for complex jobs (such as professional jobs),
while jobs with less role complexity (such as manufacturing) produced an
insignificant association between job satisfaction and job performance.
Parker demonstrated instead that the worker's perception of their job
role (role orientation) had a substantial relationship with job performance and especially for jobs that encompass a flexibility of demands and
requirements. Similarly Wright et al. (2007) illustrated that the job satisfaction and job performance relationship was non-significant for workers
with low levels of well-being. Wright et al. demonstrated that well-being
*moderated* the satisfaction–performance relationship; workers with high
well-being increased their performance as their job satisfaction levels also
increased. One implication of Wright et al.'s findings is that to improve
the job performance of workers with low well-being, interventions should
be considered that address issues such as training employees in the self-
monitoring of their well-being levels so as to enhance positive emotions
and discourage negative emotions. Finally a recent meta-analysis of the
job satisfaction–performance relationship reported that the association

was spurious and was either reduced or completely eliminated after controlling for variables such as personality traits, job control and self-esteem (Dowling, 2007). Dowling concluded 'thus organizational efforts to improve employee performance by exclusively targeting job satisfaction are unlikely to be effective' (p. 179).

## Organizational Citizenship Behaviour

The emergence of organizational citizenship behaviour (OCB) as an empirical research topic also draws upon the association between well-being and performance. Job satisfaction and OCB are strongly related: happy/satisfied workers exhibit more positive OCBs (for example helpfulness, loyalty and engaging in additional tasks) and less negative OCBs (for example stealing and absenteeism). Employees with high levels of OCB have generally been found to be more productive compared to their dissatisfied colleagues (Hanson and Borman, 2006). In a longitudinal investigation Whiting et al. (2008) demonstrated that both job performance and OCBs (specifically loyalty, voice and helping behaviours) had significant causal effects on a worker's performance ratings. Thus OCBs significantly influence both supervisors' perceptions and their objective ratings of employee performance. Happy and/or satisfied workers therefore are at least *perceived* to be higher performers in comparison with their unhappy colleagues. Research conducted by Yun et al. (2007) also confirmed this perceptual bias. Yun et al. noted that employees displaying OCBs received more recommendations for rewards from their managers and this was especially the case for employees perceived by their managers as being both good organizational citizens and highly committed workers. Employees exhibiting OCBs but with low commitment levels were not as favourably perceived. In their review Boehm and Lyubomirsky (2008) described this activation of the halo effect for employees displaying a positive attitude; such workers are generally perceived as being better organizational citizens. Boehm and Lyubomirsky noted that research has also demonstrated an objective relationship between employees' levels of job performance and the retention of workers with positive attitudes.

The direction of causality is of course very pertinent in these investigations. Do high levels of well-being lead to better performance? Or are individuals happy because they performed well? In a review of the longitudinal research exploring these questions Diener and Seligman (2004) reported that employee well-being was a stronger predictor of subsequent turnover and loyalty, as compared to (time 1) performance levels. Similarly in their review of the longitudinal research Boehm and Lyubomirsky (2008) concluded that well-being facilitates subsequent mental functioning and performance: 'Happy people are more satisfied with their jobs and report having greater autonomy in the workplace. They perform better on assigned tasks than their less happy peers and are more likely to take on extrarole tasks such as helping others' (p. 110). Research is therefore generally consistent in finding that worker well-being is associated with subsequent OCBs and job performance.

**Absenteeism, Holidays and Job Turnover**

Absenteeism from work is associated with low levels of well-being and consequently inadequate work performance. It is, however, important to note that work absenteeism (or attendance) is influenced by a number of factors and may not necessarily truly represent a worker's level of well-being. The workplace culture (monitoring/tolerance of absenteeism), family demands, financial requirements, supervisor support and external factors (such as sporting competitions) also influence work absenteeism. Most reported associations between well-being (specifically job satisfaction) and absenteeism therefore tend to be small.

In an investigation with Canadian nurses, Hackett et al. (2001) demonstrated that withdrawal from both the organization and the occupation were significantly influenced by job involvement and job commitment. Hackett et al. concluded 'it is undoubtedly useful to know that helping to enhance an employee's level of occupational or organizational commitment is likely to affect both his or her intentions to stay within the organization and within the occupation' (p. 409). Thus the interplay between well-being, job satisfaction and job commitment was demonstrated to influence withdrawal from both the organization and also from the occupation itself. In a longitudinal investigation of turnover among New Zealand police officers, Brough and Frame (2004) identified significant associations between four occupational variables (the taking of leave, paid and unpaid; supervisor support; intrinsic job satisfaction; and extrinsic job satisfaction) and subsequent turnover rates. Brough and Frame noted that improving levels of supervisor support would directly improve both the job satisfaction and retention levels of police officers. It should also be acknowledged that external factors such as local unemployment rates have also been found to influence job withdrawal and turnover rates significantly and indeed, may have as much influence as employee levels of well-being (Warr, 1999).

A more unusual method of studying well-being and job performance is via the impact of time away from work, most commonly via annual leave, days off, week-ends or holidays. Research has demonstrated that a break from work does tend to improve levels of both physical health and psychological well-being, mostly due to the avoidance of occupational stress. In a classic biopsychological investigation, Halberg et al. (1965) measured the daily level of epinephrine (a stress hormone secreted by the adrenal medulla) from one male employee for four years. Halberg et al. were able to demonstrate a clear peak in epinephrine levels at mid-week and a fall to low levels at week-ends. Other investigations have demonstrated that time away from work can significantly reduce epinephrine levels, blood pressure and heart rate, improve viral resistance, and reduce fatigue, anxiety, depression, negative mood and burnout (Frankenhaeuser et al., 1989; Glaser et al., 1985). A holiday from work can have beneficial effects on well-being and this has been demonstrated to endure for up to four weeks after the return to work, regardless of whether employees did or did not actually enjoy their holiday (Westman and Eden, 1997).

However, recent investigations have produced more ambiguous results, most probably because technology now enables many workers to transport their work (and thus much of their occupational stress) with them on week-ends or holidays. Eden (2001) for example reported that while occupational stress declined for employees over a holiday period, levels of strain remained fairly constant. Eden suggested that the high workload experienced before the holiday and a similarly high workload anticipated after the holiday resulted in stable strain levels. Eden also suggested that while a holiday provides a break from some occupational stress, the holiday period itself may evoke stressors. Holmes and Rahe's (1967) inclusion of Christmas as a stressful life event provides one example of how holidays themselves may simply provide an alternative form of stress for some workers.

## CONCLUSION

This chapter has reviewed the definitions of psychological well-being and discussed both the antecedents and consequences of well-being for workers and organizations. It is apparent that the work of both Diener and Warr primarily leads the field of occupational well-being research, and their identification of commitment, satisfaction and pleasure as core constructs of well-being continues to have a significant influence upon research. The point that both negative and positive experiences and emotions both influence and constitute well-being is now widely recognized; indeed the recent interest in happiness and positive psychology has reaffirmed the necessity of including both negative and positive constructs in occupational well-being research. The chapter discussed the key antecedents of well-being and found evidence that meaningful social relationships and employment have a stronger and more enduring impact on levels of well-being compared to financial gains. Amid the recent discussions of Western affluence it is pertinent to note that wealth bears little direct effect on well-being and that individuals with very little material wealth have comparable levels of well-being to those of very rich individuals. Similarly meaningful and satisfying employment has a greater impact on well-being than a large salary per se (although not if your salary is significantly smaller than your colleagues). Finally some evidence suggests that happy, satisfied workers have higher rates of work attendance and job performance and their supervisors certainly perceive them to be better performers, as compared to unsatisfied employees. Recent research also suggests that well-being moderates the relationship between job satisfaction and job performance, and this is considered a relevant avenue for further investigation. Workers with high levels of well-being also tend to be better organizational citizens, which in turn is likely to improve their promotion opportunities. This chapter has set the scene for the impact of psychosocial job and employee characteristics on work performance. Several of the issues raised here will be discussed in more detail within the following chapters.

# 2. Work and physical health

## OVERVIEW

An estimated 350 000 deaths, 270 million non-fatal physical accidents and 160 million work-related diseases occur in workplaces each year (International Labour Organization, 2007). Work-related injuries, diseases and fatal accidents are more prevalent in developing countries where larger numbers of workers are employed in hazardous primary labour-intensive industries such as manufacturing, agriculture, commercial fishing, mining, logging and construction. Mechanization and safety standards ensure these industries are less hazardous in developed countries although they still account for a large proportion of severe injuries and fatalities. This chapter briefly describes the common physical health outcomes associated with paid employment and reviews the associations between psychosocial work conditions and physical health outcomes. We also discuss current trends in the organization of work and the corresponding implications for improving employee health outcomes.

## OCCUPATIONAL HEALTH AND SAFETY

Prior to the 1900s employee health and safety was not a government mandated concern. During this time employees were generally considered to be expendable and injuries were perceived to be the fault of the employee (Turner et al., 2005). However, a general shift away from an employer-centric work focus resulted in the development of formal employee health and safety policies. Each industrialized nation has subsequently developed formal occupational health and safety legislation resulting in significant improvements in working conditions, particularly in relation to the physical work environment. However, recent rapid changes in the nature of work have evoked suggestions that workplaces are again becoming hazardous environments (Danna and Griffin, 1999). Employment changes such as increasing work hours, telecommuting, downsizing and the rapid implementation of new technology have been identified as the prime contributors to contemporary hazardous workplaces. Downsizing, for example, has been directly linked with higher rates of fatal injuries, musculoskeletal disorders, psychological ill health and high blood pressure among workers (Landsbergis, 2003; Vahtera et al., 1997).

The recent debates discussing *who* exactly is responsible for employee health and how health levels can be improved have identified a number of pertinent issues. It has been posited that the most effective occupational health policies and interventions are those that adopt a *systematic integrated approach* involving occupational health and safety, human resource management, productivity management and workplace health promotion (Chu et al., 2000; Sparks et al., 2001). Occupational policies and interventions focused on improving both the physical and psychological health of workers are reviewed in detail in Chapter 11.

## COMMON OCCUPATIONAL PHYSICAL HEALTH OUTCOMES

Changes to the nature of work over the past twenty years or so have resulted in a gradual decline in occupational injuries and work-related deaths in many industrialized nations. Such changes include decreased exposure to manual work due to automation, increased use of technology and the emergence of the service sector as a major employer. While this shift has meant that fewer workers are involved in physically hazardous employment, common occupational illnesses associated with the modern workplace still occur. Employee health and safety can be endangered by a variety of organizational characteristics such as the physical exposure to hazardous materials or conditions and psychological exposure to inadequate job designs (Kinicki et al., 1996). A variety of external conditions have changed employment practices resulting in a marked growth in shiftwork, night work and the casualization of labour. These employment hours and conditions have been significantly associated with deterioration in occupational health and safety standards and an increase in work-related disease and injury (Quinlan et al., 2001).

Negative physical outcomes associated with work vary from minor injuries to long-term disabilities and death. US annual estimates, for example, cited 60 000 deaths due to work-related disease, 6500 deaths due to workplace trauma, 860 000 cases of work-related illnesses and 13.2 million non-fatal injuries, producing a total annual cost of $US171 billion (Leigh et al., 1997). The costs of these injuries and illnesses include direct costs (medical treatment, rehabilitation, legal costs, insurance and compensation claims), indirect costs (lost productivity, staff replacement costs and employee medical costs), and personal traumatic costs (Boden et al., 2001). Casual workers are more likely to bear injury costs themselves, rather than the employee compensation systems. Leigh and Robbins (2004), for example, reported that in 1999 the US workers' compensation systems 'missed' approximately 93 000 work-related deaths and $23 billon in medical treatment costs.

Physical stress injuries (such as injuries caused by lifting and carrying) are common workplace health outcomes that account for approximately 40 per cent of compensation claims. Falls, trips and slips account for approximately 20 per cent of claims, followed by being hit by a moving object and exposure to noise, hazardous substances or infectious diseases (Australian Safety and Compensation Council, 2007). Both musculoskeletal injuries (such as low back pain) and chronic muscle or joint conditions (caused by repetitive work) are also common physical work-related injuries in most industrialized countries. Leroux et al. (2006) reported for example that white-collar employees with high levels of occupational stress had the highest prevalence of neck–shoulder symptoms.

Research has also clearly identified the associations between work-related exposure to hazardous elements (such as asbestos, arsenic, diesel fumes, radon, environmental tobacco smoke and carbon monoxide) and physical health outcomes such as cancer, chronic respiratory disease and circulatory diseases (Leigh and Robbins, 2004). However, clearly *proving* this association between occupational exposure and physical illnesses is more difficult (and is often fiercely resisted). For example asbestos, tobacco smoke and sunlight are considered to be occupational carcinogens; however, employees can also be exposed to these hazards in non-work settings. Furthermore the strength of the association between exposure and illness can vary: not all workers exposed to the same level of risk actually develop an illness (Ward et al., 2003). Certain lifestyle factors such as smoking, poor eating habits and alcohol consumption can also exacerbate the consequences of workplace exposure to these carcinogens (see Siemiatycki et al., 2004).

Finally the associations between physical working conditions and respiratory diseases (such as adult asthma and chronic obstructive pulmonary disease) have also been recognized as major public health issues. Approximately 30 per cent of respiratory diseases are caused by workplace exposure (Turner et al., 2005). In general these illnesses are occupationally clustered: for example, healthcare workers are more likely to come into contact with infectious diseases such as HIV, manufacturing industries with chemicals, agricultural industries with animal-borne diseases such as brucellosis, and hospitality workers with infections such as salmonella.

# PSYCHOSOCIAL WORK CHARACTERISTICS

While the exposure to physically hazardous work conditions primarily leads to the injuries and illness reviewed above, the exposure to *psychosocial* work characteristics is also associated with physical ill health. Some psychosocial work characteristics have received considerable attention: the identification of 'stress-prone' (or coronary-prone) employees in the 1980s and 1990s is one such example (Goetzel et al., 2007). Other associations such as the relationships between psychosocial work characteristics and reproductive health have more recently been identified. In this section we provide an overview of two categories of psychosocial work characteristics that have demonstrated the most significant associations with physical health outcomes.

## Job Demands and Job Control

Karasek's (1979) job strain model has been widely used to demonstrate the relationship between job demands (workload, time constraints and pacing), control (ability to participate in decision-making) and health outcomes. Much of this research has focused upon psychological health outcomes such as anxiety, strain and depression. However, research has also linked work characterized as 'high strain' (high demand and low control) with physical health outcomes such as high blood pressure and cortisol levels (Cooper and Marshall, 1976; Marmot, 1984), somatic complaints (Fox et al., 1993), musculoskeletal problems (Kushnir and Melamed, 1991) and sickness absence (Houtman et al., 1994). Amick et al. (2002) for example, demonstrated a significant relationship between the cumulative exposure to passive work conditions (for instance, low job demands and low job control) and long-term health outcomes including mortality rates. Employees who worked in low-control jobs for a long period of time had a 43 per cent increased risk of premature death as compared to employees with higher levels of job control. Similarly Cheng et al. (2000), with a longitudinal cohort study of 21 290 female US nurses, identified that low job control, high job demands and low work-related social support were associated with poor health status as well as higher rates of functional decline over a four-year period. These associations were not explained by co-morbid disease, age, marital status, educational level or reported lifestyle risk factors.

Finally in an investigation involving 6000 Netherlands workers, Schrijvers et al. (1998) also demonstrated that work characterized by high job demands, low job control and low social support was associated with poor health outcomes for both male and female respondents. It is also pertinent to note that work described as high demand–low control typically encompasses lower-level employment positions, and therefore influences the associations between blue collar workers, poor working conditions and poor health outcomes.

## Shift-work and Long Working Hours

Numerous investigations have demonstrated a direct association between shift-work and physical health outcomes such as sleep disturbance, fatigue, pregnancy complications, gastro-intestinal problems and cardio-vascular disease (Laaksonen et al., 2006). Regularly working long hours has been linked with ill health effects including hypertension, cardiovas-cular disease, musculoskeletal disorders, chronic infections and diabetes (for example Knutsson, 2003). It is somewhat ironic to note that the adverse consequences of long working hours and the push for an eight-hour working day have been recognized since at least the late nineteenth century. The call for an eight-hour day, for example, was taken up by workers in the 1870s: 'eight hours for work, eight hours for rest, eight hours for what we will' (cited in Johnson and Lipscomb, 2006, p. 992). This phrase remains highly pertinent for many contemporary employees. From their review Johnson and Lipscomb identified that US employees have the longest working hours of industrialized countries: US employ-ees work an additional *five to ten weeks per year* compared to workers in Germany, France, Sweden, Norway or Denmark.

An important question to consider is *which* workers are working long hours? Jacobs and Gerson (2004), for example, identified that working hours largely reflected social class divisions: managerial and professional workers reported the longest working hours (for instance, white collar, educated males) while production, service and manual workers tended to work shorter hours. Jacobs and Gerson referred to this as the 'time divide'. Johnson and Lipscomb (2006) in a discussion of this time divide, noted that career advancement in many professional jobs is still closely tied to long working hours. Such individuals are described as 'a relatively privileged, male group of professionals who work long hours and are intensively involved in their work, have high levels of job satisfaction, yet are also likely to suffer from exhaustion, greater job–family problems, poor general and physical health' (p. 924). These authors reported that part-time workers had fewer occupational accidents, illnesses and lower levels of work–family conflict. However, they were less satisfied with their work, and also tended to be female and less financially secure (see also O'Driscoll et al., 2007).

One recent longitudinal investigation involving over 12 000 US workers demonstrated that long working hours were associated with high rates of workplace accidents and illnesses even after controlling for confounding variables such as age, gender and occupation (Sparks et al., 1997). Dembe et al. (2005) identified that it was the increased *fatigue and stress* experienced by workers rather than the increased exposure to the working environment per se that was the primary cause of the high rates of workplace accidents. These authors reported that working more than eight hours a day or 40 hours per week, or working overtime, was directly associated with an increase in occupational injuries or illness. Dembe et al. made salient the necessity of establishing protective measures (legislation, training and education) to ensure that workers are employed in appropriate organizational environments.

One pertinent study by Eyer (1977) identified the link between prosperity and heart attacks over a 26-year period in the US: heart attacks occurred more often in periods of economic prosperity and declined during economic depressions. Eyer explained this association by the increased levels of overtime worked in the prosperous periods; this overtime in turn produced high levels of fatigue and occupational stress, and thus more heart attacks. Liu and Tanaka (2002) suggested this reasoning also explains the increased numbers of heart attacks experienced by Japanese workers in the 1980s (*karoshi* or death from overwork). These authors identified that heart disease was highest among employees working 67 hours or more per week or more than 11 hours per day and for individuals who had inadequate sleep (less than about five hours' sleep per night).

The adverse consequences of working long hours have been recognized by some statutory bodies, primarily due to the increased risk of occupational accidents. For example in 1938 the US body overseeing truck drivers (the Interstate Commerce Commission) limited driving time to a maximum of 10 hours and a minimum rest time of eight hours within a 24-hour period. In 2003 the US Accreditation Council for Graduate Medical Education restricted the hours of medical residents to a maximum of 30 hours per shift and 80 hours per week, which is surprising given that studies have shown that receiving just two hours less sleep than your body requires has a similar effect on cognitive alertness as alcohol consumption. Somewhat more progressive advances have occurred in Europe where for example, the European Union (EU) has limited medical residents to a 48-hour working week (effective from August 2009). In fact the EU has directed that *all* employees should work a maximum of 48 hours per week with a minimum daily rest period of 11 hours, although the 'opt out' option to this mandate has been adopted by a number of countries including the UK (Johnson and Lipscomb, 2006).

We next discuss the research linking employment with three specific physical health outcomes: cardiovascular disease, reproductive health and suicide. We also review the impact that employment can have on behavioural outcomes that directly influence physical health such as obesity, alcohol intake and drug use.

## Cardiovascular Disease (CVD)

While many industrialized nations have experienced recent decreases in cardiovascular disease (CVD) mortality, CVD incident rates remain comparatively high. Research suggests that *occupational stress* is largely responsible for these high incidence rates (Dembe et al., 2005). Occupational stress is attributed with producing an adverse influence on both the risk factors and the outcomes of CVD. In a recent review Belkic et al. (2004) identified a significant relationship between occupational stress and CVD and found that this association was especially strong among male workers. In a review of research from 52 countries involving approximately 25 000 workers who were compared against control samples, Rosengren et al. (2004) also reported a strong association but identified no gender differences: 'Presence of psychosocial stressors is associated with increased risk of acute myocardial infarction, suggesting that approaches aimed at modifying these factors should be developed' (p. 953). Evidence from the large-scale UK Whitehall investigations similarly reported that chronic occupational stress was associated with the risk of developing heart disease (Rosengren et al., 2004). Findings from the Helsinki Health Study also demonstrated a strong association between fatigue at work and the development of CVD symptoms (specifically angina pectoris; Kivimäki et al., 2006). In their review of this literature Siegrist et al. (2005) suggested that the experience of occupational stress (specifically effort–reward imbalance at work) was clearly associated with an increased risk of CVD. Furthermore this elevated risk was *not* influenced by medical or behavioural risk factors.

An association between working hours, shift-work and CVD has also been identified. Boggild and Knutsson (1999) for example, demonstrated that shift-workers have a 40 per cent greater risk of developing CVD compared to workers who are not employed on shift systems. White and Beswick (2003) also noted that long work hours are associated with an increased risk of CVD. Occupational stress arising from workplace bullying or unsupportive supervisors has also been linked to a higher risk of CVD. Wager et al. (2003) demonstrated differences in blood pressures among nurses according to how favourably they perceived their immediate supervisor. Similarly Kivimäki et al. (2003) reported a significant association between workplace bullying and physical ill health, including CVD.

Interestingly Hallman et al. (2003), in a Swedish investigation with a matched control group, demonstrated significant associations between psychological burnout, emotion-focused coping strategies and CVD. Hallman et al. discussed both the educational level and the perceived lack of control reported by their female respondents as being predictors of ill health. The confounding influence of socio-economic status upon the association between occupational stress and CVD has also been acknowledged. Heslop et al. (2001) noted that CVD risk factors such as being overweight, smoking, lack of exercise and alcohol consumption were associated with occupational stress levels experienced by approximately 7000 Scottish employees. Furthermore these associations withstood the correction for both age and socio-economic level. Heslop et al. remarked that whereas the associations between stress and health behaviours (exercise, cigarette smoking and alcohol intake) were *independent* of socio-economic status, the associations between stress and physical CVD risk factors (blood pressure, cholesterol levels, body mass index) were *dependent* on both socio-economic status and gender. In contrast Brunner et al. (2004) in a study of 812 employees, found that 'work stress was a robust predictor of cardiovascular mortality after controlling for socioeconomic circumstances in childhood and adulthood' (p. 1020).

**Reproductive Health**

The exposure to adverse physical work conditions has an established history associated with poor reproductive health outcomes for both men and women. Known occupational risk factors include the exposure to lead and mercury, anaesthetic gases, chemical agents, pesticides, solvents and heavy physical work. These occupational risk factors have been linked to spontaneous abortions, infertility, pre-term delivery, birth defects, reduced birth weight and disruption to menstrual cycles (Bishop et al., 2003). Examples of adverse consequences from occupational exposure to chemicals include menstrual cycle changes in hairdressers and a reduced sperm quality among metal workers (Bishop et al., 2003).

Associations between *psychosocial* work characteristics and reproductive health have also recently been demonstrated in what is a pertinent emerging research field (Cox et al., 2000a). Stressful job characteristics, such as high job demands, have been associated with gestational hypertension (Landsbergis and Hatch, 1996), pre-term deliveries (Brett et al., 1997) and low birth-weight babies (Brandt and Nielsen, 1992). Occupational stress has been demonstrated to adversely influence the physical endocrine and immune systems, altering the uterine environment and reducing the rate of successful fertilization (Figà-Talamanca, 2006). Similarly Sheiner et al. (2002) demonstrated a direct association between occupational burnout and male infertility. Shift-work and/or night-work has also been identified in some research as increasing levels of infertility, spontaneous abortions, pre-term births and low birth-weight babies, although not all of these findings have been consistently replicated (see Figà-Talamanca, 2006). Changes in circadian rhythms in both mothers and foetuses as a result of shift-work and long working hours have also recently been identified.

Work characteristics may also influence the cognitive processes (decision-making) regarding whether or not to *have* children and the *number* of children. Wood and Newton (2006), for example, compared male and female managers in terms of their marital status and childlessness. Significantly fewer female managers were in couple relationships (66 per cent) compared to male managers (89 per cent) and significantly fewer female managers had dependent children (21 per cent) compared to male managers (66 per cent). Considering the decline of national birth rates currently occurring within many Western countries, the influence of employment upon both physical and cognitive reproductive health is expected to develop into a far more active research area.

**Obesity**

Chapter 11 examines workplace health promotion schemes in detail, including schemes that aim to reduce employee obesity levels. Here we briefly review the specific associations between psychosocial work characteristics and obesity. Obesity in the workplace is becoming an issue of increasing concern for employers, largely due to the negative associations between obesity, absenteeism and job performance. Yamada et al. (2002) posited that work contributes to weight gain in three main ways: (1) job characteristics such as sedentary work, shift-work and long working hours are directly associated with fatigue, lack of exercise and poor nutrition; (2) occupational stress can alter physiological endocrine functions; and (3) the use of negative coping mechanisms such as overeating, increased alcohol, tobacco and illicit drug use. Yamada and colleagues (2001) demonstrated that the change from an eight-hour to a 12-hour shift system resulted in an average one kilogram weight gain by factory workers. The weight gain was explained by increased fatigue levels (and therefore less physical activity) arising from the 12-hour shift. Yamada et al. (2002) also provided a pertinent review of how obesity can be accurately measured within the workplace.

In an investigation involving a heterogenous sample of 12 000 workers, Ng and Jeffery (2003) demonstrated that occupational stress was directly

associated with high-fat diets, reduced physical activity and increased cigarette smoking. Additionally Overgaard et al. (2004) discussed the point
that women were more likely to overeat when stressed as compared to
men (although the evidence for this gender difference is mixed). Overgaard
et al. provided a pertinent review of the literature linking psychosocial
work characteristics and bodyweight. Kivimäki et al. (2006) also identified significant associations between stress and increased incidence of
lifestyle risk factors in a sample of 36 000 Finnish public sector employees.
Similarly Payne et al. (2002) reported that stressed employees had a high
*intention* to exercise but were actually engaged in significantly less exercise
as compared to their colleagues in low stress roles. Most recently Schulte
et al. (2007) provided an interesting review of employment discrimination
and stigmatization of overweight workers and identified, for example, that
only one US state (Michigan) currently prohibits this form of bias. Schulte
et al. acknowledged the increasing trend to associate overweight workers
with higher levels of absenteeism and decreased job performance, regardless of causal evidence.

This area of research also suffers from a myriad of methodological
problems. Researchers are reminded of the value of longitudinal studies,
objective measures of weight and body mass (as opposed to self-report
measures) and the inclusion of likely confounding variables in the statistical analyses such as gender, education and lifestyle habits (such as exercise). Chapter 11 discusses these issues in further detail.

**Alcohol and Drug Use**

The research examining the relationship between work conditions and
alcohol and drug use has produced mixed results, with some researchers
indicating little relationship between the two (Payne et al., 2002) while
others report an association between work-related stressors and alcohol
use (Harris and Heft, 1992). One reason for this discrepancy is the difficulty of linking alcohol and/or drug use with work characteristics, when
non-work factors often also play a significant role in usage rates. Thus
perceived stress arising from a mixture of work, family, relationship and
health problems is a typical cause of drug and alcohol use. Grzywacz and
Marks (2000) for example demonstrated that both occupational stress
and family problems (marital disagreement) were predictive of problem
drinking. However, it is also important to note that research in this field
suffers from methodological problems making comparability across investigations difficult. Variance occurs in the definitions of drugs being investigated, the definition of the usage period (days or months), cross-sectional
research designs, under-reporting by participants and the inclusion of

samples with a higher than average risk of drug/alcohol use. Additionally confounding variables such as age, income, education, exercise and per-ceived support may not always be adequately controlled.

Research has, however, suggested that some occupations are more highly associated with drug and alcohol use than others. For example a review of misuse amongst healthcare workers found that specific specialities were at higher risk including emergency medicine, psychiatry, anaesthetics and specialist nurses (Frone, 1999). One reason for an above-average drug use among healthcare workers is their access to substances, although this access does not account for their use of non-medical drugs. Storr et al. (1999), for example, demonstrated that nurses experiencing occupational stress were one and a half times more likely to use non-medical drugs as compared to their colleagues. This usage amounted to 10 per cent of nurses using non-medical drugs (cocaine and marijuana) at least once in the past 12 months. Storr et al. also identified that psychotropic drug use among white collar workers is an increasing concern. In one review involving nearly 7500 US workers in 14 occupations, Zhang and Snizek (2003) noted that construction, labour, sales, hospitality, executive, managerial and administrative occupations were over-represented amongst employees who reported heavy drinking behaviours. Zhang and Snizek also reported that marijuana was most commonly used by workers employed in catering, hospitality, construction, transportation and sales.

Significant changes to working conditions such as job loss have been linked with increased alcohol use. Research has also demonstrated that heavy drinking is a direct *predictor* of future job loss (Catalano et al., 1993). Zhang and Snizek (2003) demonstrated that job security had an *inverse* relationship with alcohol and illicit drug use. Furthermore, in comparisons of six job dimensions, job security was one of the more important job characteristics in the (non)use of alcohol and drugs even after controlling for gender, age, education, ethnicity and income. Similarly, job variety also demonstrated a significant inverse relationship with cocaine use: employees in jobs with high job variety were 64 per cent less likely to use cocaine, compared to workers in low variety positions. Zhang and Snizek concluded that 'regardless of personal background, workers who enjoy steady employment are much less likely to drink alcohol or use any illicit drug, including marijuana' (p. 407).

A second important issue in the relationship between job loss and alcohol use is the perception of *individual control*. Thus *voluntary* job loss appears to have little influence on increased alcohol intake, however *involuntary* job loss has a marked effect. Gallo et al. (2001) noted that individuals experiencing involuntary job loss were twice as likely to report an increased alcohol intake, with the alcohol use in this instance being employed as a coping strategy. These findings, however, contradict previous research that demonstrated that job autonomy was *positively* related to cocaine use, with employees reporting high levels of autonomy being four times more likely to use cocaine (Martin and Roman, 1996). One explanation for this unusual finding is the use of cocaine to enhance creativity and/or power for some individuals, especially workers within the film, music and entertainment industries.

**Suicide**

Reviews exploring the association between work characteristics and suicide identify a number of common research flaws including: unrepresentative and small samples, lack of matched control groups, different methods of data collection and inadequate empirical analyses (Bennett and O'Donovan, 2001). A common finding is that after controlling for demographic characteristics much of this research can be explained by social and economic factors. Work characteristics have, however, been associated with high suicide rates among specific occupations such as doctors, dentists, nurses, pharmacists and veterinary surgeons. Above-average suicide rates in these healthcare occupations, as well as in farming, military and law enforcement are partly attributed to the access to both the means and the knowledge to successfully perform suicides (drugs and firearms; Stack, 2001). High suicide rates have also been identified among low-paid workers such as labourers or semi-skilled workers (Stark et al., 2006). In a recent comprehensive review Agerbo et al. (2007) ranked 55 occupational groups by their rate of suicide. After controlling for psychiatric admissions, socio-economic indicators and demographic characteristics, the authors identified that medical doctors, nurses, factory workers and labourers had the highest suicide rates, while architects, armed forces personnel and financial personnel were ranked the lowest.

In an interesting study Feskanich et al. (2002) conducted a 14-year follow-up investigation with US nurses and demonstrated that the association between occupational stress and suicide was curvilinear such that both high and low rates of stress were associated with an increased risk of suicide. Feskanich et al. noted that nurses on medication (specifically diazepam) had a fivefold increased risk of suicide compared to their cohorts. Kahn and Nutter (2005) reviewed the evidence that veterinary surgeons as an occupational group have one of the highest reported suicide rates and concluded that the explanation for this relationship is clearly attributable to high levels of occupational stress. This stress was specifically attributed to their job characteristics: lack of job control and support, high levels of uncertainty, lack of performance feedback and appreciation, high workloads, long working hours (24-hour service), managing new technology, financial and social constraints, workplace trauma (physical injuries from animals and the public), and high rates of psychological burnout.

## FUTURE CHALLENGES

Over the past thirty years there have been significant changes to the type of employment available and the organization of work. Most developed countries have experienced a general decline in the manufacturing industries and growth in the service and knowledge industries. In addition trade deregulation and new computer technologies mean that many organizations are now competing in a global market, especially given the growth of industries in both India and China. To remain competitive many Western organizations have downsized, adopted a range of production technologies and increased their reliance on precarious forms of employment (casual contracts). These changes are exacerbated by societal and demographic developments such as an ageing workforce, tight labour market and an increase in small-to-medium-sized enterprises (SMEs). In Australia, New Zealand and the UK, for example, SMEs contribute approximately 35 per cent to the gross domestic product (National Institute for Occupational Safety and Health, 2002). However, most SMEs do not provide comprehensive employee health initiatives, often adopt informal human resource management strategies and typically lag behind larger organizations in the provision of effective employee health initiatives (Nelson et al., 2007). One challenge then for future researchers is to ensure that SME employees are at least adequately acknowledged within occupational health investigations.

Both the increasing ageing workforce and the growth of a casual workforce in many developed countries present considerable challenges to the success of many employment conditions, including occupational health and safety. Most casual job arrangements, for example, do not qualify for basic employment conditions such as sick leave, holiday loadings and the right to collective representation. The ability of these workers to formally ensure they are employed within a healthy working environment is therefore an increasing problem, especially in relation to psychosocial work characteristics. The health and well-being of an ageing workforce and the ability to retain these workers is also a growing issue for occupational health researchers. Recent economic reports estimated that the retention of at least a further 50 per cent of older workers in employment is required to meet European labour-force demands (Morschhäuser and Sochert,

2006). Thus the challenge for researchers is first to identify which work characteristics influence the physical and/or cognitive deterioration of older employees and second, to introduce working practices to ensure that older workers remain healthily and productively employed.

## CONCLUSION

This chapter reviewed the extent to which paid employment directly contributes to employees' physical health outcomes. Whilst occupational health and safety legislation has reduced many of the physical working conditions that contribute to physical injuries and disease, the influence of psychosocial work characteristics has only relatively recently been recognized. A recent European directive, for example, clearly identifies that employers are responsible for both the physical and the psychological health of their employees (discussed in Chapter 5). Examples of emerging areas for concern for employees include the exposure to infectious diseases at work and the impact of employment for both male and female reproductive health outcomes. For employers the necessity to retain high performance older workers, an increasing casual workforce, and the recognition of psychosocial work characteristics that impact on employee physical health, all have direct implications for occupational health and safety policies regardless of the size of the organization.

# 3.   Job satisfaction

## OVERVIEW

The study of job satisfaction has been prolific in industrial and organizational psychology and can be traced back to the Hawthorne studies (Roethlisberger and Dickson, 1939). Job satisfaction is by far the most frequently studied variable in organizational research; a brief search on PsychInfo using the keyword *job satisfaction* returned 15 065 results. The enduring interest in job satisfaction is due to job satisfaction being the primary variable in the debate concerning the happy/productive worker thesis (Wright, 2006). This question has dominated the landscape of industrial and organizational psychology with researchers presenting findings that have not always been consistent (Cropanzano and Wright, 2001; Ironson et al., 1989; Judge et al., 2001; Petty et al., 1984). Chapter 1 discussed the relationships between employee well-being (including job satisfaction) and job performance in detail.

The investigation of the relationships between job satisfaction and other organizational variables (such as turnover, employee absence, employee health and, more recently, work–family conflict) has proved to be of continuing interest to scholars and of practical interest to policy makers and practitioners. We begin this chapter by discussing the key points in the debate defining the job satisfaction construct and then review approaches taken by researchers in measuring it. Four theories that explain job satisfaction in relation to other variables will then be discussed. We also review the relationships between job satisfaction and key organizational and individual level variables, examine gender differences in job satisfaction and finally discuss the key methodological issues within job satisfaction research.

## DEFINITIONS

The most influential definition of job satisfaction was advanced by Locke (1976): 'a pleasurable or positive emotional state resulting from the appraisal of one's job or job experiences' (p. 1300). Although considerable subsequent organizational research has employed Locke's definition, scholars have also questioned its limited focus on affect (Brief and Roberson, 1989; Organ and Near, 1985). Researchers have argued that job satisfaction is a work attitude and have advanced a definition of job satisfaction that includes both affective as well as cognitive dimensions. Brief (1998), for example, defined job satisfaction as 'an internal state that is expressed by *affectively* and/or *cognitively* evaluating an experienced job with some degree of favour or disfavour' (p. 86). Brief suggested that affect and cognition are distinct influences on job satisfaction, and that organizational researchers have been tapping only the cognitive dimension while neglecting the affective dimension. Similarly Brief and Weiss (2002) in a major review of job satisfaction argued that it is problematic to construe job satisfaction in cognitive and affective terms but typically measure only its cognitive dimension.

## MEASUREMENT OF JOB SATISFACTION

The measurement of job satisfaction has received a significant volume of research over the past forty years and is dominated by two approaches: *global or overall measures* (Ironson et al., 1989); and *facet or composite measures* (Smith et al., 1969). Global measures estimate the respondents' overall feelings about job satisfaction, whereas facet measures cover specific job characteristics (such as pay, supervisor, co-worker satisfaction). Ironson et al. evaluated the psychometric properties of global and facet job satisfaction measures and found that global scales are *not* equivalent to the summated facet scales. Similarly Jackson and Corr (2002) tested the hypothesis that global satisfaction would represent a linear function of facet satisfaction (for example, facet description × facet importance). The hypothesis was not supported and the researchers concluded that respondents, when providing a global assessment of job satisfaction, employed a cognitive heuristic to reduce the complexity of facet description × importance calculations. The overall conclusion of the debate regarding the usefulness of global versus facet measures of job satisfaction was that each type of scale contributed unique and useful information. Hence the selection of which scale to use ought to be determined by the aims of the study.

Another contentious issue is the use of single-item versus multiple-item measures of job satisfaction. Single-item measures have been criticized because such measures cannot yield estimates of internal reliability, nor can single-item measures be used in structural equation models (Nagy, 2002). However Scarpello and Campbell (1983), in a comparative study of the two types of measures, concluded that a single-item measure of overall job satisfaction was preferable to a scale that is based on a sum of specific job facet satisfactions. Wanous et al. (1997) conducted a meta-analysis of single-item measures of overall job satisfaction and found that the mean observed correlation of single item measures with overall measures was .63. Wanous et al. concluded that the use of single-item measures should not be considered a fatal flaw in the research process. They recommended that the choice of single or multi-item measures be guided by the research question.

# THEORETICAL BASIS OF JOB SATISFACTION

Job satisfaction theories typically explain satisfaction in relation to the *process of motivation*. We discuss four such process theories in this next section.

## Equity Theory

Equity theory states that the perception of job satisfaction is based on the evaluation of inputs that employees have contributed (skills, experience, amount of time worked) and outcomes they receive as the rewards from their job (pay, promotion, recognition; Adams, 1965). Employees are satisfied if they consider the direct ratio between outcome and input as fair. Thus equity theory posits that employees determine feelings of equity by comparing their own outcome/input ratio with that of an equivalent colleague. Job satisfaction is a result of this individual appraisal of equity. Empirical evidence supporting equity theory is strong, especially with regard to how employees respond to under-reward situations (Greenberg, 1990). Recent cross-cultural evaluations of equity theory show that cultural differences do also exist. Allen et al. (2005), for example, found that Japanese workers are more likely than American workers to take overt actions to reduce their feelings of inequity. However, it can be questioned whether equity perception is primarily determined by dispositional factors or situational factors.

## Expectancy Theory

Expectancy theory proposes that work effort is directed towards behaviours that are believed will lead to desired outcomes. Job satisfaction (or dissatisfaction) results from the discrepancy between expected and actual outcomes (Vroom, 1965). Thus job satisfaction occurs when a worker perceives that an outcome noticeably exceeds his or her expectation (McFarlin and Rice, 1992). A recent test of expectancy theory showed that it predicts work effort, motivation and organizational citizenship behaviours (Haworth and Levy, 2001). However, one limitation of expectancy theory is that it fails to account for the role of emotions in employee effort and behaviour (Christie et al., 2007).

**Situational Theory**

The basic premise of situational theory is that job satisfaction is determined by situational characteristics (Quarstein et al., 1992). Situational characteristics are relatively finite and stable variables (such as working conditions, career opportunities, development, reward systems and company policies) which are usually considered by employees before they accept employment. One critique of situational theory is that it does not account for the role of personal traits in determining job satisfaction.

**Dispositional Theory**

Dispositional theory argues that internal factors (for example personality traits) are more important than situational factors in influencing job satisfaction (Judge and Larsen, 2001). In a recent review of dispositional approaches to job satisfaction, Staw and Cohen-Charash (2005) proposed that 'dispositions may influence the conditions an individual faces at work, how he or she perceives, evaluates, stores in memory and recalls from memory' (p. 73). They concluded that dispositional affect can provide theoretically and empirically robust explanations of attitudes such as job satisfaction. In an attempt to unify dispositional and situational perspectives on job satisfaction, Lent and Brown (2006) proposed the *social-cognitive model* of job satisfaction. Their model considers the specific pathways by which social, cognitive and behavioural mechanisms operate jointly with trait influences to influence individual levels of well-being. A systematic evaluation of the social-cognitive model of job satisfaction, however, is currently scarce.

## JOB SATISFACTION AND ORGANIZATIONAL VARIABLES

The associations between job satisfaction and various organizational variables has been a fertile research area. In this section we review recent research that captures the nature of the relationship between job satisfaction, with three key organizational-level variables: job performance, absenteeism and turnover.

**Job Performance**

Among the various organizational variables that have been investigated in relation to job satisfaction, the one that has generated a prolonged and substantial debate among researchers is the relationship between job satisfaction and job performance. Early investigations of the job satisfaction –job performance relationship were inconclusive and demonstrated a minimal relationship (Brayfield and Crockett, 1955), while other studies reported a moderate relationship (Vroom, 1965). The first meta-analytic review of the satisfaction–performance relationship involved 16 studies and reported a mean corrected correlation of .31 between the constructs (Petty et al., 1984). A more comprehensive meta-analytic review using 74 studies conducted by Iaffaldano and Muchinsky (1985) found an average correlation of only .17. Iaffaldano and Muchinsky's findings are widely cited as evidence that the satisfaction–performance relationship is minimal. However, this influential study had two major limitations: the first was its use of multiple correlations from a single study that violated the independence assumption of meta-analysis. The second limitation was the use of facet satisfaction to compute an overall job satisfaction score which downwardly biased the mean correlation estimate (Judge et al., 2001).

Judge et al. (2001) argued that there are seven different ways in which the satisfaction–performance relationship can be specified: (1) satisfaction causes performance; (2) performance causes satisfaction; (3) satisfaction and performance are reciprocally related; (4) the relationship between satisfaction and performance is spurious; (5) satisfaction is moderated by other variables; (6) there is no relationship between satisfaction and performance; and (7) there are alternative conceptualizations of satisfaction and/or performance. In a large meta-analytic study involving 312 samples ($N = 54\ 417$), Judge et al. found that the mean true correlation between job satisfaction and performance was .30. Unlike previous meta-analyses, Judge et al. used inter-rater reliability which is considered the most appropriate correction for contemporary meta-analyses (Hunter and Schmidt, 1990). The findings from this meta-analysis have resulted in a review of the satisfaction–performance relationship, with most scholars accepting the relationship to be a moderate correlation of .30. However, in a recent meta-analysis examining 109 studies Bowling (2007) reported that the satisfaction–performance relationship is largely spurious. Bowling noted that this relationship is partially eliminated after controlling for either personality traits or for work locus of control, and is completely eliminated after controlling for organization-based self-esteem. Bowling's findings suggest that the research controversy surrounding the satisfaction–performance relationship is likely to continue.

**Absenteeism**

Organizations are paying increasing attention to methods which reduce employee absenteeism and its associated impacts (such as reduced

competitiveness), as higher job satisfaction is noted as one of the factors
influencing an employee's motivation to be consistently present in the
workplace. However, studies on the relationship between absenteeism and
job satisfaction are inconsistent. Scholars still have no agreement as to the
exact nature of the relationship between these two variables (Goldberg
and Waldman, 2000; Wegge et al., 2007).

Böckerman and Ilmakunnas (2006) employed a recursive model to
test the mediating effect of job satisfaction on the relationship between
absenteeism and its other predictors. They found that the level of job
(dis)satisfaction did not directly contribute to the number of absences.
However, the prevalence of harm at the workplace was associated with
job dissatisfaction and with workers' sickness absences. Siu (2002) found
that the interaction of job satisfaction with other variables was statistically
significant as the predictor of absenteeism in only one of two samples of
nurses. Goldberg and Waldman (2000) employed multivariate analysis
of four variables (individual characteristics, situational factors, job satisfaction and absenteeism) from 244 nursing, clerical, technician, blue
collar, professional and managerial employees at a US hospital, and
reported negligible relationships between the three predictors and absenteeism measures. Goldberg and Waldman argued that the inconsistency
in patterns of job satisfaction and absenteeism relationships is due to the
simplistic bivariate model utilized by previous research. They suggested
employing multivariate models to examine the extent to which observed
relationships are artefactual.

The inconsistency of the research findings has implications for both
theoretical and methodological arguments. There is a possibility that job
satisfaction and absenteeism are basically two organizational constructs
that share similar explanatory variables. Thus examining their relationships can give spurious results if they are treated as two variables that
have causal relationships. Consequently job satisfaction cannot be used
both as an independent variable and as a mediating variable in relation to
absenteeism. Job satisfaction can, however, be employed as a *moderating*
variable between absenteeism and its predictors. Wegge et al. (2007), for
example, showed that job satisfaction moderated the relationship between
job involvement and absenteeism, such that job involvement affects absenteeism more strongly when job satisfaction is low.

**Turnover**

The turnover–job satisfaction nexus has gained more systematic research
attention since Mobley (1977) launched his theoretical exposition explaining the impact of job dissatisfaction on an employee's decision to quit or

stay. Mobley posited that there are several intermediate steps between job dissatisfaction and quit/stay decisions. Subsequently there have been a number of theoretical and empirical studies on job satisfaction–turnover relationships (Griffeth et al., 2000; Lum et al., 1998; Wright and Bonett, 2007). These studies confirm that a low level of job satisfaction is a predictor of turnover.

Empirical evidence examining the direct relationship between job satisfaction and turnover intention was provided by Shields and Ward (2001). They found that nurses who reported overall dissatisfaction with their jobs had a 65 per cent higher probability of intending to quit than those reporting job satisfaction. Moreover, Shields and Ward reported that dissatisfaction with promotion and training opportunities has a stronger impact than dissatisfaction with workload or pay. Evidence for a direct relationship was also noted by Kristensen and Westergård-Nielsen (2004) who found that low overall job satisfaction significantly increased the probability of quitting. They ranked job satisfaction domains according to their ability to predict an employee's decision to quit. The ranking showed, for example, that satisfaction with type of work was found to be the most important job characteristic, whilst satisfaction with job security was found to be insignificant. Moreover their findings hold across age, gender and education sub-groups.

Research has also identified that other variables influence the job satisfaction–turnover relationship. Hom and Kinicki (2001) showed that withdrawal cognitions mediated the relationship between job satisfaction and turnover, while Clugston (2000) reported that organizational commitment mediated this relationship. Wright and Bonett (2007) demonstrated that employee well-being was a moderator of turnover, such that the influence of job satisfaction on turnover was stronger when well-being was low. Finally a meta-analytical study conducted by Griffeth et al. (2000) on the job satisfaction–turnover relationship confirmed that job satisfaction correlates with employee turnover (albeit only modestly). Research therefore suggests that job satisfaction plays an important role as the predictor of employee turnover. The mediators and moderators of the job satisfaction–turnover relationship are also highly pertinent.

## JOB SATISFACTION AND INDIVIDUAL VARIABLES

From the perspective of occupational health psychology, the relationship between job satisfaction and individual difference variables are of particular significance because it provides critical information about employee well-being, which in turn affects organizational outcomes. We review in this section the relationship between job satisfaction and three individual-level variables: personality, employee health and work–family conflict.

**Personality**

The widely accepted consensus in the literature is that personality influences job satisfaction (Connolly and Viswesvaran, 2000; Judge and Bono, 2001; Judge et al., 2000; Staw, 2004). One simple typology used as a theoretical framework is the positive affectivity (PA) and negative affectivity (NA) constructs (Watson et al., 1988). Research indicates that PA correlates positively with job satisfaction while NA correlates negatively with job satisfaction (Watson et al., 1988; Connolly and Viswesvaran, 2000). The five factor model of personality (McCrae and Costa, 1996) offers a comprehensive theoretical framework in explaining the most salient personality traits relevant to job satisfaction. In a meta-analytical study involving 163 independent samples, Judge et al. (2002) found that neuroticism correlated negatively with job satisfaction ($r = -.29$), while the four remaining traits produced positive associations (extraversion $r = .25$; openness to experience $r = .02$; agreeableness $r = .17$; and conscientiousness $r = .26$). Furthermore, results showed that only the relationships of neuroticism and extraversion with job satisfaction were significant across studies. As an aggregate set, the composite of all five traits have a multiple correlation of .41 with job satisfaction. This indicates support for the dispositional source of job satisfaction when traits are organized according to the Big Five factor model.

Another personality model relevant to the study of job satisfaction is core self-evaluation comprised of self-esteem, generalized self-efficacy, locus of control and neuroticism. Scholars have found, for example, that core self-evaluations have direct and indirect effects on job (and life) satisfaction (Judge et al., 2000; Judge and Bono, 2001). Judge et al. (2005) also demonstrated that individuals with positive self-regard were more likely to have self-concordant goals and were more satisfied with their jobs, themselves and their lives overall. While in a major review of the person-situation literature, Staw (2004) proposed a new dispositional model of job satisfaction that incorporates recent advances in cognitive sciences. Staw and Cohen-Charash (2005) argued that dispositional affect can provide theoretically and empirically robust explanations of job attitudes, including what is experienced in the workplace and how it is evaluated and stored and retrieved from memory. Bowling et al. (2006) also found that affective dispositions play an important role in the change of job attitudes across time.

**Employee Health**

With rapid technological advances transforming work environments and as the notion of 'work anytime, anywhere' becomes a reality for a growing number of individuals, there is growing interest in investigating the relationship between job satisfaction and employee health. Some recent evidence suggests that employment conditions in several industrialized countries have deteriorated and job satisfaction levels have also declined in the past decades (Fischer and Sousa-Poza, 2008). These developments have identified that the relationship between job satisfaction and employee health is an important concern for employers, primarily due to the impact on employee productivity and healthcare costs. Research indicates that job dissatisfaction is associated with employees' mental ill health, depression, job burnout and low self-esteem (Faragher et al., 2005; Fischer and Sousa-Poza, 2008).

In a systematic review and meta-analysis of 485 studies, with a combined sample size of 267 995 individuals, Faragher et al. (2005) found that job satisfaction had a direct impact on employees' psychological and physical health. This review reported that the overall correlation between job satisfaction and all health measures was positive ($r = .31$). Moreover, the review revealed that job satisfaction was more strongly correlated with psychological than physical health. The strongest relationships was found for burnout ($r = .48$), followed by self-esteem ($r = .43$), depression ($r = .43$) and anxiety ($r = .42$). The correlation with subjective physical illness was modest ($r = .29$). The study concluded that dissatisfaction at work can be hazardous to employee mental health and well-being, as a modest decrease in job satisfaction levels was associated with an increase in the risk of psychological burnout.

Much of the research investigating the link between job satisfaction and health suffers from two difficulties: the use of cross-sectional data which cannot confirm causality and secondly, the scarcity of objective measures of health. A recent study by Fischer and Sousa-Poza (2008) using the German Socio-Economic Panel, overcame these two difficulties through the use of objective health measures (such as Body Mass Index) and by controlling for unobserved individual characteristics (such as affectivity). Fischer and Sousa-Poza's analysis uncovered an increasing effect of job dissatisfaction on health, corresponding to the conclusions drawn from previous cross-sectional studies. Fischer and Sousa-Poza demonstrated that over time improvements in job satisfaction exert a 'healing effect' with respect to health measures, such as a decrease in the number of self-reported impediments to daily activities, frequency of depression, and a decrease in the number of doctor visits and hospital stays.

More than three decades of job satisfaction research therefore provide evidence of direct, indirect and reciprocal links between job satisfaction and employee health, which is a matter of concern for organizational practitioners and policy makers. What are now required are well-designed organizational interventions that can demonstrate the efficacy of remedial measures that organizations can deploy to deal with this issue.

**Work–family Conflict**

There is growing evidence in the literature indicating a negative relationship between work–family conflict (WFC) and job satisfaction. Aryee et al. (1999) in a longitudinal investigation demonstrated that parental overload led to family–work conflict (FWC), which in turn lowered job satisfaction. In a study that measured job satisfaction from several different facets, Howard et al. (2004) found that increased levels of conflict were negatively related to different facets of employee job-related satisfaction. However, their results indicate that WFC is generally more powerful as the predictor of job satisfaction than FWC. A comprehensive study undertaken by Bruck et al. (2002) found that WFC and FWC each have a significant effect on both facet and global job satisfaction, but their relationships are significantly stronger to facet job satisfaction than to global job satisfaction. Using samples drawn from five Western countries (US, Canada, Australia, Finland and New Zealand) Lapierre et al. (2008) found that employees' perceptions of their organization family-supportiveness was related to six different dimensions of WFC which, in turn, predicted both job and family satisfaction. It is therefore evident that one consequence of work–family conflict is a reduction in both domain-specific and overall job satisfaction. Research with a wide variety of occupational samples has demonstrated that increased WFC results in reduced job satisfaction.

# GENDER DIFFERENCES IN JOB SATISFACTION

Research exploring the role of gender on job satisfaction mostly focuses on the gender–job satisfaction paradox (Jung et al., 2007; Sousa-Poza and Sousa-Poza, 2000; 2003). Although male workers typically have higher pay and job status compared to female workers, women consistently report higher levels of job satisfaction (Clark, 1997). Clark explained this paradox as a function of lower expectations due to women historically having held lower-level jobs. However, Clark also found that gender-based job satisfaction differences disappeared for younger and higher-educated workers, professionals, managerial-level employees, workers whose mother had a professional job and those working in male-dominated workplaces. Clark therefore suggested that the phenomenon of the gender job satisfaction paradox may be transitory and not permanent. The results of a recent cross-country study undertaken by Kaiser (2005) also supported the findings of Clark. Investigations by both Gazioglu and Tansel (2002) and Bender et al. (2005) confirmed that women report higher job satisfaction than men. Bender et al. also reported that women working in female-dominated workplaces have higher levels of job satisfaction.

However, evidence also indicates that the generality of the gender–job satisfaction paradox is not valid for all countries. Sousa-Poza and Sousa-Poza (2000) found that women report higher job satisfaction levels than men in only eight of the 21 countries studied. Furthermore in only four countries (Great Britain, US, Hungary and New Zealand) was the difference larger than 5 per cent. A recent study conducted in Korea (Jung et al., 2007) found no systematic difference in job satisfaction between female and male workers. Furthermore gender-based inconsistencies in satisfaction with job security, personal development, salary and human relations were reported. These findings suggest that gender influences may depend on specific job facets.

More recent studies have confirmed Clark's (1997) prediction that gender differences in job satisfaction may be transitory. Sousa-Poza and Sousa-Poza (2003) analysed job satisfaction differences between UK men and women and showed that the positive job satisfaction differential between women and men halved during the past decade. While men's job satisfaction remained constant through the decade, the reduction in the job satisfaction differential was attributed to the sharp decline in women's job satisfaction during this period.

## METHODOLOGICAL ISSUES

There are a number of methodological issues that need to be addressed to advance empirical research in job satisfaction. In the beginning of this chapter we referred to the controversies surrounding the definition of job satisfaction; reaching a consensus among scholars on an agreed definition of job satisfaction has been problematic. This difficulty has manifested itself in the development of numerous scales to measure the construct. The first question from a construct validity perspective is 'do all these scales measure the same phenomenon?' In a systematic review of 29 instruments used in job satisfaction research, van Saane et al. (2003) found that only seven instruments met their psychometric quality criteria (internal consistency, convergent validity, discriminant validity and content validity).

The most frequently used measure of job satisfaction, the Job Descriptive Index (JDI; Smith et al. 1969), did not meet several of the quality criteria. This is a problem because the use of measures that are not reliable and valid indicators of the intended theoretical construct can result in inconsistent findings.

As was identified earlier in this chapter, the use of facet job satisfaction scores to compute a single unitary score for job satisfaction is problematic. For instance many researchers have used the procedure of summing the five subscales scores on the JDI to compute an overall unitary score for the job satisfaction construct (Ironson et al., 1989). This practice is problematic because the JDI subscales were constructed to measure five distinct areas, and so these subscales represent five distinct factors. Edwards and Parry (1993) stated that combining conceptually distinct elements into a single index score precludes clear interpretation; a composite index conceals the contribution of each element to the overall score. Edwards and Parry argued that the elements combined do not contribute equally; the contribution of each element is determined not by its weight, but by the variances and co-variances of the element measures. The implication of this point is that there may be considerable conceptual ambiguity in interpreting the scores of combined indices.

A third methodological issue pertains to the use of cross-section designs in job satisfaction. Most studies in job satisfaction employ a quantitative methodology. By using this method researchers are able to test the existing theory and make predictions based on the level of generality obtained from the results. However, these advantages can only be obtained if the data used in the analysis is appropriate and the research instruments used in obtaining the data are valid and reliable (Schwab, 2005). In reality most job satisfaction studies use cross-sectional data based on self-reporting survey instruments. This type of data is considered inadequate if it is used as the basis for making generalizations of job satisfaction in other organizational settings or for predicting future job satisfaction conditions. Excessive reliance on self-report measures tends to overestimate the magnitude of observed correlations and is complicated by problems of common method variance (Spector, 1994). The use of different methods and sources of data, in combination with self-reported data, is important in reducing problems arising from this subjective measurement.

Finally the issue of causality and spurious relationships between job satisfaction and other variables are also crucial in job satisfaction research. These problems usually arise if the theories and models used in the research are not rigorous and the results from prior studies do not provide a consistent direction. However, the use of strong theory and clear models is insufficient if the research only uses cross-sectional data: 'simultaneity bias' obstructs the identification of actual causality among variables (Fischer and Sousa-Poza, 2008). Even the use of structural equation modelling cannot overcome these problems (Spector, 1994). The issue of causality can be better addressed if the data has longitudinal or panel characteristics (Ferrer-i-Carbonell and Frijters, 2004; Fischer and Sousa-Poza, 2006).

## CONCLUSION

This chapter reviewed the recent literature on job satisfaction. We discussed difficulties in reaching a consensus in the definition of job satisfaction and the common measurement issues surrounding the construct. The review showed job satisfaction remains a widely used construct within organizational research. We explicated the key tenets of four theories of job satisfaction and reviewed the empirical support for these theories. We also reviewed the relationship between job satisfaction and three organizational-level variables (job performance, turnover and absenteeism) and three individual-level variables (personality, employee health and work–family conflict). In the final sections of the chapter we discussed gender differences in job satisfaction and some methodological issues that continue to hamper the potential contribution of the job satisfaction construct in advancing scientific knowledge within industrial and organizational psychology.

From the perspective of occupational psychological health, this review of job satisfaction has produced three core conclusions. First, theoretical models that integrate dispositional and situational factors hold promise for furthering the theoretical understanding of job satisfaction. Second, the relationships between job satisfaction and job performance, absenteeism and turnover confirm the role of job satisfaction in influencing sustainable long-term organizational performance. Finally, research on the relationships between job satisfaction and employee health, personality, and work–life balance suggests that improvements in working conditions would increase employee productivity and well-being, and reduce healthcare costs.

## ACKNOWLEDGMENT

We thank Jerry Marmen Simanjuntak for assistance with the literature review for this chapter.

# 4.  Job support and job control

## INTRODUCTION

In previous chapters we have outlined the fundamental processes involved in the development of personal well-being, and have discussed various work-related factors which can contribute to well-being (and its converse, strain), including both dispositional and situational variables. Two variables which we have not to this point discussed in detail, but which have received considerable attention from both researchers and practitioners, are the amount of social support the individual experiences in their work environment and the level of control that they feel they can exert over that environment. Job-related support and control have been regarded as two highly influential variables, so this chapter is specifically devoted to a discussion of their role in the development and maintenance of positive well-being and the alleviation of work strain. Given that the preponderance of research has focused on strain, rather than more general well-being, for simplicity we will describe the impact of support and control on strain rather than well-being, although the mechanisms and impact are the same (albeit in opposite directions).

Both support and control can function in a variety of ways but there are two major mechanisms by which they influence strain (or well-being). First they can exhibit a direct relationship (correlation) with psychological strain – the more support or control the person experiences, the lower the level of strain they report. Numerous empirical studies have confirmed this direct relationship. Alternatively social support and job control can exert a moderating effect on the relationship between environmental stressors (such as work demands, role conflict, role ambiguity) and psychological strain. This *buffering* effect of these variables is depicted in Figure 4.1.

A moderator is a third variable which influences the relationship between two other variables, serving either to increase or decrease the correlation between the predictor variable (such as stressors) and the criterion variable (such as psychological strain). Hence the relationship between the predictor variable and the criterion variable depends on the level of the moderator (support or control). Moderator effects are typically assessed as the interaction between predictor and moderator variables. Although several different kinds of moderators have been examined in research on

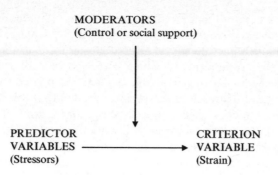

Figure 4.1    *Moderating effects of job control and social support*

work-related strain and well-being, our focus will be on social support and job control.

By and large, research on job control and job support has built upon a model of stress proposed by Karasek (1979). Karasek's model is referred to as the *demand–control* model of strain but also known as the *demand– discretion* model or the *decision latitude* model (Fox et al., 1993). The original model proposed that although excessive job demands (such as workload) are associated with higher levels of psychological strain and even physiological health outcomes (such as cardiovascular disease; Kristensen, 1996), the effect of these demands on the person will be alleviated by the perception that one has control over them. Indeed highly challenging or demanding work combined with a high level of control is regarded by Karasek as reflecting an 'active' job which has beneficial outcomes for the person. Conversely, where a job contains high demands but there is little or no perceived control over these demands, the individual will experience a considerable amount of psychological strain.

The rationale underlying the demand–control model has been clearly explicated by Fox et al. (1993), among others. High work demands are stressful because they create anxiety not only about job performance but also about the consequences of not being able to complete one's work within the necessary time period. This anxiety can be ameliorated if the individual (a) has the power to make decisions about their work (referred to as *decision authority*); and (b) can use a variety of skills in their work (*skill discretion*). These two factors have normally been combined by researchers into a single construct referred to as *decision latitude* or *control*. In essence the extent of control that individuals feel they can exert over important elements of their work, especially their workload, will function as a buffer against the negative impact of these work elements. There is consensus among researchers that appropriate levels of perceived control over the work environment are important for an individual's well-being, especially in terms of stress reduction and even physical health status (as we discussed in Chapter 2).

However, the mechanisms by which perceived control exerts its influence are less clear, and the available evidence is not consistent. From their own research Karasek and associates argued that job demands and control have interactive effects on well-being: that is control functions as a moderator of the relationship between work demands and psychological strain. However, in some research the extent of control was not measured directly but was inferred from formal occupational classification profiles: this can create uncertainties as to whether such profiles provide an accurate reflection of the amount of control any individual *actually* possesses, or whether they *perceive* that they have control over their work. This latter issue is critical as it has often been suggested that objectively defined levels of control are not the most important predictor of worker reactions, but rather of how much control the person *thinks* or *perceives* they can exert.

Johnson and Hall (1988) later expanded the demand–control model to include social support as another potential buffering variable. Their model became known as the *demand–control–support* model. In brief Johnson and Hall suggested that social support (especially from work colleagues, supervisors or managers) will function as a further moderator of relationships between job demands and worker well-being, and that the buffering effects of control will be most evident when individuals receive support from their work environment. In effect the demand–control–support model posits a three-way interaction: job demands × job control × social support.

We next examine the role of job control in the maintenance of worker well-being. As noted above, research on this topic has predominantly used the demand–control model as a theoretical platform although other theoretical approaches have also been tested. We will focus on social support. Our intention here is to review relatively recent research to illustrate prominent themes, rather than providing an exhaustive review of the extensive literature on each of these two variables. We conclude the chapter with some integrative comments concerning control and support.

## JOB CONTROL

As already mentioned, one of the situational factors which has consistently been demonstrated to ameliorate the negative impact of work-related stressors (such as high work demands, lack of time, role conflict and role ambiguity) on the amount of psychological strain an individual experiences, is the degree of autonomy or control a person feels they have over their environment. We regard perceived control as a *situational* factor (rather than a dispositional variable) because it reflects the individual's perceptions of their environment rather than a trans-situational disposition. In other words a person may believe that they have a high level of autonomy and control in one situation but not in another. This aspect differentiates perceived control from the more generalized *locus of control*, which is defined as a dispositional tendency to perceive events and outcomes in one's life as being under one's own control or as being controlled by sources such as luck, fate or other people (Rotter, 1966).

A substantial volume of research has been published over the past 25 years demonstrating that appropriate levels of perceived control can make a substantial difference to a person's well-being, although there are circumstances (which we examine later) where increased control may in fact have negative repercussions. As discussed above, Karasek's demand–control model has been the starting point for much of the research on this topic. However, there is still debate about whether the effects of control are direct or indirect. Here we present a selection of studies that have investigated the possible functions of perceived control.

A comprehensive review of predictions from Karasek's (1979) job demand–control model was presented by de Lange et al. (2003) who noted that the demand–control model 'has been a leading work-stress model in occupational health psychology since the 1980s' (p. 282), but that previous reviews have reached indefinite conclusions about the role of control. De Lange and colleagues suggested that there is no doubt that control is important and that it can have direct (negative) relationships with strain; the real issue is whether or not it also has buffering effects and if so, under what conditions. Unfortunately, as noted by de Lange et al. much research in this field has been cross-sectional in design, which therefore limits our ability to draw conclusions about cause–effect relationships. For this reason the researchers constrained their review to studies which incorporated a longitudinal design. This resulted in a selection of 45 studies published between 1979 and 2000. Of these 45 papers only 19 (42 per cent) met the criteria established by the authors for inclusion in the review: (a) two or more waves of data collection; (b) based on the demand–control or demand–control–support models; (c) self-report measures of demands, control and support were collected; and (d) the study was published before or in 2000. Their review of these articles led de Lange et al. to question the validity of the demand–control model proposed by Karasek; only modest support was found for the strain hypothesis (that a combination of demands and control predicts strain better than either variable alone), and few interaction effects (demands × control) were observed across studies. Lack of multiplicative (interaction) effects does not necessarily undermine the importance of job control – it simply implies that it may not always function as a buffering variable.

Bakker and Demerouti (2007) conceptualized control as one of many resources that an individual may be able to mobilize to combat the impact of stress on their well-being. They noted that autonomy or control can be beneficial because the person can decide for themselves how to deal with work demands and hence develop a coping strategy that is most appropriate for them personally. However, empirical support for the buffering effect of control is far from consistent, potentially indicating that control 'is only partly able to buffer the impact of job demands on employee well-being' (p. 310). Bakker and Demerouti's Job Demands–Resources (JD–R) model represents an expansion of the demand–control–support model, incorporating other resources (physical, psychological, social or organizational) which individuals might utilize in their efforts to deal with work stressors. The JD–R model is discussed in detail in the following chapter (Chapter 5).

Boswell et al. (2004) noted that stressors can be classified as either *hindrance* stressors or *challenge* stressors. Hindrance stressors are those which potentially impede a person's work performance or functioning and which may be (perceived as) threatening to their psychological or even physical well-being. Challenge stressors, on the other hand, are 'work-related demands or circumstances that, although potentially stressful, have associated gains' for the person (Cavanaugh et al., 2000, p. 12). Boswell and her associates found that control only served as a moderating variable in the relationship between hindrance stressors and psychological strain (anxiety and emotional exhaustion); there was no significant interaction between challenge stressors and job control. One possible limitation in this study, however, was that hindrance and challenge stressors were pre-defined by the researchers (using items developed by Cavanaugh et al.) and there was no assessment of whether the various work demands were perceived by individuals themselves as being a hindrance or a challenge, which would be necessary for a comprehensive test of this hypothesis.

Mikkelsen et al. (2005) speculated that one of the reasons for the burgeoning interest in control during the 1980s and early 1990s was that in Europe at least, there was an increased emphasis on providing workers with more control over their work environments. In the late 1990s, however, increases in job control 'have levelled off or have declined slightly' (p. 154) and one survey cited by Mikkelsen et al. suggested that about one third of workers reported having little or no control over their work. Mikkelsen et al. attributed this trend (toward reduced control) to the changing economic and market environment in which today's organizations need to operate and which has led to greater time constraints, higher work intensity, a tightening of controls and reduced autonomy for individual employees. They observed that new technologies require different skills and place different demands on workers compared with the demands Karasek and others considered within the demand–control model. Specifically Mikkelsen et al. suggested that 'new technologies in production and communication increase the requirements for *cognitive* abstract qualifications, for example, decision-making, more profound understanding of complex organizations, and the ability to analyse and solve problems in unexpected situations' (2005, p. 155). They added that in some occupational sectors such as human services, emotional labour demands (dealing with clients or customers) can also have a significant impact on the person (as we discussed in Chapter 2).

The implication of this reasoning is that the type of demands impinging upon workers may extend beyond simple quantitative workload, which has been the primary focus of the demand–control model. In addition there needs to be differentiation between the types of control that individuals can exert. Mikkelsen et al. (2005) distinguished between *horizontal (task) control* and *vertical (more general) control*. While task control is constrained to particular situations or job roles, vertical control refers to the extent to which the individual has influence over broader organizational decisions and changes. Both forms of control may be important, and it is critical to examine each of these separately and in combination. Hence Mikkelsen and colleagues tested an extended version of the demand–control model which examined how different dimensions of job demands interact with both task control and decision authority. Mikkelsen et al. did find some evidence of moderating effects for control, although these effects were relatively weak and the number of significant demand × control interactions was small (less than 20 per cent of the total number of interaction terms tested). Nevertheless Mikkelsen et al. cautioned against abandonment of the interaction hypothesis, suggesting that 'it is useful to know that skill discretion may moderate the relationship between emotional demands and adverse health effects' (p. 172). In other words it is likely that certain types of control may indeed buffer the negative impact of various forms of demands, highlighting the need for research to discriminate further between both types of control as well as demands.

It is also important to ensure a match between the demands and forms of control investigated. Over 12 years ago Wall and his colleagues (Wall et al., 1996) noted that research on the demand–control model often investigated global measures of both demands and control, which may account for the lack of demand × control interaction effects obtained. Wall et al. argued that there needed to be a correspondence between the form of control and the demand. For instance if a person is confronted by extreme pressure to perform a task rapidly and accurately, having control over when they start and finish work may be irrelevant to the strain they experience as a consequence of these demands. In their research Wall et al. found that when control was linked to the specific demands there was a greater likelihood of obtaining a significant moderation effect on three well-being indicators (job satisfaction, anxiety and depression). With a few exceptions (for example Mikkelsen et al., 2005), research has, however, continued to utilize more generic measures of demand and control, and the matching hypothesis has not been consistently examined in empirical studies.

Another consideration is that there may be other variables which function as moderators. This possibility was explored by Schaubroeck and Merritt (1997) who examined the role of self-efficacy in the context of the demand–control model. Schaubroeck and Merritt suggested that individuals with high dispositional self-efficacy have more confidence in their ability to exercise control, which can in turn lead to more beneficial outcomes in high-demand/high-control situations. Conversely, lower levels of control in demanding situations may induce less strain for people with low self-efficacy because they do not feel personally responsible for the situation. Under these circumstances affording low self-efficacy employees more control may be counterproductive, leading to an exacerbation rather than an alleviation of job-related strain. A corollary of this idea is that it may be as important to elevate self-efficacy (and self-esteem) as it is to increase control.

De Witte et al. (2007) also noted that the demand–control model may be applicable to some groups of workers more than others. Their research sampled young (<23 years old) workers in their first job on the assumption that job characteristics may have more impact on this group of workers, compared to older and more experienced workers. De Witte et al. obtained evidence for both additive and multiplicative (interactive) effects of job demands and control in this sample, with autonomy buffering the negative consequences of high workload on job satisfaction. One implication of these findings is that future research should examine age and levels of experience as possible moderators in tests of the demand–control model.

Control may also be differentially important to people at various levels within an organization. For some individuals such as those in managerial roles, having a high level of autonomy and control may be an extremely important dimension in terms of both their job performance and their personal well-being. A recent study by Wong et al. (2007) supported this notion. Wong et al. found that task interdependence (having to work collaboratively with others) had a substantial impact on reducing managers' role stressors (role ambiguity and role conflict). Specifically job control was associated with lower role ambiguity when task interdependence was low (the manager could function relatively independently of others), but not when there was high interdependence. This suggests that the buffering effect of job control may be contingent upon other factors, especially the extent to which managers are required to work interdependently.

Research such as that reported by Schaubroeck and Merritt (1997) and Wong et al. (2007) is important because it suggests that simplistic models may be inadequate to account for the complexity of stressor–strain relationships. Further work is needed to tease out whether other dispositional variables in addition to self-efficacy, contribute to the interaction between job demands and job control. Other situational variables such as the nature of the task performed could also be considered.

## SOCIAL SUPPORT

As with perceived control a substantial proportion of research on social support and strain has built upon the (expanded) demand–control–support model (Johnson and Hall, 1988) which suggests that like control, social support (from work colleagues, supervisors and other significant people) will buffer the impact of stressors on strain and other indicators of well-being. This is known as the *stress-buffering hypothesis* and has been the subject of empirical investigation for over 30 years. Numerous investigations have illustrated the important role that social support from other people can play in the alleviation of job-related strain and the enhancement of positive well-being. Less clear, however, is whether support functions as a buffering variable.

Before discussing the potential functions of social support it is important to differentiate between the various kinds of support that may be available to a person in their work environment. Several definitions of social support have been proposed by social scientists, but in the field of organizational research the conceptualization articulated by House (1981) has been most frequently adopted:

1. *Instrumental support* (providing practical help to solve a problem)
2. *Emotional support* (showing an awareness and understanding of the other person's situation, along with caring and empathizing with that person's difficulties)
3. *Information support* (giving information which may help the person deal with their problems – this is sometimes viewed as a sub-category of instrumental support)

4.  *Appraisal support* (providing feedback on the other person's function-
    ing that may enhance their self-esteem).

These different forms of support can have differential effects on individual levels of stress and well-being, depending on the type of support that
(a) might be most applicable in the situation and (b) that the individual
would like to receive. Some efforts have been made to examine the different types of support. For instance Lawrence et al. (2007) developed an
inventory which assesses three sources of support (supervisor, colleague
and non-work support) and four distinct support functions (emotional,
informational, instrumental and appraisal). Unfortunately researchers
have not often examined the *kind of support desired* when they have
explored the impact of social support on psychological strain and well-
being, and as we discuss below, there is an implicit assumption that more
support (irrespective of its desirability) will contribute to reduced strain.

A related issue is the distinction between support which is perceived to
be *available* and that which is *actually used*. Research has not always clari-
fied which of these variables is being investigated and there is sometimes
a confusion between them. The issue of whether available support or utilized support is the more critical variable has not yet been fully resolved.
On the one hand simply having support available in times of need may be
sufficient to alleviate strain (at least to some extent) because the person
feels that help, advice or emotional support is there if they need it. On the
other hand full stress buffering may require support to actually be utilized.
A resolution of this issue has yet to be confirmed empirically.

Finally there is considerable debate in the literature on the difference
between *perceived* social support (that is, the amount of support an individual believes they have available or that they are using) versus *objective*
support (typically as judged by others). The question here is which is more
important – what the person believes they receive or some 'objective'
measure of the amount of support available/received. From Lazarus's
transactional perspective (Lazarus, 1966; Lazarus and Folkman, 1984)
individual perceptions are paramount in determining the level of strain
experienced, but relatively few studies have compared perceived versus
objective support.

With these observations in mind we now summarize some of the
research literature on the effects of social support on work-related strain
(and by implication, well-being). Our focus here is on work stressors and
work-based social support rather than more general (non-work) forms of
support, although this non-work support can also be salient to the reduction of work-related strain. Social support may be influential in at least
three distinct ways. First it may directly reduce strain, irrespective of the

number or intensity of stressors encountered. This is perhaps the simplest effect of the three and can be illustrated by a significant zero-order correlation between support and (reduced) strain. One explanation for this main effect is that support may increase a person's self-esteem and feelings of self-worth, making them less vulnerable or susceptible to the negative impact of stressors. A recent study by Escriba-Aguir and Pèrez-Hoyos (2007) examined the effect of the psychosocial work environment (including both job control and social support from supervisors and co-workers) on levels of psychological strain and emotional exhaustion among Spanish doctors and nurses. These investigators found that low job control and low social support were directly associated with reduced well-being among doctors, but that low social support (from their supervisors) was linked with low mental health in doctors and greater emotional exhaustion among nurses.

A second mechanism reflects a mediational effect (see Figure 4.2) where encountering stressors induces the person to mobilize their resources, including social support, in an effort to combat stressors. Thirdly, as depicted in Figure 4.1, social support may serve as a moderator of the relationship between stressors and strain – this is the classic *stress-buffering hypothesis*. That is, when individuals utilize social support, the link between stressors and strain is diminished because support protects or shields them from the potentially adverse effects of the stressors, either directly (in the case of practical help) or perhaps indirectly (modifying their perceptions of the stressors). Of course it is possible that all three of the above mechanisms may be in operation even though research has concentrated predominantly on the direct and the moderating (buffering) effect.

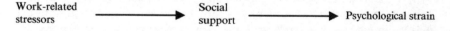

Work-related stressors ⟶ Social support ⟶ Psychological strain

*Figure 4.2  Social support as a mediator between work stressors and strain*

As noted earlier most research on social support in work environments has been developed (either explicitly or implicitly) from the expanded version of the demand–control (support) model, although only a minority of studies have concurrently assessed both control and support as moderator variables. In an innovative assessment of stress-buffering, Jones and her colleagues (Jones et al., 2007) examined the relationship of daily events with changes in mood and physical health among workers in a government organization. Jones et al. noted that the *iso-strain* hypothesis, which is reflected in the expanded demand–control–support model, has been partially confirmed in previous investigations; however, one limitation is that this research may have focused on distal rather than proximal stressors.

Jones et al. also argued that it is important to examine within-person fluc-
tuations in experiences (on a daily basis) to test the iso-strain hypothesis
adequately. In their investigation these authors found that daily variations
in mood and work hours were more predictive than distal characteristics
(demands, control, support) of health behaviours, and that 'individuals may
adapt to daily variations in affect and work hours in diverse ways depending on the constraints and freedoms offered by their job' (p. 1738). This
conclusion does not undermine the salience of control and social support,
but places these variables in context. As commented above it is important
to consider the forms of support and the person's desire for support, not
simply whether support is available. As Jones et al.'s findings illustrate, it
is also important to examine variations within the person, which requires a
longitudinal approach to the assessment of stress-buffering.

Beehr et al. (2000) examined job stressors and social support from work
colleagues in relation to both psychological strain and job performance
among university students who worked full-time as door-to-door sales-
persons during the summer. They found that the amount of functional
support received from co-workers was directly linked with reduced strain
(although not so much with performance) but support did not moderate
relationships between generic and job-specific stressors and strain. Beehr
et al. noted that the failure to obtain significant moderator effects may be
due to methodological issues and hence the search for possible buffering
effects of social support should not be abandoned.

A relevant consideration when examining the role of social support in
reducing work-related strain and promoting well-being is the *matching*
hypothesis (referred to earlier) which suggests that support that is appropriate to the stressor should have more beneficial effects than support
that is unrelated to the stressor. For example if a person is confronted by
excessive workload, practical help in reducing that workload or perhaps
information on how to manage the workload better may be more advantageous than simply being empathic (emotional support). In other cases,
however, emotional support may be more salient to the person than direct
assistance. Thus support should also be matched with specific outcomes.

Luszczynska and Cieslak (2005) examined this idea along with the potentially moderating role of two dispositional variables (hardiness and emotional
reactivity) in a sample of managerial personnel. They hypothesized that hardiness would moderate the impact of social support on psychological distress
such that hardy managers would have less need for social support than their
counterparts who were less hardy. Conversely among managers with high
emotional reactivity (more intense reactions to emotion-generating events),
higher social support was predicted to function as a buffering variable. These
predictions were confirmed; buffering effects occurred when managers were

low on hardiness and high on emotional reactivity. These findings suggest that dispositional variables may themselves function as moderators of the moderating effect of social support. There is clearly a need for further assessment of other factors (both situational and dispositional) that may condition the buffering impact of social support.

While some researchers (for example Sargent and Terry, 2000) have obtained the predicted interaction between social support and job-related stressors, confirmation of the buffering hypothesis is by no means universal. Other studies have either found no interaction effect at all or in some cases a *reverse buffering* effect has been observed. Reverse buffering occurs when the presence of social support exacerbates rather than alleviates the negative impact of a stressor. This (seemingly counter-intuitive) phenomenon was identified by LaRocco et al. (1980) and observed directly by Kaufmann and Beehr (1986), who found that under certain conditions, higher levels of social support were associated with more rather than less psychological strain. This may occur when other people confirm the person's beliefs about the aversive nature of a work environment (for example 'We talk about the bad things in our work') which then leads the individual to experience even more strain. Deelstra and associates (2003) also noted that sometimes individuals might not want help or support from their work colleagues as the provision of help can undermine their feelings of competence or self-efficacy. Although reverse buffering is not the most prevalent effect of social support, its occurrence indicates that the impact of support is neither simple nor unilinear (Cooper et al., 2001).

Other research findings suggest that as with job control, the effects of social support may be additive rather than interactive. That is, the additive combination of low levels of stressors and high support contributes to reduced strain rather than the stressor × support interaction (McClenahan et al., 2007; Morrison and Payne, 2001). Although from a practical viewpoint this may not be a significant issue, it has considerable implications for theoretical models (such as the demand–control–support model) that endeavour to explain *how* support functions to alleviate strain.

In summary numerous questions remain about the role that workplace social support plays in the reduction of psychological (and even physical) strain. On balance the weight of evidence favours a direct effect: the availability and usage of support can alleviate levels of strain and enhance a person's overall well-being irrespective of the presence of work stressors. Whether or not there is also a moderating effect of social support appears to depend on a variety of other factors. Under certain conditions buffering would appear to occur, especially if (a) the individual wants to receive support; (b) the type of support is matched with the stressor/s; and (c) it can actually assist the person in dealing with the stressful work environment (either directly or indirectly). However the 'wrong' types of support or inappropriate (unwanted) levels of support can induce *more* rather than less strain, resulting in a reverse buffering effect.

More research is needed to tease out other factors that may influence the effects of social support on strain and well-being. For instance it is clear that dispositional variables (such as negative affectivity, emotional reactivity and self-efficacy) may themselves function as moderators of relationships between support and strain. We also suggested above that situational factors may also impinge upon these relationships. In addition it is critical for researchers to disentangle various sources of support. For instance a worker may welcome practical help from a colleague but resent the same help being offered by their supervisor (due to perceptions of incompetence). There are also situations in which excessive support may be overwhelming for the person and (again) be viewed as a lack of faith in their ability to complete the job. All of these factors need to be considered when research on social support and its impact is being conducted.

## CONCLUSION

To summarize the issues that we have discussed in this chapter, it is evident that (perceived) control over the job and work environment along with social support from one's colleagues, supervisor and other people can play a very significant role in the determination of levels of psychological strain and consequent well-being. The research discussed here illustrates that control and support are important variables, which have both theoretical and practical relevance. Obtaining the right 'mix' of these variables can have major implications for individuals and organizations as they endeavour to enhance their quality of work life and (indirectly at least) maintain or increase productivity. A huge amount of research has been conducted over the past 30 years or so on both job control and social support. A large proportion of this research has been derived from Karasek's (1979) job demands–control model and expanded by Johnson and Hall (1988) into the demands–control–support model. These theoretical models posit interactions between demands, control and support. However, evidence for these interactions has been far from consistent and in many cases additive rather than interactive effects have been observed from control and support. In addition too much control and too much support can be counterproductive, leading to increased rather than ameliorated strain. From a practical perspective the key is to ascertain appropriate levels of these factors as well as the right 'types' of control and support.

# 5. Occupational stress and coping

## OVERVIEW

This chapter reviews some of the recent advances in the research concerning occupational stress, and coping. We begin by discussing the Job Demands–Resources model which has recently emerged as an occupational stress theory. We also review advances in coping research including the focus on positive emotions in the coping process and we evaluate some current issues surrounding the definitions and measurements of psychological burnout. Finally we discuss the rather limited progress made by stress management intervention research and we identify the characteristics included in effective organizational interventions.

## RECENT ADVANCES IN OCCUPATIONAL STRESS AND COPING THEORIES

Fifty years or so of occupational stress research has produced a number of theories describing the antecedents, consequences or the processes involved between occupational stress, individual and organizational outcomes and the variables which influence these associations. The theories still in common application today include, for example, Karasek's (1979) Job Demands–Control model and its extension to the Job Demands–Control–Support model (Johnson and Hall, 1988; described in Chapter 4), the Person–Environment Fit model (French et al., 1982), the Vitamin Stress model (Warr, 2005), and the Work Stress model (Cooper, 2005). These theories are widely described within the literature (for example O'Driscoll et al., 2008) and we will not therefore replicate these discussions here. In this chapter instead we review some of the newly defined occupational stress and coping theories, with a view to evaluating their current or potential contribution to this field. We focus specifically upon the Job Demands–Resources theory (Demerouti et al., 2001), adaptive coping (Folkman and Moskowitz, 2003) and psychological burnout (Kristensen et al., 2005; Maslach et al., 1996).

## The Job Demands–Resources Model

The Job Demands–Resources model (JD–R; Demerouti et al., 2001) proposes that all occupations contain job demands and resources that influence individual and organizational outcomes. The JD–R model is thus a specific application of Hobfoll's (1989) *Conservation of Resources theory* (COR) which similarly proposed that 'people strive to retain, protect and build resources and that what is threatening to them is the potential or actual loss of these valued resources' (Hobfoll, 1989, p. 513). Hobfoll defined resources as properties in the environment that can be utilized such as personal characteristics, time, money, knowledge, objects (home, car and other material possessions) or support. Hobfoll described stress as occurring when resources are lost in the process of coping with the demands of both work and non-work life. This (potential or actual) loss results in life dissatisfaction, job dissatisfaction, depression, anxiety and stress. Behaviours such as absenteeism and turnover occur in order to replace or protect the threatened resources, otherwise individual resources may become so depleted that burnout or depression ensues (Grandey and Cropanzano, 1999).

The JD–R theory contains a similar proposition to the COR theory in that occupational stress is defined as resource gains or losses. The JD–R theory proposes two processes by which this stress–strain relationship occurs (see Figure 5.1). First an *energy process* exists whereby demands perceived as stressful and threatening produce exhaustion, ill health and burnout. Second a *motivational process* exists whereby a lack of resources further exacerbates job demands leading to withdrawal and disengagement from work. The JD–R theory defines *resources* as aspects of the work environment that promote positive outcomes (for example employee engagement) by reducing the impact of high job demands, stimulating personal growth and development, or by facilitating the achievement of work goals. Thus resources include job control, qualifications, participation in decision-making, task variety and support from colleagues, family or friends. *Job demands* are the 'physical, social or organizational aspects of the job that require sustained physical or mental effort and are therefore associated with certain physiological and psychological costs' (Demerouti et al., 2001, p. 501).

Note the JD–R theory is formally defined as a theory of burnout (Demerouti et al., 2001); however, we have described it here as being a new development in occupational stress research. We acknowledge that the JD–R model can be employed to measure occupational stress that may or may not result in psychological burnout. Hence the JD–R model is being included in occupational stress research more generally than was

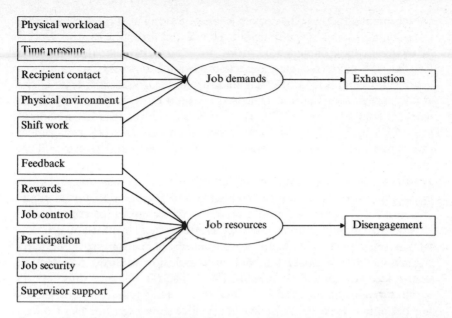

*Source:*    From Demerouti et al. (2001). Reproduced with permission from the publisher.

*Figure 5.1    The Job Demands–Resources model of burnout*

perhaps its initial intention and also as an expansion to occupational stress models such as the Job Demands–Control–Support model (Johnson and Hall, 1988).

Although the JD–R theory is a relatively new description of occupational stress and burnout, the work of the theory's authors in the Netherlands has resulted in a substantial number of applications of this model. Bakker et al. (2003), for example, applied the JD–R model to employees of a Dutch call centre and demonstrated that job demands such as work/task pressures, computer problems and emotional pressures significantly predicted employee health and sickness absenteeism. Job resources (such as social support, supervisor support, job control and performance feedback) were each significantly associated with job involvement and negatively associated with turnover intentions.

The robustness of the JD–R model across different occupations and nationalities has also been demonstrated. Llorens et al. (2006), for example, reported that the JD–R model was applicable across Dutch and Spanish samples in tests with different occupational groups and with different data-gathering techniques (pen and pencil versus computerized surveys). Llorens et al. demonstrated that job resources influenced organizational commitment directly via increasing levels of job engagement and indirectly by reducing psychological burnout. Hence the focus on *positive* aspects of the work environment (increasing job resources) as well as *negative* job characteristics (reducing job demands) appears to enhance employee health and commitment. Similar findings were produced in tests of the JD–R model with Finnish dentists (Hakanen et al., 2005) and Finnish teachers (Bakker et al., 2007). These two latter investigations supported the proposition that job resources increase levels of work engagement during periods of high job demands. Finally Lewig and Dollard (2003) demonstrated in a sample of Australian call centre employees that the JD–R model was a stronger predictor of both job satisfaction and emotional exhaustion, as compared to either the Job Demands–Control model (Karasek, 1979) or the Effort–Reward Imbalance model (Siegrist, 1988).

More recent applications of the JD–R model have included objective as well as self-report assessments, a web-based application providing users with immediate personal feedback and inclusion in stress intervention studies (see Bakker and Demerouti, 2007). The JD–R model thus appears to be a promising advance in occupational stress research, demonstrating both theoretical and applied applications among samples of different occupations and nationalities. We predict the popularity of this new occupational stress theory will continue for some time.

### Advances in Coping Research

Significant progress in both the theoretical and applied aspects of occupational stress has occurred over the past few decades, as was discussed above. However, coping research has generally achieved far more modest outcomes. Discussions continue concerning the most appropriate definitions, measurements and taxonomies of coping. Indeed coping has become such a 'difficult' construct to research that it is often excluded from stress investigations. This exclusion is in stark contrast to the recognition of the centrality of coping to the stress process as was originally defined by Folkman, Lazarus and colleagues. The transactional stress and coping theory (Lazarus, 1966) and more recent theories such as Edwards' (1988) cybernetic coping theory defined coping as an individual response maintaining a state of equilibrium and thus preserving well-being. Exactly *how* these coping responses fit within the psychological stress process and how coping should be best measured remains under discussion.

Several decades of coping research have succeeded in drawing our attention to the identification of coping as a *state-based* or a *trait-based* individual response and the corresponding qualitative and/or quantitative measurement techniques which accompany these responses (see O'Driscoll et al., 2008). However, it is noticeable that many researchers fail to identify the basic type of coping they propose to assess, and this oversight partly explains the lack of adequate progress in coping research. Some recent discussions suggest, for example, that *future-oriented proactive coping* may be a significant advancement to coping research (Folkman and Moskowitz, 2004). Future-oriented coping identifies ways in which individuals can best cope with an anticipated future stressor such as an examination, medical procedure or work restructure. Hence the focus in future-oriented coping is training individuals to cope with *future* stressors, as opposed to evaluating the coping strategies individuals used to manage past stressors. Common proactive coping strategies which can be 'stored' in readiness to cope with a future stressor include recognition and appraisal of the stressor, preliminary coping responses, building resources (temporal, social or financial) and requesting feedback about one's efforts (Aspinwall, 2004). Training individuals in the use of future-oriented proactive coping may be a useful method for increasing the impact of organizational stress management programmes.

A second interesting area of coping research focuses upon positive coping, defined as the occurrence of positive emotions within the stress and coping process (Folkman, 2008; Folkman and Moskowitz, 2004). Folkman argued that both positive and negative coping responses may occur in reaction to a stressor, and furthermore that positive and negative coping elicit distinct processes, behaviours and resource use. Negative coping is the traditional form of coping and focuses on reducing distress. Positive coping in contrast focuses on the meaningfulness of situations/ life to each individual and has been termed a 'health protector' (Folkman, 2008, p. 4). Folkman cited evidence demonstrating that positive coping responses contributed to improved outcomes (even individual survival) as compared to negative coping responses.

In a revision of the Lazarus and Folkman (1984) stress and coping model (see Figure 5.2) Folkman (2008) suggested that 'there is now substantial evidence that positive emotions are a normative aspect of the stress process and that they help restore physiological and psychosocial coping resources' (p. 11). Folkman also acknowledged that the role of positive coping extends the observation made 30 years ago, that individuals often attribute some positive meaning to a stressor in order to experience a positive moment or a 'breather' (Lazarus et al., 1980). Recent work on the role of *individual resilience* also overlaps with discussions of positive emotion within the stress and coping process (for example Fredrickson et al., 2003). One obvious implication of the positive coping research is the training of individuals in the use of coping strategies that reduce negative emotions and enhance positive emotions.

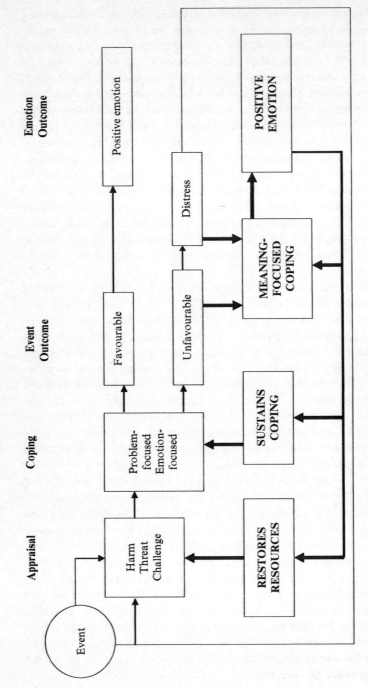

*Note:* New positive coping process highlighted in bold capitalized text.

*Source:* From Folkman (2008). Reproduced with permission from the publisher.

*Figure 5.2 Revised stress and coping model*

Research involving positive coping has also identified the existence of *meaningful coping*. Meaningful coping stems from the positive reappraisal process reported by Lazarus and Folkman (1984): 'Meaningful focused coping is, in its essence, appraisal-based coping in which the person draws on his or her beliefs (e.g., religious, spiritual, or beliefs about justice), values (e.g., "mattering"), and existential goals (e.g., purpose in life or guiding principles) to motivate and sustain coping and well-being during a difficult time' (Folkman, 2008, p. 7). Meaningful coping therefore focuses on the *individual growth* resulting from a stressor, although it is not yet clear exactly how this growth can be accurately measured. We consider these recent developments in coping research to be pertinent and a significant advance in this somewhat stagnated field. We look forward to the more detailed insights produced by subsequent occupational stress and coping research that includes future-oriented proactive coping, positive coping and/or meaningful coping.

**Psychological Burnout**

Since Maslach et al. (1996) published their definition of psychological burnout it has become a popular measure of excessive strain, especially for workers within high-stress occupations. Psychological burnout is defined as an extreme consequence of occupational stress that develops over time from excessive job demands, particularly those that involve interactions with other people in the work environment (human-service occupations). Recent research, however, acknowledges that workers employed within non-human-service occupations may also experience burnout (Maslach et al., 2001). Burnout differs from strain in that burnout is a state of *chronic resource depletion*. Maslach et al. (1996) originally described three components of burnout: *emotional exhaustion, depersonalization* and *reduced personal accomplishment* and these components were subsequently revised as *emotional exhaustion, cynicism* and *professional efficacy* (Maslach et al., 2001). Emotional exhaustion concerns the depletion of an individual's emotional resources and is the central component of burnout. Cynicism refers to the negative or indifferent attitudes held by workers and their attempts to distance themselves from their customers/clients/patients. Professional efficacy describes depleted personal accomplishment: workers perceive both their work accomplishments and interactions with their clients negatively and as being unlikely to improve. Burnout is said to occur when all three components are experienced, with the source of the stressor being the interaction between worker and clients. More recent research has queried this tripartite structure of burnout (Taris, 2006; Winwood and Winefield,

2004). Kristensen et al. (2005), for example, demonstrated that emotional exhaustion, cynicism and professional efficacy are three distinct and unrelated dimensions.

The development of burnout is linked with situation factors (job, occupation and organizational characteristics) as well as personal factors (demographics, personality and job attitudes; Maslach et al., 2001). Job demands, working time, social support and control are all associated with the aetiology of burnout. Burnout has been demonstrated to significantly influence organizational citizenship behaviours, productivity and performance (Taris, 2006), job satisfaction and turnover intentions (Lee and Ashforth, 1996), mental health (Shirom, 2005), colleague support, decision-making and skill utilization (Neveu, 2007).

In discussions of gender differences in burnout, a consistent finding is that males tend to score more highly on measures of cynicism and lower on emotional exhaustion than females (Maslach et al., 2001). For example Morgan et al. (2002) demonstrated that male correctional officers reported higher levels of cynicism than female officers. Morgan et al. also noted that hours of work, prison security level and inmate contact were not significantly associated with burnout. In contrast Carlson et al. (2003) in their investigation of occupational stress and burnout also with correctional officers, identified no significant gender differences for cynicism. Instead Carlson et al. demonstrated that female officers reported higher levels of personal accomplishment as compared to their male colleagues. For a recent review of occupational stress and burnout specifically experienced by police officers and correction workers see also Brough and Biggs (2009).

The Maslach Burnout Inventory (MBI) is the most widely employed measure of burnout within the published literature, although other measures such as the Copenhagen Burnout Inventory (CBI; Kristensen et al., 2005) have recently emerged. The CBI is based on the premise that burnout is a state of physical, mental and emotional exhaustion and fatigue that occurs as a result of chronic exposure to situations that are emotionally taxing. The CBI also distinguishes between three specific domains of burnout: personal burnout, work-related burnout and client-related burnout, potentially providing valuable information for stress intervention research. In empirical investigations comparing the CBI and the MBI, the CBI exhibited more robust psychometric properties and a stronger association with criterion variables (Kristensen et al., 2005; Winwood and Winefield, 2004; Yeh et al., 2007).

Considerations for the future developments in the theorizing and measurement of psychological burnout include such issues as the influence of *individual emotions* in the development of burnout, especially

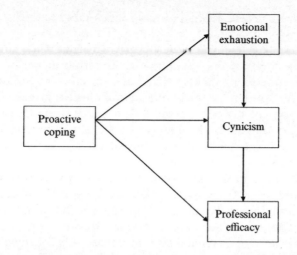

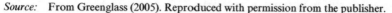

*Source:* From Greenglass (2005). Reproduced with permission from the publisher.

*Figure 5.3 Proactive coping and psychological burnout*

among workers whose work includes a high level of emotional labour (for example Enzmann, 2005). This perspective revives Maslach's original focus concerning the occurrence of burnout by workers encountering the public in human-service type jobs. The influence of *proactive coping* (reviewed above) on the burnout process is also receiving some recent attention. It is hypothesized, for example, that the use of resources activated during proactive coping may help to offset the depletion of resources that occurs during burnout (Greenglass, 2005). This relationship is depicted in Figure 5.3 and appears to be supported by some initial investigations.

Finally research has recently also renewed its interest in *work engagement*, which is the antithesis of burnout. Engagement was included in the original models of burnout (Maslach et al., 1996) but has received renewed interest most noticeably by the Job Demands–Resource model (described above; Demerouti et al., 2001). Schaufeli et al. (2002), for example, defined engagement as 'a positive, fulfilling work-related state of mind that is characterised by vigour, dedication, and absorption. Rather than a momentary and specific state, engagement refers to a more persistent and pervasive affective-cognitive state that is not focused on any particular object, event, individual, or behaviour' (Schaufeli et al., 2002, p. 74). The influence of engagement in the relationships between job resources, job demands and burnout is the focus of some current occupational stress investigations by the authors of this book.

# STRESS MANAGEMENT INTERVENTIONS

Although we have enjoyed twenty years of occupational stress research since Murphy (1988) first identified his tripartite model of stress management interventions (SMIs), the dearth of effective SMIs remains of pressing concern. Unlike many other psychological investigations, SMIs suffer in general from poor research designs, ensuring that the evidence of their effect is diluted. There remains a scarcity of investigations which include objective criteria such as control groups, longitudinal research designs, pre-intervention and post-intervention testing (Caulfield et al., 2004; Zapf et al., 1996). One popular criticism of the stress management training and EAP (Employee Assistance Programmes) approaches to SMIs concerns their *individualistic* approach which typically ignores (or is unable to address) the actual occupational stressors. It is of limited value for example to train or rehabilitate employees only for them to return to the same stressful working environment.

The three-pronged approach to managing occupational stress remains the core model for effective SMIs. Cartwright and Cooper (1997), for example, suggested that by adopting three approaches targeting the prevention and management of stress at work, organizations could achieve a comprehensive strategic framework. Cartwright and Cooper's three approaches reflect Murphy's (1988) original classification: *primary prevention* (stress reduction: redesigning the task or the working environment; participative management; establishing fair employment policies including career development and goal setting; sharing rewards; building cohesive teams; and providing social support), *secondary prevention* (stress management: increasing awareness of occupational stress via individual training and educative activities such as cognitive coping skills; work/lifestyle modification skills; time management courses and assertiveness training), and *tertiary prevention* (the treatment, rehabilitation and recovery of individuals experiencing ill health caused by occupational stress, primarily through the use of employee assistance programmes and workplace counselling; see also Cooper, 2006).

The management of occupational stress achieves the most attention within organizations by focusing on the financial costs of (untreated) stress (such as lost productivity and performance, employee replacement costs, long-term sick leave and rehabilitation costs, costs of litigation and so forth). Ensuring a working environment is both psychologically and physically 'safe' for employees is therefore the focus of many organizations. In the UK, for example, the Health and Safety Executive (HSE) has identified occupational stress as a health problem for a number of decades. The HSE recommends a *risk management approach* as an organizational

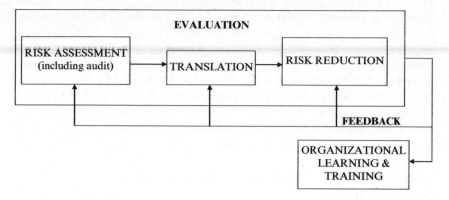

*Source:*   From HSE Report (Cox et al., 2000b). Reproduced with permission from the publisher.

*Figure 5.4    Model of risk management framework for occupational stress*

framework for the effective management of occupational stress. This framework is illustrated in Figure 5.4 and includes the seven core steps for the management of health and safety risks (including stress):

1.   Identification of hazards
2.   Assessments of associated risks
3.   Design of control strategies (interventions)
4.   Implementation of control strategies
5.   Monitoring and evaluation of the effectiveness of control strategies
6.   Feedback and re-assessment of risk
7.   Review of information needs and training needs of employees (Cox et al., 2000b).

The risk management approach recommends the tailoring of stress audits to the specific sample (rather than the use of standardized stress surveys) and a focus at the group-level rather than the individual-level of analysis (thus emphasizing that occupational stress is most effectively addressed as an *organizational* problem rather than an individual issue). This risk management approach has been adopted by various formal bodies, organizations and union groups within the UK, European Union and the US, with the aim of improving the recognition and management of occupational stress (Cox et al., 2000b). Palmer et al. (2004), for example, described a revised work stress model based on the HSE recommendations. The revision acknowledged the influence of organizational culture throughout the six main predictors (potential hazards) of occupational stress: job demands, control, support, relationships, role and change. However, the adoption of this work stress model and of a risk management approach remains grounded in the original tripartite model of SMIs. Palmer et al. stated that 'the main emphasis should be on reducing or eliminating hazards and not solely on stress management courses or training. . . Realistically, in a comprehensive well-being or stress prevention programme, employee counselling, coaching and stress management training have very important roles to play' (p. 5). Thus Murphy's (1988) recommendation for a mixed approach that incorporated two or even all three of the SMI's structures (primary, secondary and tertiary prevention practices) remains as the currently recommended best practice for effective stress management.

Some recent reviews of SMIs have produced pertinent although largely disappointing news. Caulfield et al. (2004), for example, in a review of recent SMIs in Australia, identified only one intervention (from a total of six) that achieved the 'gold-standard' in terms of evidence-based research, that is: 'evidence obtained from a properly conducted study with pre and post measures and a randomized control group' (p. 155). Caulfield et al. also identified that only one of the six interventions was organizationally-focused; the rest adopted individually-focused stress management strategies. Richardson and Rothstein (2008) in their international review identified 38 articles describing SMIs published since 1976 that had appropriate research designs (employee samples, random assignment to treatment and control conditions, appropriately reported statistics and so forth). Only eight of these 38 investigations were focused at the organizational-level of intervention (primary prevention) mainly aimed at improving employee participatory decision-making or social support. Richardson and Rothstein identified that SMIs that included cognitive-behavioural training (increasing perceptions of control, training in proactive coping skills and adaptive behaviours) had the most impact. However, the most *popular* form of intervention (treatment) in these 38 investigations was relaxation training or meditation. These authors also recommended that SMI research include *organizational outcome variables* (stress costs, absenteeism and performance levels) as well as the more popular psychological criterion variables (psychological strain, satisfaction and commitment) so as to improve the evaluation of intervention studies.

In a broad review Hurrell (2005) concluded that SMIs which focused primarily on psychosocial work characteristics (such as increasing levels of control or support) had minimal (long-term) effects. Although interventions that focused on managers and supervisors (such as increasing managerial role clarity, improving leadership skills) did demonstrate some positive effects. Hurrell, however, noted that SMIs that improved the socio-technical job characteristics (workload, work schedules, work hours, job redesign and technical training) produced 'consistent and robust evidence for the efficacy of the intervention' (p. 636). The socio-technical SMIs also tended to have more appropriate research designs (control groups, random allocations) and included objective as well as subjective outcome measures. Hurrell concludes with the observation that 'primary prevention interventions that focus on a few stressors and those that don't try to introduce too many changes too quickly appear to have been most successful' (p. 641).

## CONCLUSION

This chapter focused on recent advancements in occupational stress, coping and burnout research and briefly reviewed the impact of stress management interventions. We noted that whilst being a relatively new theory of occupational stress, the Job Demands–Resources model (Demerouti et al., 2001) has already proven popular and appears to demonstrate fairly robust findings. The measurement of stress in terms of job demands and resources has both theoretical and practical benefits, while the inclusion of both positive and negative pathways has considerable face validity for employees, employers and researchers. We noted that the JD–R model has a number of similarities to theories such as the Conservation of Resources theory (Hobfoll, 1989) and the 'quality of working life' approach to employee health and well-being. This chapter also briefly reviewed recent advances in coping, which is refreshing to acknowledge after considerable stagnation within coping research. Recent research by Folkman in particular (Folkman, 2008; Folkman and Moskowitz, 2004) has resulted in new avenues for exploration such as future-oriented proactive-coping and positive coping strategies. Thus coping theory, like the JD–R model, is now re-focusing on the measurement of positive as well as negative pathways by which individuals can alleviate stressful experiences.

Similarly psychological burnout research has also recently acknowledged that its polar opposite (work engagement) should not be ignored in evaluating extreme individual health reactions (Schaufeli et al., 2002). We acknowledged that the structure and measurement of burnout is currently under discussion with alternatives to Maslach's Burnout Inventory now also being employed in research investigations. Finally we briefly reviewed the stress management intervention research and acknowledged the ongoing dearth of scientific studies in this area. Whilst many researchers are aware of the characteristics of a 'good' intervention study (such as random allocation, control groups, pre and post-testing, primary-level intervention), the willingness of organizations to endorse such testing is rare and this partly explains the small number of published investigations in this domain. The risk management approach for the effective prevention and management of occupational stress (Cox et al., 2000b) may be one strategy that investigators can successfully adopt to achieve benefits for organizations (stress reductions) and for research (systematic testing). Therefore rather than being in a state of stagnation, this chapter has identified that occupational stress and coping research has recently embraced a number of new initiatives. Such advances bring new life to this research area and suggest that occupational stress and coping research will continue to remain a fruitful avenue for further investigation.

# 6. Work–family balance

## OVERVIEW

This chapter reviews current research concerning work–family balance. We define the types and directions of work–family balance and discuss why both employers and workers are becoming increasingly concerned about an effective 'work–family fit'. We review the research evidence concerning the primary predictors of work–family *im*balance (or conflict), the individual and workplace consequences of prolonged imbalance and the moderating factors which have been found to have the greatest influence on this balance relationship. Finally we evaluate some of the popular work–family balance organizational policies and provide recommendations for their usage.

## DEFINITIONS

The accurate evaluation of individual health and performance should acknowledge the multiple life roles most individuals have. Hence the interest in evaluating health and performance in both the work and family (and other non-work) domains, which is characterized by the work–family balance literature. The bidirectional influence of work upon family-life and of family upon work-life is generally accepted as having both a *positive influence* (inter-role enhancement) and a *negative influence* (inter-role conflict) upon outcomes of health and performance (Brough and O'Driscoll, 2005). It is also evident that the two directions of conflict (work-to-family interference (WFI) and family-to-work interference (FWI)) are influenced by different antecedents and consequences. For example work can enhance family-life via the provision of financial resources and perceptions of achievement. However, work can also *negatively* influence family life through excessive demands such as overwork, shift-work and occupational stress. Similarly having a supportive personal relationship may enhance an individual's work performance, but excessive demands caused by dependants may result in absenteeism from work. Work–family balance research, similar to occupational stress research, has largely focused upon the negative *inter-role conflict* relationship and seeks to minimize the impact of family-life upon work performance. However, as is described subsequently, current work–family research also includes the positive *inter-role enhancement* relationship in order to provide a more accurate evaluation of work and family relationships.

Greenhaus and Beutell (1985) defined three types of inter-role conflict: *time-based conflict, strain-based conflict* and *behaviour-based conflict*. In their formulation, these three forms of conflict combine to pose challenges for individuals endeavouring to manage the demands and responsibilities of work and family commitments simultaneously. However, empirical research distinguishing between these three types of inter-role conflict is scarce and the majority of published research includes only two types: time-based conflict and strain-based conflict (Allen et al., 2000; Brough and Kelling, 2002; Noor, 2002a). Inadequate construct definition and measurement are the principal reasons for the exclusion of behaviour-based conflict. Carlson et al. (2000) however, successfully addressed this point and provide one of the rare assessments of all three types of bidirectional work–family conflict (that is, six conflict constructs).

One important current topic of discussion is the actual definition of work–family *balance*. While the term 'work–family balance' is increasingly employed within the literature, an agreed definition of this specific term has not been achieved. Kalliath and Brough (2008) recently reviewed six definitions of balance commonly employed with the literature; briefly these definitions consist of:

1. *Work–life balance defined as multiple roles.* The recognition that non-work demands may carry over into the working day and adversely influence individual health and performance at work (Weinberg and Cooper, 2007).
2. *Work–life balance defined as equity across multiple roles.* The suggestion that the *equality* of time or satisfaction across an individual's multiple life roles constitutes work–life balance (Greenhaus et al., 2003).
3. *Work–life balance defined as satisfaction between multiple roles.* The importance of *individual satisfaction* with multiple roles (Kirchmeyer, 2000).
4. *Work–life balance defined as a fulfilment of role salience between multiple roles.* The perception that multiple roles vary in individual importance (or salience) over time, due to for example a work promotion, new baby or a sick spouse/parents (Greenhaus and Allen, in press).
5. *Work–life balance defined as a relationship between conflict and facilitation.* Work–life balance defined as an absence of conflict and a presence of facilitation (Frone, 2003).

6.   *Work–life balance defined as perceived control between multiple roles.*
     Work–life balance as construed as the degree of perceived autonomy
     over multiple role demands (Fleetwood, 2007).

Each of these definitions contains limitations primarily concerning the
validity of the measures they promote (Brough et al., 2007). Work on
an accurate definition and measure of work–family balance is currently
underway. Kalliath and Brough (2008), for example, proposed a definition
of work–family balance which incorporates individual perceptions of both
the *balance* of their work and non-work roles and the *current salience* of
these roles: 'Work–life balance is the individual perception that work and
non-work activities are compatible and promote growth in accordance
with an individual's current life priorities' (p. 326).

# ANTECEDENTS OF WORK–FAMILY BALANCE

A number of theoretical models of work–family balance have been developed to describe the primary antecedent and consequences of work–family
balance. In the next section we discuss in detail two common antecedents
of work–family balance: resources and demands.

## Work and Family Resources

A significant proportion of work–family balance research is based on the
theory of *role strain* (Greenhaus and Beutell, 1985). Role strain theory
stipulates that individuals have finite amounts of psychological resources,
time and physical energy. Each life role of an individual exerts demands
on these finite resources. Strain occurs when the demands of multiple
roles exceed the individual's resources, time and energy, resulting in negative consequences in both the home and work domains. The role strain
hypothesis accounts for the suggestion that demands and strain from
one domain may spillover to affect health and performance in the second
domain. A principal characteristic of the role strain hypothesis is the
*salience* or value of each role to an individual. A high value placed upon
family-life requires the devotion of time and energy to the family domain.
If these preferences are blocked (such as by job demands) then work–
family conflict will occur.

The influence of work and family roles as an antecedent of work–family
conflict can also be explained by the *Conservation of Resources model*
(COR; Hobfoll, 1989; described in Chapter 5). The COR model classifies
variables such as gender, marital status, age, job tenure, job rank and status

as resources. Employees with low job rank, status and tenure typically have fewer resources than their high-rank colleagues, and therefore would be expected to experience higher levels of both occupational stress and WFI. Grandey and Cropanzano (1999) suggested that this explains why some research has shown that employed women tend to experience higher levels of work–family conflict than employed men. In contrast to the more traditional role theory model (Kahn et al., 1964) the COR theory posits that having a spouse/partner is an additional resource to be drawn upon. This perspective was supported by Grandey and Cropanzano (1999) who found that married/partnered individuals experienced lower self-reported family stress than individuals without a spouse or partner. Brough and Kelling (2002) also reported significant associations between having a partner and low levels of both WFI and FWI. Similarly the number of dependants an individual has at home is associated with a corresponding loss of the resources of time and energy, again resulting in stress and FWI. The COR model therefore also explains why research has identified the number of dependants as an antecedent of work–family conflict (discussed below).

**Work and Family Demands**

Work demands have been consistently identified as a antecedent of WFI. Grandey and Cropanzano (1999), for example, demonstrated that occupational stress was directly related to WFI, while stress at home was directly related to FWI. More recently Boyar et al. (2003) demonstrated that work conflict, overload, and ambiguity all positively predicted WFI, while family responsibilities (personal responsibilities and dependant characteristics) predicted FWI. Importantly while both work and family demands respectively predicted WFI and FWI, the work demands to FWI relationship is consistently found to be the stronger relationship. Thus work demands typically have a stronger influence on work–family imbalance and the consequential outcomes as opposed to family demands (O'Driscoll et al., 2004; Parasuraman and Simmers, 2001).

The primary family demand that influences work–family balance is the presence of *dependants*. Dependants tend to increase levels of inter-role conflict and this is especially relevant for women rather than for men (Noor, 2002b). The presence of dependants increases home demands and often entails a corresponding reduction in paid employment time. The number and ages of children, particularly the age of the youngest child, are considered to increase parental demands, with children of infant or pre-school age generally producing the highest demands (Major et al., 2002; Parasuraman and Simmers, 2001). The presence of dependants has been found to increase levels of psychological strain and to consistently reduce work–life balance (Tausig and Fenwick, 2001). Nordenmark (2002) concluded that employed fathers experienced higher levels of psychological strain compared with employed non-fathers. Similarly Beatty (1996) found that employed mothers had increased levels of work–family conflict and negative health outcomes, compared with employed non-mothers. Additionally mothers who received little spousal support also had higher levels of depression. Brough and Kelling (2002) noted for example that single parents experienced higher levels of psychological strain compared to parents with a partner.

A major predictor of behavioural involvement in both family and work domains is *time demands*. As time demands in one domain increase, the level of behavioural involvement in that domain also increases, resulting in less involvement in the second domain and thus producing work–family imbalance or conflict (Frone et al., 1997). The number of hours worked is a classic time demand. Carlson and Frone (2003), for example, demonstrated that as the time spent at work increased, so too did the experience of WFI. Interestingly these authors also demonstrated that increased family involvement was associated with FWI, such that thoughts about family life while in the work domain interfered with work performance. Similarly Major et al. (2002) demonstrated that long work hours were predictive of work–family conflict and that work time mediated the relationships between work and family characteristics and WFI. Brough and Kelling (2002) compared the work hours of women with and without dependants and found the former group were employed for significantly fewer hours (36 hours compared to 40 hours per week, respectively). Nordenmark (2002) also found that the number of children in a family was linearly associated with the desire for both parents to reduce their working hours and to spend more time with their children. However, it is the total number of hours worked in *both* paid employment and on household/ family tasks that is most pertinent to the conflict debate and is associated with negative health outcomes. Noor (2002b) suggested that the total hours worked each week for individuals in family groups (three or more dependants) consisted of 90 hours for women and 70 hours for men – an average gender difference of about two and a half hours per day.

## CONSEQUENCES OF WORK–FAMILY BALANCE

A review of the consequences of work–family conflict (Allen et al., 2000) suggested three core groupings: *work-related outcomes* (such as job satisfaction, commitment, absenteeism, and job performance), *non-work-related outcomes* (including marital, family and life satisfaction, and leisure) and *stress-related outcomes* (such as psychological strain, physical health, depression, burnout, and substance abuse). We discuss four of these consequences here.

**Psychological Well-being**

Associations between work–family conflict and psychological distress have been widely explored and suggest a strong positive relationship: increased conflict is associated with increased psychological distress (Major et al., 2002; Stephens et al., 2001). Associations between increased inter-role conflict and levels of depression have also been demonstrated, generally with few evident gender differences (Frone et al., 1996; O'Driscoll et al., 2004). In a longitudinal investigation Bacharach et al. (1991) demonstrated that work–family conflict predicted burnout to a similar extent within two samples of nurses and engineers. In their study, burnout was composed of strain from both the work and home domains. Kelloway et al. (1999), employing cross-lagged analyses, demonstrated that the experience of strain predicted *subsequent* work–family conflict. Kelloway et al. concluded that as well as predicting strain, inter-domain conflict is also influenced by prior stress experiences.

**Physical Health**

Research has also reported an association between high levels of work–family conflict and adverse physical health. Lee (1997), for example, found that the dual demands of both paid employment and care-giving (for elderly parents) were associated with the classic physical stress–strain symptomology: weight loss or gain, headaches, drowsiness and insomnia. The strain produced by work–family conflict has also been linked to coronary heart disease (Haynes et al., 1984), decreased appetite and energy levels, increased fatigue and anxiety (Allen et al., 2000), and increased cholesterol levels and somatic complaints (Thomas and Ganster, 1995). Associations between inter-role conflict and alcohol consumption have also been documented: Frone et al. (1996) reported that WFI was positively linked to heavy alcohol use. This finding is not surprising as the occupational stress and coping literature has long recognized the use of alcohol as an avoidant coping strategy (O'Driscoll and Brough, 2003).

**Satisfaction**

Research has consistently demonstrated associations between inter-role conflict and reduced levels of job and family satisfaction: WFI is associated with reduced family/marital satisfaction and FWI can adversely influence job satisfaction. The relationship between FWI and job satisfaction also appears to be more consistent than the relationship between WFI and family satisfaction (Aryee et al., 1999). It is notable that job satisfaction can be influenced to a large extent by organizational and/or supervisor support, especially in terms of the perceived support with family demands. Thompson et al. (2006) for instance demonstrated that having a supervisor who was supportive and sympathetic to family demands resulted in employees reporting low levels of work–family conflict and high levels of job satisfaction. The adoption of a number of 'family-friendly' initiatives by organizations also does tend to reduce employees' experiences of work–family imbalance and improve satisfaction and health levels. Brough et al. (2005), for example, demonstrated that the use of organizational 'family-friendly' resources positively predicted both employee family satisfaction and job satisfaction over time, with a stronger relationship documented for family satisfaction.

## Absenteeism and Withdrawal Behaviours

Work–family conflict is positively related to work absenteeism (Thomas and Ganster, 1995) and to turnover intentions (Netemeyer et al., 1996). More specifically Gignac et al. (1996) found that only WFI predicted workplace absenteeism while FWI did not. Similarly Greenhaus et al. (2001) also demonstrated that WFI had a greater impact on withdrawal behaviours than did FWI. Greenhaus et al. suggested that career involvement moderates the conflict–withdrawal relationship, such that individuals who have lower levels of career involvement exhibit higher levels of work withdrawal behaviours. This finding suggests the influence of role salience which we described above.

Comparing the effects of both WFI and FWI on turnover intentions, Boyar et al. (2003) found that while both forms of conflict positively predicted turnover intentions, WFI produced a stronger relationship. MacEwen and Barling (1994) reported that both directions of work–family conflict predicted withdrawal behaviours from both the work and family domains. Furthermore the influence of inter-role conflict on withdrawal behaviours occurred within each domain and applied to both men and women (that is WFI was positively associated with family withdrawal behaviours and FWI was positively associated with workplace withdrawal). Allen et al. (2000) in their meta-analysis also found a strong relationship between work–family conflict and turnover behaviours. Interestingly this relationship was stronger than the association between job satisfaction and work–family conflict which is more commonly investigated.

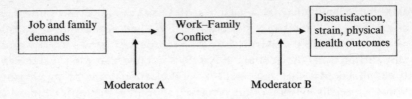

*Figure 6.1    Moderation effects in relationships between job/family
demands, work–family balance and outcomes*

## MODERATORS OF WORK–FAMILY BALANCE

A moderator effect is obtained when the relationship between the predictor and criterion variables varies for different levels of a third variable (discussed in Chapter 4). It has been suggested, for example, that the relationship between work-related demands and WFI, and that between family demands and FWI, varies for males and females. Specifically it has been posited that women experience greater FWI resulting from family demands, whereas men report more WFI due to work demands. Hence gender may be a possible moderator of the relationship between demands (work or family) and work–family balance (WFI or FWI).

Figure 6.1 depicts two mechanisms by which moderators can affect relationships involving work–family balance. In the first, labelled moderator A, the moderator is predicted to influence the association between stressors (work or family demands) and levels of work–family balance. The example given above for gender illustrates this type of moderation effect. A second form of moderation (depicted as moderator B in Figure 6.1) occurs when the moderator variable affects the relationship between work–family balance and outcomes such as job satisfaction, family satisfaction or psychological strain. For instance social support from work colleagues or family members may reduce the negative impact of work–family balance on an individual. We discuss four specific variables found to act as moderators in the work–family balance process below (social support, gender, coping behaviours and neuroticism).

### Social Support

Social support has been found to have a moderating influence upon work–family balance relationships, similar to the more widely acknowledged role of support within the occupational stress process (described in Chapters 4 and 5). Social support (from home and/or work sources) has been found to moderate the relationship between work/family demands and various outcomes, although some of this research reports mixed findings. Carlson and Perrewe (1999), for example, identified no significant moderating effects of work based social support on the relationship between work demands and WFI, nor of family-based social support on the relationship between family demands and FWI. Instead a model which positioned social support (from work and family) as a direct antecedent of reduced work–family conflict produced a better fit to their data. However, both Matsui et al. (1995) and Aryee et al. (1999) demonstrated that spouse social support buffered the relationship between family demands and FWI. That is when perceived spousal support was high, the association between overload and FWI diminished. However, these researchers found no evidence that spousal support moderated the relationship between work overload and WFI. The mixed results concerning the moderating role of social support suggest further investigations are required. Research specifically assessing the role of support over time, the most beneficial types of support and the quality of support provided by family members, work colleagues and others, would be most valuable.

**Gender**

Numerous comparisons have been conducted of male and female experiences of work–family balance. It is suggested that social pressures (such as gender role socialization) remain a strong influence on the accepted 'normal' values and behaviours for both men and women, and that 'deeply ingrained norms' (Major, 1993, p. 150) continue to emphasize a woman's family responsibilities and a man's income-generating responsibilities. Such reasoning is used to explain why inter-role conflict is highest for women in the work-to-family direction, while family-to-work conflict is generally stronger for men (Frone and Yardley, 1996). However, other research has begun to challenge this view, coinciding with the change in social expectations for achieving an overall improved quality of life for both women and men. Carr (2002) suggested that the strategies employed by both men and women for dealing with work and family responsibilities are converging (and thus gender differences are diminishing), evidenced by increasing family responsibilities adopted by each new male generation. Barnett and Hyde (2001) also observed that regarding work–family balance 'psychological gender differences are not, in general, large or immutable' (p. 784). Despite this trend female workers in general continue to shoulder a greater proportion of family responsibilities, particularly through the temporary withdrawal from paid employment.

**Coping**

Research has also investigated the influence of individual difference variables as moderators of relationships between work–family balance and affective reactions. Behson (2002), for example, examined the stress-buffering effects of a form of *coping* which he referred to as 'informal work accommodations to family' (IWAF). He noted that little empirical research has been conducted on the informal strategies used by individuals to help balance their work and family lives, such as arranging leave from work to attend to family matters, taking care of household tasks while at work and working through lunch so that one can go home early. Behson constructed a set of 16 such coping behaviours and found that the total IWAF score was a significant moderator of the relationship between FWI and negative emotional reactions to work experiences. Further research is required to assess if specific work–family balance coping behaviours are valid and can account for significant reductions in the outcomes associated with work–family conflict.

**Neuroticism**

Finally, in keeping with the more general literature on stressor–strain relationships, *neuroticism* has also been investigated as a moderator in the relationship between work–family balance and psychological strain. Individuals who score highly on neuroticism are presumed to be more vulnerable and less resistant to work/family demands and more likely to employ ineffective coping mechanisms. This expectation was confirmed by Stoeva et al. (2002) who observed a significant moderating effect such that family demands were associated with FWI for individuals who were high in neuroticism. However, no significant moderating effect of neuroticism on the corresponding relationship between work demands and WFI was identified. We suggest that the moderating role of neuroticism, and other individual differences such as conscientiousness, have been largely overlooked within work–family balance investigations, and we recommend this as a fruitful area for future research.

# ORGANIZATIONAL POLICIES TO ENHANCE WORK–FAMILY BALANCE

We discuss in this next section two organizational policies which are most widely employed to reduce the adverse effects of work–family conflict: flexible working hours and paid parental leave.

**Flexible Working Arrangements**

It appears to be logical that flexible working arrangements would function to reduce inter-role conflict and subsequently increase both individual and organizational health and performance outcomes. A substantial volume of research suggests this is indeed the case. Flexible working arrangements have generally been found to lower the perceived experiences of work–family conflict significantly. Kropf (2002), for example, reported that part-time and flexible working arrangements are organizational practices that significantly reduce levels of employee work–family conflict. Nordenmark (2002) found that more women (31 per cent) than men (19 per cent) considered reducing their work hours to part-time employment, in order to allow more time for family responsibilities. This was especially the case for women both with children and a spouse/partner, and for women in the higher ranks of an organization. A longitudinal study of 691 New Zealand managers (Brough et al., 2005) demonstrated that flexible working hours was the most frequently utilized organizational policy for managing work–family balance. Importantly Brough et al. demonstrated that the use of 'family-friendly' workplace practices such as flexible working hours, predicted levels of both job and family satisfaction over time.

In qualitative interviews with working mothers in Hong Kong, Lo (2003) also reported that flexibility of work hours and the ability to work shorter hours were two of the three most highly rated job characteristics of 'women-friendly work arrangements', while Kropf (2002) identified that a substantial number of employees are likely to use *both* full-time and part-time working options at different points in their career and life stages. Finally, Brough et al. (2008) discussed how the use of organizational work–life balance policies is strongly influenced by social norms, but that the provision of such policies is essential for organizations experiencing difficulties with labour supply.

**Parental Leave**

Employer-sponsored paid parental leave is one of the more contentious family-friendly provisions. Some governments and organizations consider an employee's non-work life (including dependant responsibilities) to be 'external' to their primary interest in the employee and therefore solely the responsibility of the individual. The US and Australia are two Western countries who do not have statutory policies on paid parental leave. Other countries and organizations consider employee performance within a more holistic framework and suggest there are advantages in assisting workers with their non-work responsibilities. Such advantages include internal benefits such as attracting and retaining staff with dependants, aiming to enhance the health and well-being of these employees (to ultimately enhance levels of attendance and performance), and external benefits such as contributing to a shared society-level responsibility for child raising, elder-care and other dependant responsibilities (O'Driscoll et al., 2007).

Countries with generous parental leave policies are often cited as 'extreme examples' of good practice. Sweden, for example, is considered to have one of the most generous statutory parental leave policies (Hyde et al., 1996). Paid parental leave for all Swedish employees was introduced in 1974 (non-paid maternity leave was available since the end of World War II) and entitles new parents to a total of 480 days' leave, of which 390 days are paid at 80 per cent of their salary. Each parent has a legal right to take 50 per cent of this leave and may transfer some leave entitlement to the other parent. However, 60 days of leave is not transferable at all. These 60 days are referred to as 'mother months' and 'father months', and exist to encourage the sharing of childcare between both parents (Berg, 2004). Norway is also recognized as having a generous parental leave policy; paid leave constitutes 52 weeks with 80 per cent of salary or 42 weeks with 100 per cent of salary, plus one year of unpaid parental leave for each parent. Norway also strongly encourages *paternal* leave based on the expectation that 'fathers are obliged to take leave from work to care for the child' (Brandth and Kvande, 2002, p. 191). Approximately 92 per cent of Norwegian working fathers use some form of paternal leave entitlement.

In 2002 the UK revised its maternity leave policy to 26 weeks' paid leave plus an additional 26 weeks of unpaid leave (totalling one year of maternity leave). Paid paternal leave of two weeks was also introduced. The UK justified these provisions by recognizing the importance of work–life balance to benefit working parents, employers, and children: 'the Government's Work–Life Balance Campaign actively encourages businesses to adopt best-practice and to offer work–life balance opportunities across the workforce' (Department of Trade and Industry, 2003, p. 1). New Zealand has also recently introduced national paid parental leave of 14 weeks (New Zealand Department of Labour, 2004).

In an evaluation of the social, physical and psychological outcomes of parental leave amongst US working mothers and fathers, Hyde et al. (1996) demonstrated that the actual number of hours worked per week (rather than the duration of leave taken by new working mothers) was associated with high levels of anxiety. However, short periods of maternity leave (six weeks or less) together with relationship problems were risk factors for depression amongst these women. Short maternity leave was also associated with negative maternal–infant interactions and with a greater occurrence of physical health problems for biological mothers.

Hyde et al. identified financial consequences as the primary reason for the length of leave taken, but recommended that longer maternity leave (12 weeks minimum) provides a buffering effect against adverse physical and psychological outcomes. These authors also observed that most new fathers (91 per cent) took leave with an average of five days' duration. However, this leave was classified as recreational or sick leave rather than paternal leave per se. The stigma associated with the taking of parental leave remains much stronger for men than for women. Allen and Russell (1999), for example, noted that US fathers taking paternal leave 'were less likely to be recommended for rewards than were males who had not taken a leave of absence' (p. 166).

We also acknowledge the existence of other family-friendly organizational policies that we have not discussed here, including telecommuting, workplace child-care provisions, and job sharing (see Brough and O'Driscoll, 2005). The literature commonly demonstrates that the use of such family-friendly strategies reduces levels of work–family conflict, stress, absenteeism and turnover, and increases employee health and satisfaction outcomes (Allen et al., 2000; Brough et al., 2005; Kossek et al., 2006; Voydanoff, 2002). The successful implementation of family-friendly strategies largely depends on the prevailing corporate and national cultures as was briefly discussed above. Most organizational structures and cultures continue to reward uninterrupted full-time employment and long working hours. It will be of considerable interest to see if employment practices over the next few years change in response to pertinent social issues such as the continual increase in female workers, decreasing national birth rates, and increasing employee demands for work–family balance.

## CONCLUSION

In this chapter we reviewed the current discussions concerning work–family balance. We discussed the current different perceptions of how work–family balance can best be defined and we anticipate that forthcoming research will clarify this definition. The chapter identified that changes in both employment and social traditions continue to shape our perceptions of work–family balance. This may lead, for example, to the emergence of different views of how balance is experienced by male and female workers. We also considered how gender, social support and personal dispositions can influence individual experiences of balance. Finally the chapter examined the issue of responsibility for employee dependants and the different national approaches adopted to acknowledge this responsibility. We predict that it will be of considerable interest for researchers to evaluate the long-term impact of this national legislation in terms of levels of employee health and work performance, organizational recruitment and retention, as well as wider issues such as immigration, occupational reproductive health, and national child-birth rates.

Finally we end this chapter with a comment from Poelmans et al. (2008) who reviewed the current state of work–family balance research and reinforced the need for improving our definitions and measurement of this construct:

> The 'bottom-line' of work–life balance research is whether we can improve working conditions and subsequent levels of work–life satisfaction in employees in order to attract, motivate and retain personnel. If we don't have means to assess progress in organizations, our research lacks the most fundamental justification and credibility. In order for comparative studies to generate useful data though, we need both good measures and sound research designs, and in the actual state of affairs, both are still lacking. (p. 228)

# 7. Work addiction

## Co-authored with Dr Aline Masuda, Escuela de Alta Dirección y Administración (EADA)

## OVERVIEW

> The workaholic is the man with the bulging briefcase who arrives at the office before anyone else has gone home. He eats lunch while working at his desk and spends weekends and holidays at the office catching up. He's a fountain of information whose projects are always done ahead of time. He's adored by top management and often viewed with suspicion by his colleagues and sub-ordinates. Workaholism may undermine his family and marriage, weaken his friendships, or destroy his health. And it's bad for his company too. (Stevens, 1972)

Some readers may have recognized themselves in the first lines of this quote, but may have experienced a growing feeling of unease when reading the second half. In the article 'Beware of the work addict' Stevens paints a gloomy picture of the workaholic. We should not underestimate the number of people that lead these busy lives, but are considered as heroes; they are the innovating entrepreneurs, the industrious small shop owners, the successful executives, the thriving artists, the dedicated doctors, the engaged politicians. It is this paradox that has fascinated scholars from a variety of disciplines including economics, clinical and occupational psychology, philosophy, management, medicine and health sciences, and sociology. Researchers in these fields have studied this phenomenon with a view to finding the answer to the central questions: how and when exactly does spending more time at work become unproductive, or unhealthy for the individual, the group, the organization or society? What exactly is the distinction between the *positive side* of working hard (including motivation, job engagement, commitment and organizational citizenship behaviour) and the *negative side* (such as obsessive-compulsive person-alities, work–family conflict, work addiction, occupational stress and psychological burnout)? European and British governments, for example, have discussed the standards and reinforcement of a European Council

Directive on working time (93/104/EC), delimiting what is considered to be healthy and unhealthy working schedules (Cooper, 1996).

This concern is understandable if we consider the number of technological and socio-economical trends that have emerged in a relative short time span throughout history. The major technological and socio-economical trends include the intensification of work (fewer people doing more work), advances in information and communication technologies (employees working at various locations and times), globalization (need to travel and work with colleagues in different time zones), competition for talented employees, and the integration of women in the labour market (Messenger, 2006). Some workers are expected to be available and responsive 24 hours a day and ready to accommodate their personal lives with that of clients and colleagues located in different time zones. Dual-earner couples, for example, are an increasing norm, representing 54 per cent of US married couples (US Census Bureau, 2000). Many dual-earner couples spread their time between work and caring responsibilities and tolerate the intrusion of work into their personal lives. Conciliating family and work has become a significant contemporary challenge faced by many individuals, as we discussed specifically in Chapter 6.

This chapter focuses on the study of work addiction or workaholism. Scholars in this field have advanced interesting suggestions of where and how we can 'draw the line' concerning what is a workaholic. Over the last two decades research has accelerated rapidly in this domain and workaholism has featured in both journal special issues and dedicated books (for example Burke, 2006; Robinson, 2007). Research has made progress in defining the concept of work addiction (Aziz and Zickar, 2006; Harpaz and Snir, 2003) and identifying different types of workaholics (Buelens and Poelmans, 2004; Scott et al., 1997). Several authors have also provided reviews and meta-analyses of work addiction research (Ng et al., 2007). In this chapter we focus on what makes working long and hard an unhealthy work habit. We conceptualize work addiction as a maladaptive working habit with negative consequences for individual health, productivity and relationships.

## WORKAHOLISM: SHORTCOMING OR MERIT?

While workaholics have been portrayed in a positive light by some researchers (Korn et al., 1987; Sprankley and Ebel, 1987) the majority of scholars have adopted a pathological view to describe work addiction. Oates (1971) who coined the term workaholism defined it as 'one's addiction to work, the compulsion or the uncontrollable need to work incessantly' (p. 1). Similarly Fassel (1990) presented a morbid view of workaholism arguing that it is 'a progressive, fatal disease in which a person is addicted to the process of working' (p. 2). Research to define the construct of workaholism has differentiated between workaholic behaviours, identifying which specific behaviours lead to positive or negative consequences for both individuals and their organizations. Scott et al. (1997), for example, described three dimensions that categorize workaholics: (1) the tendency to spend time at work sacrificing family and social life; (2) the tendency to have obsessive thoughts about work when not at work; and (3) the tendency to work long hours above and beyond organization performance expectations or financial needs. Based on these three dimensions Scott et al. identified three types of workaholics: *compulsive dependent workaholics* (someone who cannot control their desire to work even when they are confronted with social problems and who suffer withdrawal symptoms when not working); *perfectionist workaholics* (individuals who work long hours because they have a strong need to be in control of tasks and to attain perfection); and *achievement oriented workaholics* (who work long hours because they are motivated by competition and attaining long-term goals).

However, the most commonly employed conceptualization of workaholism was proposed by Spence and Robbins (1992). These authors suggested that a workaholic is someone who 'feels driven or compelled to work, not because of external demands or pleasure in work, but because of inner pressures that make the person distressed or guilty about not working' (p. 161). Spence and Robbins classified individuals based on how highly psychologically involved they are with work (work involvement), how much they enjoy their job (work enjoyment) and how much they perceive an inner pressure to work (work drive). The first three profiles described in Table 7.1 (workaholics, work enthusiasts and enthusiastic workaholics) are described as being 'classic workaholics'. They each have high levels of

*Table 7.1   Types of workaholics*

|  | WI (Work Involvement) | D (Drive) | E (Enjoyment) |
|---|---|---|---|
| (Non-enthusiastic) workaholic | High | High | Low |
| Work enthusiasts | High | Low | High |
| Enthusiastic workaholics | High | High | High |
| Unengaged workers | Low | Low | Low |
| Relaxed workers | Low | Low | High |
| Disenchanted workers | Low | High | Low |
| Reluctant workaholic | High | Low | Low |

*Note:*   Adapted by Buelens and Poelmans (2004). Reproduced with permission.

work involvement and drive for work and it is this high level of drive that causes stress. Specifically *enthusiastic workaholics* are described as those individuals who work long hours because they are passionate about their job. While *non-enthusiastic workaholics* work long hours because they feel an uncontrollable inner drive or pressure to work, but they do not necessarily enjoy their work. Research has identified little difference in levels of satisfaction between these two types of workaholics. In fact McMillan et al. (2002) suggested that the work involvement factor proposed by Spence and Robbins was largely redundant and should be excluded. McMillan et al. instead classified workaholics on just two factors: *drive* and *enjoyment*.

Buelens and Poelmans (2004) replicated the research reported by Spence and Robbins (1992) with 6644 full-time workers and found support for a three factor model of work addiction. Buelens and Poelmans identified a new type of workaholic: the *reluctant hard workers* who are high in involvement, low in drive or motivation and low in work enjoyment. Reluctant hard workers can be portrayed as those who are high in psychological involvement with work only because of external pressures related to the work environment. However, these individuals would prefer to work less and are typically unhappy with their job. They represent the underpaid, highly pressured and unhappy worker. Interestingly these authors found that this type of workaholic is most prominent in the fields related to education.

While Spence and Robbins (1992) characterized workaholics based on the degree of drive and enjoyment of their work, other researchers have developed typologies specifically focused on behaviours. Robinson (2007) proposed that different types of workaholics can be classified based on their work initiation and likelihood of completing their work task (see Table 7.2). Robinson's framework is interesting because it focuses on performance criteria and describes how the different types of workaholics use their time: while relentless workaholics tend to initiate and complete

*Table 7.2    Four groups of workaholics*

|                                | Work initiation | Work completion |
|--------------------------------|-----------------|-----------------|
| Relentless workaholics         | High            | High            |
| Bulimic workaholics            | Low             | High            |
| Attention-deficit workaholics  | High            | Low             |
| Savoring workaholics           | High            | Low             |

*Source:*   Reproduced with permission. Copyright 2007 by Bryan Robinson, Ph.D. (2007). *Chained to the Desk: A Guidebook for Workaholics, their Partners and Children, and the Clinicians who Treat Them.* New York: New York University Press.

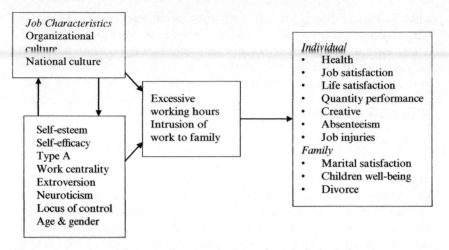

*Figure 7.1   Antecedents and consequences of workaholic behaviours*

their work, other workaholics have a lower level of work initiation and completion. These definitions can be employed to determine which specific type/s of workaholic behaviour is encouraged or most prominent within organizations. Most recently Ng et al. (2007), in a comprehensive review, suggested a definition of workaholism that included *behaviours*, *cognitive* and *affective* components. Based on clinical definitions of addiction, Ng et al. defined workaholics as 'those who enjoy the act of working, who are obsessed with working, and who devote long hours and personal time to work' (p. 114). It is therefore apparent that most authors agree that the criteria for defining workaholics include the existence of an internal pressure to work hard. However, there remains disagreement for other criteria such as the necessity for an enjoyment of work or the existence of external pressures. We next review the common antecedents of work addiction and the consequences both for individual employees and organizations. Figure 7.1 illustrates the variables most often identified as antecedents and consequences of work addiction.

## ANTECEDENTS OF WORKAHOLIC BEHAVIOURS

Although the causes of workaholism are commonly discussed, few empirical studies have actually been published that clearly define these antecedents. In their review, Andreassen et al. (2007) located only 17 published articles based on empirical data that examined the causes of workaholism. Similarly, of the 131 articles reviewed by Ng et al. (2007) only 40 were published in academic journals and only 28 reported empirical studies. This research indicates that despite the growing interest in this topic, few investigations have been conducted that empirically examine the causes of workaholism. We discuss the two primary groups of individual and organizational antecedents here.

**Personality Characteristics**

It is generally accepted that some individuals are predisposed to addictive behaviours (Eysenck, 1997) and evidence suggests that several personality traits are associated with work addiction. Individuals with *low self esteem*, for example, are more likely to become workaholics because they may find social activities more threatening than work activities (Burke, 2004; Ng et al., 2007; Robinson and Kelley, 1998). Individuals with *high self-efficacy at work*, characterized by confidence in job performance and career success, are also likely to develop workaholism for similar reasons (Burke et al., 2006). Ng et al. found that individuals with high self-efficacy at work and low self-efficacy for family activities, choose to spend more time working because they are more comfortable and successful in their professional roles and less confident in their family roles. There is also evidence that employees with *Type A behaviour* (impatience, hostility, time urgency) are more likely to work long hours (Ersoy-Kart, 2005; Harpaz and Snir, 2003; Robinson, 1999). Individuals high on *work centrality*, which are those individuals who give high importance to their work roles, are also more likely to work long hours compared with individuals low on work centrality (Snir and Harpaz, 2006). Finally evidence also suggest that *neurotic* employees (individuals who experience high levels of anxiety) are more likely to feel internal pressure to work, while *extroverts* are more likely to work because they experience high levels of work enjoyment and involvement (Burke et al., 2006). These findings therefore provide support for the contention that different types of workaholics engender either healthy or unhealthy traits.

**Demographic Characteristics**

Some specific demographic variables are also commonly associated with workaholism. For instance *gender, age, marital status* and *family dynamics* have each been associated with the probability of becoming addicted to work. Harpaz and Snir (2003), for example, demonstrated that men have a higher tendency to become workaholics compared with women, although other research has failed to demonstrate this gender difference (Burke, 1999). Snir and Harpaz (2006) demonstrated that while married women work *fewer* hours than unmarried women, married men work *more* hours than unmarried men. In an investigation examining the association between workaholism and age, Kanai and Wakabayashi (2001) found that age significantly influenced the level of work overload. Specifically these authors observed that overloaded employees younger than 34 years experienced high degrees of enjoyment and drive, while those older than 35 years experienced high degrees of drive but low degrees of work enjoyment. They also found that employees between the ages of 39 and 49 were the most driven but also experienced the highest levels of job stress. Interestingly Robinson (2007) proposed that children of workaholics have a higher probability of becoming workaholics themselves because their working habits are learnt from their parents' behaviours.

**Contextual Antecedents**

Consider this scenario: Company A rewards employees for the amount of hours they work, while in Company B employees are allowed the autonomy and flexibility to work anywhere and anytime. If a group of workaholic employees were moved from Company A to work at Company B, where would they work more hours? Where would job performance be highest? Below we discuss how several contextual variables promote workaholism in organizations and influence employee well-being and performance.

**1. Job characteristics**
The characteristics of the job itself can promote workaholism. For example Kanai and Wakabayashi (2001) found that employees who experience work overload, both in terms of quality and quantity of load, had the highest levels of work drive. Enriching jobs, which are those that promote autonomy and inspire employees by providing them with a sense of purpose, can engender enthusiastic workaholic behaviours, while less enriching jobs are more likely to breed non-enthusiastic workaholics (Hackman and Oldham, 1975). Workaholic behaviours are generally more frequent in managers, self-employed individuals and employees of private sector companies (Snir and Harpaz, 2006). Interestingly Buelens and Poelmans (2004) found that the disenchanted worker is over-represented in public administration and the unenthusiastic work addict is over-represented in banking and insurance.

**2. Organizational culture**
The organizational environment can also directly promote workaholic behavi   . For instance employees working in an organization with a family-supportive culture that values the integration of employees' work

and family demands, are more likely to cope with work–family conflict and more likely to divide their time between both personal/family activities and work activities (Allen, 2001; Thompson et al., 1999). Some 'family responsible' companies have started taking action to discourage workaholic behaviours. For example at *Caja Madrid* in Spain, excessive working hours are controlled by switching off all lights at 8.00 pm and an obligatory notification is required if employees plan to work over the weekend. Similarly *Sony* reports on an MBA student who worked excessive hours and had his promotion suspended due to concerns that his working style would be taken as an example of how to succeed. Sony management suggested that this employee should learn to work more efficiently and leave work earlier (Chinchilla et al., 2004). Employees who perceive their organizations to be supportive of long work hours are more likely to work overtime more often (Lambert, 2000; Rhoades and Eisenberger, 2002). This is consistent with the finding that employees who have a trusting relationship with their supervisors are more likely to work additional hours out of feelings of obligation (Ilies et al., 2007).

Cooper (1996) suggested that some organizations have a 'workaholic culture', that is a culture with the common belief that working long hours leads to higher productivity. Managers may endorse this culture by perceiving that working extra hours is an indication of commitment and organizational citizenship. This in turn may cause employees to feel guilty when leaving work at their formal finishing time. In fact most organizational reward systems create a competitive environment in which employees feel the necessity to work additional hours in order to stand out and gain promotion. It is therefore essential to ensure that an organizational culture encourages healthy levels of commitment without pushing employees to adopt workaholic habits. The research therefore indicates that while perceived organizational support elicits hard work and productivity, organizational initiatives are required specifically to promote work–life balance and to avoid excessive working hours and unhealthy working habits.

### 3. Country characteristics
National or cultural factors can also influence workaholism. For example in Japan *karoshi* (death by overwork) was officially used to describe a fatal illness that leads to approximately 10 000 deaths each year (Babbar and Aspelin, 1998). Snir and Harpaz (2006) conducted a cross-cultural study investigating workaholism in employees from Belgium, Israel, Japan, the Netherlands and the US. Consistent with previous findings, the Japanese employees worked more hours per week compared to the other workers. Snir and Harpaz found that across nations, individuals with high levels of

work identification worked more hours per week, compared to employees with low work identification. This raises the question: is there a healthy limit to the level of identification with the organization? We can observe excessive identification by employees who suffer from the delusion that they are *vital* to the organization's aims and performance, or that their work *is* their life, leading to behaviours that are literally lethal for their organization or themselves (Finkelstein, 2003). Kanai (2006) argued that economic and employment conditions should be considered as contextual factors responsible for the *karoshi* phenomenon. In countries with uncertain economic conditions and high competition for jobs, individuals are often forced to work long hours out of necessity. It is therefore apparent that research of workaholism should include cultural variables such as the national socio-economic status.

# CONSEQUENCES OF WORKAHOLIC BEHAVIOURS

### Health Consequences

The most widely recognized consequence of workaholic behaviour is the negative effect on the workaholics' physical and mental health. Research indicates that non-enthusiastic workaholics are less satisfied with their lives and have a lower sense of purpose compared with enthusiastic workaholics (Bonebright et al., 2000). Similarly Andreassen et al. (2007) found that individuals who work long hours and enjoy their work are less likely to report job stress, burnout and subjective health complaints compared with individuals who feel pressurized to work long hours. However, it remains unclear whether workaholics are more satisfied or less satisfied with their jobs, with mixed findings reported in the literature (Burke, 2001a; Ng et al., 2005; Peiperl and Jones, 2001).

### Personal Relationships

Working excessive hours not only has negative consequences for the workaholic but also adversely affects their families. Workaholics in general may have problems with intimacy, marriage and other personal relationships. Burke (2001a) found that professionals who report high levels of workaholism are less satisfied with friends, family and their community. Similarly Robinson et al. (2001) demonstrated that spouses of workaholics are more likely to report marital estrangement and lower positive affect compared with spouses of non-workaholics. In contrast, McMillan et al. (2004) failed to find a significant relationship between workaholism and low satisfaction with personal relationships. These mixed findings suggest the possibility of unidentified factors that intervene or buffer the negative consequences of workaholism.

**Job Performance**

Finally workaholism may impact career success and job performance. There is evidence that those working an excessive amount of hours are more likely to achieve higher salaries and better promotions (Ng et al., 2005). This is not surprising given that organizations tend to recognize and reward employees who spend more time at work (see also the discussion of organizational citizenship behaviour and job performance in Chapter 1). Although workaholics may be more financially successful and more likely to advance in their careers, it is unclear if they are actually also the best performers. It is suggested, for example, that workaholics may perform better than non-workaholics in the short-term but that their performance declines over the long-term (Ng et al., 2007). This may be because workaholism tends eventually to produce poor health outcomes, which inhibits a continued high level of productivity.

## CONCLUSION

This chapter has reviewed the mixed research relating to work addiction and health. Under a certain threshold there exists a grey zone where working long hours can be positive or negative, indicative of healthy or unhealthy working patterns and attitudes. What seems to matter in this grey zone is not the mere quantity of work or how many hours people work, but the *quality* of how people work. The key concept of influence here is the perception of individual job control. This can constitute a lack of individual control (incessant drive, obsessive-compulsive behaviour or addiction) or a lack of control over the working environment (pressure, expectation or obligation to work long hours). Individuals who perceive it is their own choice to work hard may actually enjoy and thrive on the workload, as working is then associated with positive outcomes for both themselves and their organizations. However, working excessive hours against personal preferences is often detrimental (as we also discussed in Chapter 4). Thus issues such as self-management, people management skills, supportive management, role-modelling, training and coping skills are important in ensuring that employees have some job control. Organizations with workaholic leaders, for example, will breed workaholic employees. Organizational cultures require measures that support employees in coping with the removal of the natural boundaries between work and family, through the development of self-management skills and coaching. In other words organizations should promote employees not to 'work hard' but to 'work smart' instead.

Ideally managers and coaches should also be trained to be aware of the different 'workaholic' types, to distinguish healthy from unhealthy work patterns and to be aware of the diverse reasons concerning why people work long hours. Situational leadership and coaching is required to turn non-enthusiastic workaholics into enthusiastic and committed employees by helping them to enjoy work, instead of feeling anxious and obligated to do so. Targeting workers' intrinsic motivation, coaching workers to ensure that the job matches their skills and values (job–person fit), or redesigning the job to make it more meaningful and challenging, are some of the tactics that can be used to generate enthusiasm.

# 8. Workplace violence and aggression

## OVERVIEW

The changing nature of work, increased diversity of the workforce, longer opening hours, economic globalization and work intensification caused by downsizing and work restructuring, has resulted in increased pressure on workers. The increase of temporary and other precarious forms of labour arrangements (such as contract, outsourcing and casual positions) has also resulted in declining perceptions of job security and worker control. These economic changes are placing pressure on the work environment, and when these changes are poorly managed, tension and conflict flourish. While physical assault in the workplace receives the most press, it is actually the more insidious psychological abuse that is the most common threat to workers. This chapter describes the prevalence and nature of occupational violence and provides a review of the consequences to individuals, organizations and society. We also discuss interventions to reduce aggression and violence within the workplace.

## DEFINITIONS OF WORKPLACE VIOLENCE

The precise meaning and definition of workplace violence have been repeatedly discussed and can include experiences ranging from psychological harassment to fatal physical assault. In this chapter we adhere to the definition of violence and aggression recommended by the European Commission: 'Incidents where persons are abused, threatened or assaulted in circumstances related to their work, involving an explicit or implicit challenge to their safety, well being or health' (Wynne et al., 1997, p. 14). Neuman and Baron (1998) provided an important distinction between violence and aggressive acts: *workplace aggression* encompasses all forms of intentionally harmful behaviour experienced at work, while *workplace violence* refers only to direct assaults. Howard (1996) also suggested a useful taxonomy of workplace violence and aggression based on the relationship between the perpetrator and the victim:

1. Type I (criminal intent). The perpetrator has little or no relation-ship to the organization or the employees. The perpetrator is usually committing a crime that can result in violence, such as robbery and trespassing. This category accounts for most of the violent workplace deaths.
2. Type II (customer/client). The perpetrator is a client/customer of the organization and becomes aggressive or violent while receiving a service or being served. Clients/customers include patients, students, inmates and members of the public. Most Type II incidents involve verbal threats or non-fatal assaults.
3. Type III (worker on worker). The perpetrator is an employee or past employee of the organization. Attacks can be made directly on other employees (for example verbal abuse) or against the organization itself (for example arson).
4. Type IV (personal relationship). The perpetrator has little or no relationship with the organization, rather they have a personal rela-tionship with the intended victim at the workplace. This form of aggression and violence usually stems from the spillover of interper-sonal disputes (such as domestic violence). Other employees may be harassed or assaulted as well as the intended victim.

The 2000 European Working Conditions Survey reported that the incidences of occupational aggression and violence experienced across the European Union have significantly increased since 1996, especially within the healthcare and educational sectors. Whether this increase represents an escalation in the actual *number* of incidents or an increase in the *aware-ness and reporting* of these workplace experiences is, however, not clear. However Heiskanen (2007) also reported that workplace violence has increased significantly in Finland since the early 2000s, a period marked by an increase in service jobs in health, education and social work. Heiskanen suggested similar trends have also occurred in Sweden and Norway. Rather alarmingly LeBlanc and Kelloway (2002) also reported an increase in US workplace violence such that an average of 20 US employees are murdered and 18 000 workers are assaulted *each week* whilst at work. These statistics constitute approximately one in every six violent US crimes being commit-ted in the workplace (Paetzold et al., 2007).

The individual, organizational and societal costs associated with occupational violence are also difficult to estimate accurately. In some instances this is because occupational violence is perceived to be 'part of the job' and goes unreported, for example among nurses (Gates et al., 2006; Jackson et al., 2002), police officers (Kraus, 1987) and sex workers (Church et al., 2001). Individual costs range from personal injury and emotional distress, financial costs such as loss of income or costs associated with medical treatment, plus indirect costs such as the burden to families. Organizational costs include sickness absence, premature retirement, turnover costs, compensation, and damage to the plant and equipment. One significant consequence of workplace violence and aggression is the experience of occupational stress. In fact 'interpersonal conflict at work' is commonly cited as an occupational stressor (see Chapter 5 for further details). Stress experiences typically enhance the consequences of workplace violence and aggression, resulting in work withdrawal behaviours (absenteeism and sick leave), poor psychological health (anxiety, depression and victimization) and poor physical health (sleep problems, fatigue and colds).

# THEORETICAL MODELS OF WORKPLACE VIOLENCE AND AGGRESSION

This section reviews three theoretical approaches which are commonly employed to study workplace violence and aggression: social identity theory, social interaction theory, and the cognitive/frustration perspectives.

### Social Identity and Social Interaction Theories

Social identity theory (Tajfel and Turner, 1979) describes the formation of in-groups and out-groups and has been applied to explain incidents of workplace violence and aggression. Although social identity theory was not purposefully devised for its application to occupational settings, its core premises do have relevance for organizational researchers. Thus employees who threaten the in-group status in some way either through their performance (such as being overly productive), their individual characteristics (for example gender or race) or representation (for example from a competing branch) are identified as an out-group and are hence vulnerable to workplace violence and aggression. Another common scenario is for workers to form the in-group and for managers and supervisors to comprise the out-group, which may subsequently expose the latter group to upwards bullying and harassment (described subsequently) from workers.

A second social psychology theory focusing specifically on a *social interaction* perspective has more recently been employed to investigate workplace violence and aggression. Baron (2004) emphasized that the *context* surrounding the aggressive incident should be acknowledged. Hence aggressive/violent incidents can be best explained by considering the individual, situational, organizational, and environmental characteristics of each incident. Douglas et al. (2008) suggested a specific interactionist model that accounts for the 'differential influences of attributions, attitudes, and affects in aggression-related processes while also considering individual, situational, organizational/environmental, and temporal factors' (p. 425). The model proposed by Douglas et al. describes how aggressive incidents occur via three pathways: *attributions* (attributing experiences as external and stable in nature elicits individual anger); *attitudes* (attitudes based on social experiences or stereotypes may elicit negative behaviours); and *emotions* (emotions influence individual judgements and behaviours). Hence the model emphasizes both the cognitive and behavioural processes which operate in these aggressive situations. The model also acknowledges that negative experiences within the work environment (for example aggression) influence trigger events. Both the exposures to these trigger events, and the resulting scale of these events, are influenced by individual personality characteristics. Hence Douglas et al. suggested that individual personality traits have an influence over employees' exposure to aggressive and/or violent incidents in the workplace; for example workers with high levels of neuroticism or Type A behaviour are likely to experience a greater number of negative events than their colleagues.

**Frustration–aggression**

Spector (1997) updated his original model of organizational frustration (Spector, 1978) to incorporate cognitive processes and individual differences. The modified organizational frustration model consists of six components: sources of frustration (role ambiguity, interpersonal conflict, workload); cognitive appraisal; frustrated emotions (anger, irritation, rage); behavioural reactions (increased effort, goal change, aggression); moderators of the frustration and cognitive appraisal relationship (for example goal importance); and moderators of the emotional and behavioural relationship (perceived control, fear of punishment). The model therefore describes the antecedents and moderators of aggression; sources of frustration are appraised as such and produce frustrated emotions, these emotions in turn result in behavioural reactions (which may include aggressive behaviours). The scale of these outcomes is moderated by the intensity of the frustrations and the importance of the blocked goals to each individual.

Based on this and other cognitive/frustration perspectives, Snyder et al. (2005) recently developed a social interactional model of workplace aggression. This model includes individual and organizational antecedents, cognitive appraisal, emotional and behavioural reactions, individual and organizational consequences, organizational interventions, and various moderators of these relationships. Snyder et al. therefore suggested that aggressive behaviours are caused by adverse organizational characteristics, frustrated emotions and blocked goals: 'High levels of frustrating job characteristics, including organizational constraints, role ambiguity and conflict, workload, and sense of control, are likely to be related to increased frustrated emotion, which may in turn trigger aggressive behaviours at work' (2005, p. 24). Snyder et al. also reviewed the most pertinent frustrating job characteristics associated with workplace aggression including organizational justice, culture and change.

## NATURE AND PREVALANCE OF WORKPLACE VIOLENCE AND AGGRESSION

### Physical Violence

Occupations at a high risk of physical violence include retail stores, hospitality and service-related business (Castillo and Jenkins, 1994). Workplace characteristics which increase the likelihood of experiencing violent assaults include: the exchange of money, having one employee working alone, and having opening hours at night or on the weekend (Loomis et al., 2001). Occupations which are precarious in nature (such as prostitution) and whose focus is to protect businesses from crimes (police officers and security guards) also report higher than average incidents of workplace homicide (Rosen, 2001). However, the extent of this violence at work is often under-reported, due to data collection methods, fear of repercussions and a reluctance to identify a criminal occupation (such as prostitution; Salfati et al., 2008). For example Potterat et al. (2004), in a study of US female prostitutes, found that the leading cause of death was homicide, while Church et al. (2001) reported that 50 per cent of sex workers had experienced workplace violence perpetrated by their clients. It should also be noted that it is not only employees who are at risk of occupational homicide. A recent US study of retail stores and late-night service businesses identified that *customers* were more likely to be injured than employees during a violent crime (Peek-Asa et al., 2006).

## Workplace Aggression

Schat and Kelloway (2005) defined workplace aggression as 'behaviour by an individual or individuals within or outside an organization that is intended to physically or psychologically harm a worker or workers and occurs in a work-related context' (p. 191). Conceptualizations of workplace aggression are diverse and include aggression as a retaliatory behaviour and as a deviant response (Hershcovis et al., 2007). Neuman and Baron (1998) proposed a model of workplace aggression based on three factors: *expression of hostility* (ridicule of a co-worker, rumour-spreading, and verbal sexual harassment); *obstructionism* (intentionally ignoring telephone calls or emails from a co-worker, sabotaging their work and being late for their meetings); and *overt aggression* (physical attacks and assaults, theft or destruction of a co-worker's personal property and destroying a co-worker's mail or messages). Expressions of hostility are reported to occur most frequently. Neuman and Baron reported that 32 to 69 per cent of workers in various investigations reported to have experienced either direct or vicarious workplace hostility. Acts of obstructionism have also received recent interest within the organizational citizenship behaviour literature (discussed in Chapter 1). Obstructive behaviours can hence also be described as *anti*-citizenship behaviours. Neuman and Baron suggested that social factors, situational factors, personal determinants, internal states and cognitive appraisals all predict the occurrence of an aggressive response.

A meta-analysis of workplace aggression by Hershcovis et al. (2007) commented on the distinction between workplace aggression aimed at individuals and aggression aimed toward the organization. Hershcovis et al. reported that *interpersonal aggression* is predicted by situational factors such as interpersonal conflict and distributive injustice, while procedural injustice, job dissatisfaction and situational constraints predict *organizational aggression*. These authors recommended that research should clearly distinguish between interpersonal and organizational aggression, and investigate both the individual and situational predictors for each respective type of aggression.

The antecedents, consequences and moderators of workplace aggression overlap considerably with those of harassment and bullying (discussed below). Thus both individual and situational variables (and an interaction of the two) are commonly described as antecedents of aggression and include, for example: demographic characteristics, neuroticism, trait anger and anxiety, organizational climate (tolerance for aggression), and organizational changes. Consequences of aggression may include individual reactions such as anxiety, fear, depression and avoidance behaviours, and organizational consequences such as reduced performance and turnover. Variables identified as moderators of aggression include social support, job control and previous exposure to aggression (Schat and Kelloway, 2005). The impact of workplace aggression obviously also depends on who is the perpetrator, thus aggression experienced from a co-worker or a manager can result in quite different outcomes for the targeted worker.

**Workplace Harassment**

Workplace harassment is commonly defined as 'any experiences that encompass verbal aggression, disrespectful, or exclusionary behaviour, isolation/exclusion, threats or bribes, and physical aggression, without explicit reference to duration of experiences, perpetrator motivation, or power relationship between perpetrator and target' (Rospenda et al., 2006, p. 379). Bowling and Beehr (2006) defined workplace harassment simply as: 'interpersonal behaviour aimed at intentionally harming another employee in the workplace' (p. 998). Harassment behaviours commonly take the form of belittling comments, shouting, threats or silent treatment. However, significant associations have been reported between harassment and physical violence (Rospenda and Richman, 2005), indicating the often simultaneous multiple forms that workplace aggression may take. Rospenda and Richman also suggested that harassment describes micro behaviours, while discrimination represents these behaviours more generally. Hence for example, the net effect of sexual harassment is sexual discrimination. In a telephone survey examining the prevalence of perceived discrimination reported by approximately 3000 US adults, Kessler et al. (1999) reported that racial discrimination was most common (reported by 37 per cent of respondents), followed by discrimination against their gender (33 per cent), appearance (28 per cent) and age (24 per cent). Discrimination attributed to religion, sexual orientation or disability was reported infrequently (by less than 7 per cent of respondents). It is also pertinent to note that many of the respondents reported experiencing *multiple* types of discrimination, thus being a target for one specific form of workplace discrimination may also result in more generalized types of harassment.

Organizational culture/climate and human resource systems are considered to be at least partially responsible for workplace harassment via the creation of a harassment-tolerant workplace environment (for example by not adequately punishing harassers). Bowling and Beehr (2006) reported that the presence of stressors in the work environment (such as role conflict and role ambiguity) were significant predictors of workplace harassment. In their meta-analysis of sexual harassment, Willness et al. (2007)

described three aspects of organizational climate commonly associated with harassment: the risk to victims for complaining, a lack of sanctions against offenders, and the belief that complaints will not be taken seriously. Indeed Willness et al. found that organizational climate had the largest effect size in their prediction of sexual harassment. Rigid hierarchical organizational structures have also been found to directly influence the prevalence of a harassment-tolerant workplace culture. Brough and Frame (2004), for example, reported that harassment was the only organizational variable to predict both job satisfaction and turnover intentions within a sample of New Zealand police officers. Brough and Frame concluded that these findings are of particular importance to organizations such as the police services, as they aim to increase their retention of female workers. It is also clear that having a prominent antidiscrimination organizational policy is effective in reducing workplace harassment and ensures that any reported experiences are investigated seriously (Rospenda and Richman, 2005).

The majority of workplace harassment research has focused on the psychological and behavioural impact of harassment on individual victims (such as stress, physical ill health and psychological burnout). However, recent multi-level research has demonstrated that harassment can also negatively affect team productivity and performance. Raver and Gelfand (2005), for example, reported that sexual harassment was positively related to team conflict, such that teams who reported higher levels of harassment also experienced more conflict, reduced cohesion and reduced performance. Willness et al. (2007) also reported that harassment adversely influences workgroup productivity via worker absenteeism, withdrawal and inhibited performance. Furthermore these negative individual reactions also vicariously influence the productivity of the other workgroup members.

## Workplace Bullying

Workplace bullying includes behaviours ranging from incivility to hostile and violent behaviours. Salin (2001) described workplace bullying as: 'repeated and persistent negative acts towards one or several individuals, which involve a victim–perpetrator dimension and create a hostile work environment' (p. 425). Similarly Einarsen et al. (2003) defined bullying as 'harassing, offending, socially excluding someone or negatively affecting someone's work tasks' (p. 15), and furthermore they noted that bullying behaviour has to 'occur repeatedly and regularly (e.g. weekly) over a period of time (e.g. six months)' (p. 15). Most authors agree that bullying is defined as frequently occurring hostile incidents which the target finds difficult to avoid or defend against. Reports suggest that for approximately 10 per cent of workers bullying is a regular part of their working day. However, some organizations report considerably higher rates: Langan-Fox and Sankey (2007), for example, identified that 53 per cent of workers in a UK University Business School had experienced bullying, and 78 per cent of staff had witnessed bullying from colleagues.

Bullying research tends to focus on either the individual characteristics of the victim, the perpetrator, or on the situational characteristics in which the incident/s occurred. In their review, Jennifer et al. (2003) noted that victims of bullying may be shy *or* over-confident and are typically not well-liked by other colleagues. Aquino et al. (1999) suggested that victims of bullying comprise two groups: the *submissive* worker and the *proactive* employee. Characteristics of the submissive worker include: anxiety, low self-esteem, low social confidence, introversion and a lack of friends. Proactive workers are typically anxious, aggressive, annoying and hold unrealistic views of their abilities and resources. Research focusing on the perpetrator suggests that bullying behaviours exhibited as a child at school may simply continue into the work (and home) environments. In their review Langan-Fox and Sankey (2007) reported that a lack of social competence, empathy and emotional control are common characteristics of the bully.

Characteristics of organizations that foster bullying behaviour have also been scrutinized. Large organizations structured around rigid hierarchies and bureaucracies are often susceptible to a culture of bullying. Thus services such as the military, police, fire and corrections tend to experience more bullying than organizations with more informal (flatter) structures. Bullying is also commonly associated with organizational characteristics such as leadership, autonomy, conformity, workload, poor information flow, conflict and insufficient empowerment. Indeed in some organizations such as the military services, bullying can become an ingrained social norm or a 'tradition' exemplified by new recruits experiencing bullying as a rite of passage and as a test of their loyalty to the unit/organization (Langan-Fox and Sankey, 2007). Changes to organizational working conditions that promote uncertainty, suspicion or competition are also found to be predictive of bullying incidents. Langan-Fox and Sankey reported that most bullying occurs when changing jobs or when acquiring a new manager. Jennifer et al. (2003) noted that workplace bullying occurs due to a combination of negative situational characteristics such as: unfair management practices, organizational uncertainty or change, role ambiguity, unsupportive work culture, interpersonal conflict, or general discontent and job dissatisfaction. This point reflects the similar proposition reported by Hershcovis et al. (2007) described above; it is apparent that neither workplace aggression nor bullying operate in a vacuum and that situational and organizational characteristics significantly influence the occurrence, duration and management of these deviant behaviours

Branch et al. (2007) noted that whilst workplace bullying is tradition-ally perceived to occur in a downwards direction (by a manager against an employee), *horizontal bullying* may also occur (staff against staff) as well as *upwards bullying* (by an employee against a manager). Branch et al. reported that the 'bullied boss' is becoming an increasingly common phe-nomenon. Statistical accounts support this prediction: Zapf et al. (2003) reported that upwards bullying has a prevalence rate of up to 27 per cent in Europe. Hoel et al. (2001) reported that 15 per cent of their sample of UK managers had experienced upwards bullying from their subordinates or clients. Similarly McCarthy et al. (2003) demonstrated that university academics are experiencing increasing rates of bullying from both their students and subordinates, with approximately 17 per cent of academics reporting these incidences of upwards bullying.

An important point of interest about upwards bullying is that it signifies that organizational position or rank is not necessarily a protection against workplace aggression. Indeed reports from female senior managers indi-cate that bullying from male subordinates does occur and is especially common in male-dominated occupations such as the military, policing or corrections (see Branch et al., 2007). Hence traditional gender-norm behaviours may override formal organizational rankings and positional power circumstances. In their review Branch et al. suggested that bullying consequences may also be experienced *vicariously* by workers who witness the bullying of a colleague. Hence such workers may experience anxiety about whether they themselves will also subsequently become a target to be bullied. Branch et al. reported: 'This climate of fear is likely to impact upon the organization through loss of productivity, increased absentee-ism, intention to leave and turnover, as well as the cost of intervention programmes' (p. 95).

Some recent attention has also been paid to *mobbing*, defined as the bul-lying of an individual by a group of workers/peers. Mobbing has recently been formally recognized in some European countries (such as the UK, the Netherlands and Scandinavia) as a deviant workplace behaviour distinct from bullying. Other countries such as the US, Australia and New Zealand currently define mobbing as a form of bullying. Shallcross et al. (2008) defined mobbing as consisting of 'covert forms of rumour, gossip and innuendo that are used to discredit and demonise targeted co-workers until they are forced to leave their employment' (p. 3). Shallcross et al. reported that the resignation/termination of the mobbing victim is a discrete aim by the perpetrators and that the psychological consequences experienced by the victim may continue in the form of post-traumatic stress, social exclusion, or suicide after the bullying has ceased. Shallcross et al. also reported that women tend to outnumber men in both the victim and perpetrator categories of mobbing.

# VARIATIONS OF RISK

This section discusses in further detail four common antecedents of workplace violence and aggression: occupation, gender, age and union membership. Although not specifically discussed here we also acknowledge that several individual dispositional characteristics have also been associated with (perpetrating) workplace violence and these include, for example: negative affectivity, trait anger, agreeableness, conscientiousness, narcissism, locus of control and communication skills (for a review see: Snyder et al., 2005).

## Occupation

Although the degree of exposure to violence varies considerably across occupations, jobs that entail close contact with clients and customers commonly exhibit a higher risk of violence (Hogh et al., 2003). The majority of these industries include service employees who have high levels of contact with the general public, work in isolation, handle cash or pharmaceutical drugs, or those who work in custodial, security or legal employment (Beech and Leather, 2006). An analysis of the British Crime Survey identified that police and other security employees had the highest probability of experiencing occupational violence, followed by publicans, nurses and other allied health professionals (Budd, 1999). Thus workers within occupations that regularly encounter clients with a mental illness, or who are on medication or other drugs, are at an especially high risk of experiencing workplace violence and aggression (Brough, 2005b; Brough and Biggs, 2009). Recent research also recognizes the risks of workplace violence to employees within sales roles (such as call centre employees, sales representatives and telemarketers) who often experience aggression from customers (Grandey et al., 2004).

The recognition that healthcare professionals in particular are experiencing significant increases of workplace violence has received recent attention. The UK National Health Service Executive, for example, reported approximately 65 000 violent incidents occurring in 1998 against National Health staff. Consequences of this violence included: poor morale, staff recruitment and retention problems, staff absenteeism, and high levels of occupational stress and psychological strain (Occupational Safety and Health Service, 2004). Pozzi (1998) also reported that 90 per cent of US pre-hospital service providers had experienced verbal and/or physical violence during their careers. The pervading impact of verbal violence as well as physical violence was also reported by Brough (2005b) within a sample of Australian paramedics. Brough noted the distressing impact of regular (daily) verbal violence reported by these paramedics and the widespread under-reporting of these incidents. Similarly Heiskanen (2007) found that nurses, doctors and allied health professionals in Finland reported more workplace violence incidents than workers in other occupations. The consequences of these encounters adversely affected individual health and well-being and directly increased organizational human resource costs. Interestingly Spector et al. (2007) suggested that the *perceived violence climate* within a hospital was directly linked to the prevalence of aggression and violence experienced by nurses. Spector et al. suggested that 'the emphasis and support given by organizational management to employee safety' (p. 117) constituted a violence climate. Therefore management could take action to directly reduce this perception of a violence climate and the subsequent incidents of violence. This violence climate construct builds on the harassment-tolerant workplace construct discussed previously.

## Gender

The existence of significant gender-differences concerning both the perpetration and receipt of workplace violence and aggression has not been clearly identified. Research has indicated that male workers are both more at risk of *being targeted* for work-related violence and are also more likely to be the *perpetrators* of workplace aggression, than females (Hershcovis et al., 2007; Schat et al., 2006). In a detailed analysis Hewitt and Levin (1997) noted that while female workers experienced more non-fatal physical assaults than males, male employees were more likely to be the victim of occupational homicide. In contrast recent Finnish data reported that *women* are more likely to experience physical violence at work as compared to males, although earlier Finnish reports had cited more men experiencing violence (Heiskanen, 2007). Heiskanen suggested this change was due to the growth in service occupations and the decline in industrial labour occupations in Finland since the early 2000s.

Some gender results are, however, confounded by occupation (such as nursing and the military) which produces difficulties in measuring workplace violence and aggression strictly along gender lines. One French study of 7000 employees found that more females than males reported being bullied in the previous 12 months (Niedhammer et al., 2007), while a study of Finnish prison officers found no significant difference in the prevalence of bullying for male and female employees (Vartia and Hyyti, 2002). Research suggests that the *type* of assault experienced is gender-specific in that females tend to experience more sexual harassment than males (Vartia and Hyyti, 2002). The recent increase in the employment of women especially within the service sectors with the high exposure to customers, partially accounts for some of the mixed results that are now being produced. Organizational education and training programmes have also reduced the prevalence of workplace aggression (especially harassment) within some of the occupations which used to tolerate such aggression informally (such as the police and fire services; Brough and Biggs, 2009).

**Age**

The research generally indicates that younger employees experience more workplace violence and aggression than their older colleagues. Schat et al. (2006) noted, for example, that younger employees were more likely to be exposed to both physical and psychological aggression at work, and that this exposure increased until age 30 (after which it decreased). An Australian study of young employees in the fast-food industry reported that 48 per cent of employees had been verbally abused, with the majority of this abuse emanating from clients rather than co-workers or supervisors (Mayhew and Quinlan, 2002). Data collected by the US Bureau of Labor Statistics revealed that the cause of death for 19 per cent of young workers was occupationally-related homicide and that approximately 75 per cent of these cases occurred within the retail industry (Janicak, 1999). Mayhew and Quinlan suggested that young workers are disproportionally employed on a casual basis within the retail and hospitality industries especially, where they typically receive limited training concerning occupational violence.

Not only are young workers at a higher risk of workplace violence, they are also more likely to be the perpetrators of violence. Dupré et al. (2006) reported that approximately 25 per cent of US teenage employees in their sample had been involved in workplace aggression, with most of this aggression directed at supervisors. Similarly Cleary (2000) found within a US school setting that 39 per cent of teenagers had perpetrated aggressive or violent acts targeted at other students and/or at teachers. The research therefore indicates that young employees are exposed to more occupational violence than older employees. Prevalence rates are, however, significantly influenced by occupation and also reflect the fact that young individuals within society are generally more often involved in aggressive acts.

**Union Membership**

The most frequent cause of workplace violence in the US between 1950 1970 was caused by strike action (especially via picket lines), followed by renewal of contracts and internal union dissention (Brinker, 1985). In their review of US incidents, Thieblot et al. (1999) reported an annual average of 432 incidents of union and strike-related violence. Importantly Thieblot et al. noted that while union membership and strike-related incidents had decreased since 1955, the occurrence of violence during an industrial strike had increased. Thieblot et al. also reported that highly unionized industries characterized by hazardous and physically demanding working conditions and minimal education (such as coal mining) produced the highest level of violence. More recently Schnabel and Wagner (2007) reported that union membership and the propensity to violence depends considerably on the industry, the country and union member characteristics. The recent emergence of 'women only' unions in countries such as Japan and Korea, for example, has been associated with a decrease in the incidents of union violence (Broadbent, 2007).

## INTERVENTIONS TO REDUCE WORKPLACE VIOLENCE AND AGGRESSION

As discussed earlier in this chapter, violence in workplace settings can be manifested in different forms, including physical aggression, verbal aggression, bullying and harassment. One challenge in developing strategies to address these different kinds of violence is that the most effective approach will depend on the nature of the violence, as well as on its consequences (for both individual workers and the organization). Another issue which has impeded our understanding of effective violence-reduction strategies is that frequently organizations turn a 'blind eye' to specific incidents of aggression toward employees and may have no formal mechanism for attending to the problems which arise from aggressive acts. Finally the source of violence can vary considerably, from work colleagues to supervisors/managers to clients/customers of the organization. Reducing the incidence of violence attributable to these different sources therefore requires different approaches. For instance Runyan et al. (2000) commented that 'interventions must be developed for multiple types of circumstances' (p. 124) and tailored to address not only the specific types of violence perpetrated but also the situations in which violence occurs in different organizations. In other words, there is no one-size-fits-all solution. However, there is no doubt that many organizations recognize the seriousness of the problem and that efforts are now being made to reduce both the level and frequency of violent behaviour towards workers, as well as the impact on individuals in work contexts. In addition several countries are beginning to recognize various manifestations of violence in their national health and safety legislation (McCarthy and Mayhew, 2004; Peek-Asa et al., 2001; Schat and Kelloway, 2003). As we have commented previously, the consequences of workplace violence for individual health and well-being, as well as organizational productivity and societal functioning, are receiving more prominent attention.

Although there are several examples of interventions implemented by organizations in their efforts to reduce the incidence of violence toward workers and its effects, unfortunately there is little systematic empirical research on the impact (especially long-term) of these efforts. Interventions may also be described as reactive responses to occurrences of violence, rather than being systematic and integrated into organizational policy and procedures (McCarthy and Mayhew, 2004). This has resulted in a somewhat fragmented understanding of what is effective and what is not. A viable starting point for violence-reduction policies and practices is to develop an understanding of how violence emerges in workplaces (this is similar to the notion of a *stress audit* to identify sources of work-related stress and their effects). Although it is tempting to attribute aggressive behaviour to the personal characteristics of perpetrators, and there may be valid arguments for such attributions, by itself this focus is too constrained and overlooks important environmental contributors to such behaviour, as we discussed above.

Much like stress-management interventions, strategies to combat workplace violence can be grouped under three broad categories: primary, secondary and tertiary interventions. Primary interventions are preventative and proactive, whereas secondary and tertiary interventions are more reactive, endeavouring to minimize the negative impact of violence rather than directly addressing its antecedents. Another classification has been proposed by Peek-Asa et al. (2001), who described interventions as environmental (focusing on the workplace situation as a potential contributor), behavioural (managing the behaviours of the individual person), and managerial (including organizational policies and procedures). These broad perspectives provide useful frameworks for considering violence intervention strategies.

As noted previously in this chapter, many interventions relating to aggression occur within healthcare settings. Several studies have assessed the beneficial effects of strategies such as staff training to handle violent clients (Beech and Leather, 2006), feedback to communicate with workers following their experience of violence (Arnetz and Arnetz, 2000), peer support (Rains, 2001), and the provision of organizational support (both instrumental and informational) to victims (Schat and Kelloway, 2003). Each of these strategies has been demonstrated to exhibit some benefits and positive outcomes, especially in helping workers contend with the aftermath of a violent incident. Also, with the possible exception of staff training in how to diffuse violence, the majority of these strategies can be classified as secondary (reactive) rather than preventive (proactive) interventions. Other specific strategies which have been suggested include improved monitoring and surveillance, for instance the installation of cameras in potentially hazardous work areas, and improvements in the physical environment, such as levels of lighting and making areas physically secure from outside intrusion (Loomis et al., 2002). These strategies may be beneficial in preventing some forms of violence, especially from outsiders, although clearly they will not be appropriate in all circumstances.

At a more general level it is evident that dealing with violent behaviour, whether from work colleagues or from outsiders, is a joint responsibility of both management and workers themselves. One significant factor which we discussed above is the influence that the organizational culture can exert on worker behaviours (Runyan et al., 2000). It is critical for each organization to develop and promote norms about appropriate interpersonal responses. These may vary considerably from one kind of work setting to another, but a core issue is that all people should be treated with respect and dignity, and that this embraces both physical and psychological elements of interpersonal interactions. Along with this basic element, it is also clear that organizations must establish and promulgate very clear rules about how individuals may behave toward each other, especially what kinds of behaviour are unacceptable, along with definitive procedures for sanctioning violations of these norms and rules (Runyan et al., 2000). Ultimately a reduction of interpersonal violence (in all its forms) requires an integrated and consistent approach from management, accompanied by systematic evaluations of the effectiveness of specific interventions.

A possible moderator of the psychological consequences of violence experiences is perceived social support. The receipt of optimum types and levels of social support has been established as moderating the occupational stress–strain relationships, primarily through Johnson and Hall's (1988) Job Demand–Control–Support model (JDCS). Recent investigations of both the sources and the types of workplace social support have considered the implications for organizational supervisor/management training (Brough and Frame, 2004). Such training interventions have been found to reduce occupational stress consequences significantly, as predicted by the JDCS. Beaton et al. (1997), for example, investigated the influence of workplace social support in samples of paramedics and firefighters. Beaton et al. demonstrated that these workers cope with inherently dangerous and stressful occupational demands by seeking social support from colleagues, friends and family members. Furthermore because of the shift-work nature of their job, these emergency service workers commonly develop a high degree of dependence on their colleagues, relying on them for both practical and emotional support when encountering violent situations.

## CONCLUSION

This chapter reviewed the nature and prevalence of occupational violence and aggression. We discussed three theoretical models commonly employed to describe the onset of aggressive behaviours. These theoretical models described how situational characteristics, organizational climate and individual-cognitive processes each directly influence the occurrence of aggressive behaviours. The chapter also reviewed the prevalence of the common types of workplace violence, specifically: physical violence, aggression, harassment, bullying and mobbing. The recent recognition of upwards bullying, for example, has significant implications for the continued advancement of senior managers who are not white and male. We also discussed the common characteristics associated with workplace violence such as age, gender, occupation, casual employment and union membership. The significant growth of employment within the healthcare and service industries explains a large proportion of the recent increases in violence reported by workers who are female, young, and/or casually employed. Finally we reviewed organizational interventions that are commonly employed to manage workplace violence. While the most effective interventions are tailor-made to suit the specific characteristics of each organization, some common intervention components were identified and these included: organizational policies, staff training, effective reporting, surveillance, peer-support and organizational support. We also acknowledged that the propensity for organizational change such as downsizing, relocating and restructuring, as well as the increase in precarious forms of labour arrangements such as contract and casual workers, are fuelling the incidents of workplace violence and aggression. Technological changes have also influenced the method of workplace aggression; increased reports of *cyberaggression* for example, suggest that this insidious method of workplace aggression will become more prevalent (Weatherbee and Kelloway, 2006). The recent interest in researching the 'dark side' of employee behaviours such as stealing, retaliatory behaviours, incivility and negative politics (see for example Griffin and O'Learly Kelly, 2004), also attests for the growth in studying other non-productive organizational behaviours that have many similarities with violence and aggression.

# 9. Psychological health and technological change

## INTRODUCTION

The relationship between psychological health and the implementation and usage of technology has been the subject of considerable debate and empirical research for many years. It is recognized that technological changes, both at work and more generally, have had an enormous impact on people's lives and that much of this influence has been constructive and beneficial. For instance information and communication technologies (ICTs) have significantly affected the way in which work is carried out, especially through providing greater (and more timely) access to information and speeding up the transmission of information between people and organizations. In addition new technology has created a more 'mobile' workforce and increased use of telecommuting. These changes can yield positive benefits for individuals as well as their organizations. On the other hand, there is also growing concern over the 'dark side' of new technologies (especially ICT) and their potential negative impacts on individual and societal well-being.

This chapter provides an overview of the impact of technology on the psychological health and well-being of individual workers. This is not intended to diminish the importance of physical health considerations, which have been discussed in detail by other commentators (Beckers and Schmidt, 2003; Coovert and Thompson, 2003; Coovert et al., 2005), but simply to concentrate on the psychosocial influences of technology. Secondly our aim is not to offer a comprehensive review of all the empirical research which has been conducted in this domain, but rather to highlight some of the key issues which impinge upon individuals in their working lives. The main focus will be on information and communication technologies (ICTs) as these are the most prominent forms of technology now used by many workers. Finally although this chapter concentrates on individual well-being, teams also can experience many of the pros and cons of technological advances. For instance in many organizations today teamwork has become 'virtual' using a wide array of different communication systems that enable people to work together without actually being together physically. There is growing evidence that the welfare of teams is an important consideration in the implementation of technology (Marshall et al., 2007), and clearly team experiences are pertinent to the link between technological change and individual psychological health. However, the effects of ICT on teamwork will not be dwelt upon here.

Although the concept of 'technology' has a variety of definitions, our attention in this chapter is focused on information and communications technology (ICT). Vyhmeister et al. (2006) noted that ICT 'is commonly used in reference to a wide set of techniques and tools that link information systems with people, denoting e-mail, video conference systems, Internet, groupware and corporate intranets, mobile telephony, electronic personal devices, among many other applications' (p. 39). In sum, ICT refers to a diverse range of technologies that increase communication and information modification and sharing, with a view to enhancing performance. In the present context we will consider ICT as it relates to workplace functioning and performance.

## TECHNOLOGICAL CHANGES IN THE WORKPLACE

It is evident that ICT usage is becoming more pervasive in workplaces, with increasing numbers of workers relying (either exclusively or predominantly) on this technology to perform their work tasks. For instance Gustafsson et al. (2003) reported that approximately one-third of Swedish workers spent 50 per cent or more of their work time using a computer, and around 80 per cent of the Swedish population had access to mobile phones and similar devices. Lazar and his colleagues (Lazar et al., 2006) noted findings from a US National Telecommunications and Information Administration survey report in 2002 which indicated that 73 per cent of US workers used a computer in their work. Similar rates have been reported in other countries, reflecting the high usage of ICT for work-related purposes.

Several commentators have documented changes that have occurred over the last 40 years in the utilization of computer-based technologies in work organizations. Coovert and Thompson (2003), for instance, noted that since IBM introduced desktop computers in 1981 there has been an explosion of new ICTs. Although there have been numerous significant benefits of these new technologies, one issue of concern raised by Coovert and Thompson (and others: Bessière et al., 2006; Ceaparu et al., 2004) is that the increasing sophistication of ICT has not always been matched by appropriate implementation and support for users. New technologies can be perceived by end-users as adding unwanted complexity and requiring them to learn new systems and develop skills and knowledge that they believe are non-essential to the effective performance of their work. Despite attempts to construct interfaces which better match human needs and capabilities, the anxiety and frustration associated with utilizing ICT are widespread (Bessière et al., 2006) resulting in a negative impact on individual well-being. The impact of ICT on individual users' well-being depends very much on the manner in which the technology is implemented and the influence which it has on the psychosocial environment at work.

Major changes in ICT have occurred in recent years in both their design and implementation. For example there has been substantial growth in the use of PCs, laptops, Blackberries, and various other mobile computing devices, which have increased work flexibility and worker mobility, as well as enabling organizations to respond more rapidly and effectively to changes in global economic and technological conditions. The positive benefits of adopting these forms of technology have been described in detail (Vieitez et al., 2001) especially with regard to their impact on organizational productivity (Mamaghani, 2006). As noted above, our interest here is not so much in the benefits for organizations, although these can have trickle-down effects on individuals, but rather the relationship between technological changes and individual well-being. Technology that is more effective has the potential to enhance the capacity of people to achieve their work goals and to reduce anxiety due to lack of goal achievement. Despite this promise of a better quality of working life, in practice, however, research has illustrated that for many workers anxiety, frustration and strain arise from their interactions with new technologies, referred to as 'technostress'. This phenomenon was first described over twenty years ago by Brod (1984) as 'a modern disease of adaptation caused by an inability to cope with the new computer technologies in a healthy manner' (p. 16).

**Electronic Mail**

One very pervasive form of ICT that has had a substantial impact is electronic mail (email), which is now considered by many to be an indispensable tool at work and in life generally. Much has been said about the influence which email (and its more recent analogue, cell phone texting) has exerted over people's lives. At its inception in the 1980s email was used predominantly as an adjunct communication mechanism alongside memos, the telephone and even face-to-face conversation. Email communication systems were initially slow and unwieldy to operate, and lacked the capacity to send large amounts of data. With continuing sophistication, however, email has become a primary mode of communicating with other people (and organizations) and is much more than simply 'electronification of the traditional mailed letter' (Hair et al., 2007, p. 2791). As with other technological developments this has led to both positive and negative outcomes. On the positive side there is no doubt that email has speeded up interpersonal communication and enables almost instantaneous exchanges across the globe. It also permits the immediate transmission of documents and other information that previously may have taken days or weeks to convey to recipients. Hence as an information-sharing procedure, email has many significant advantages.

On the negative side concerns have been raised in many quarters about the manner in which email is being used in some circumstances, and about the overall time which individuals are now devoting to email communications – sometimes at the expense of other work-related activities. Hair et al. (2007) noted, for instance, that 'there is mounting evidence of the intrusiveness of email' (p. 2792), with reports of up to 30 per cent of work time being devoted to either initiating or responding to email messages. Not only is this of potential concern from a work productivity perspective (due to time lost on email usage), but various psychosocial implications have also been alluded to by researchers. For example it has been suggested that the continuous 'switching' from email to other tasks can lead to systemic overload and stress as the individual becomes increasingly pressured by both the perceived need to respond instantaneously to email messages and by the demands of (other) task-completion (Bellotti et al., 2005). Bellotti et al. suggested that email demands can become overwhelming and addictive, and that organizations and individual workers need to develop strategies for managing email usage. Although some organizations have proposed the notion of an 'email-free' day, this apparently has not been universally successful.

As noted above, email is just one of many forms of ICT whose implementation and usage has become widespread in organizations. In the discussion which follows, we will not focus on specific forms of ICT but rather on the overall psychosocial impact that implementation of such technology can exert on individual well-being. Our goal is not to offer an exhaustive review of all relevant areas but to highlight some key issues that have been demonstrated by research to be of significance. For further recent reviews of the literature we recommend Bessière et al. (2006), Coovert et al. (2005), and Thomée et al. (2007).

## PSYCHOSOCIAL RESPONSES TO TECHNOLOGY

As noted already in this chapter ICT and related technologies have been found to have a substantial effect on the well-being of individual users. Our interest here is specifically in work-related use of technology, rather than more general usage (for example at home or in leisure pursuits), and our attention will focus on the effects of technological changes within work environments on worker psychological health. We adopt a psychosocial perspective rather than others which are also pertinent in this context, such as ergonomic, human–computer, managerial or economic perspectives. From a psychosocial perspective responses to technology (and technological change) can be classified as *cognitive* (perceptions and beliefs about technology), *affective* (emotional and evaluative reactions), and *behavioural* (usage or withdrawal). Most research has centred on cognitive and affective (emotional) responses. Positive outcomes can arise when individuals are able to utilize technology effectively and feel that it enables them to acquire a sense of goal achievement and that it improves their work performance.

However, significant psychosocial difficulties can arise when individuals believe they are unable to master the technology, experience frustration with its usage and ultimately perceive that the technology is impeding, rather than enhancing, their goal achievement. While acknowledging the positive benefits of technology the present chapter focuses predominantly on potential negative outcomes which individuals can experience, especially anxiety, frustration and feelings of reduced efficacy.

**Technostress**

As mentioned above, the term *technostress* has been in existence for some time (Brod, 1984) and has been used to describe a variety of stress-related symptoms associated with exposure to and usage of new technology, especially ICT (Sami and Pangannaiah, 2006). These symptoms include anxiety, frustration, feelings of incompetence, perceived lack of control over the technology, sense of lack of achievement of one's goals, and ultimately even depression. Physiological changes, such as increased levels of adrenaline and noradrenaline, have also been aligned with technostress. Stressful experiences in relation to technology usage can ultimately produce 'technophobia' (Sami and Pangannaiah, 2006) where the individual is not simply anxious in respect of the technology but develops avoidant behavioural patterns. All of these manifestations may contribute to a decline in psychological health and well-being, hence attention to their antecedents and consequences is highly salient to psychosocial perspectives on technology and technological change. The present coverage focuses on four major elements: anxiety, frustration, feelings of incompetence (lack of mastery or self-efficacy), and perceived lack of control. While there are clearly several other relevant variables, these four have received considerable attention in the research literature.

**Technological Anxiety**

There is now substantial evidence on the effects of anxiety on individuals' reactions and ability to utilize ICT. This is sometimes referred to as 'computer anxiety' although it may be more appropriate to designate it as 'technological anxiety' since the feelings which people experience are not necessarily limited to computers and can extend to other forms of ICT (such as cell phones, iPods, and so forth). There have also been suggestions (Morgan and Cotten, 2003; Thomée et al., 2007) that anxiety about technology use can be coupled with depression, although this linkage is not inevitable and the evidence concerning long-term depression is not consistent. From the multitude of studies that have been conducted on this topic, it is evident that anxiety over the use of ICT is an issue of significant concern to a relatively high proportion of individuals (Smith and Caputi, 2007) and that such anxiety is a major psychosocial contributor to suboptimal usage of ICT (Thorpe and Brosnan, 2007).

Anxiety comprises several different, albeit related, characteristics including fear, apprehension, nervousness, worry and tension (Beckers et al., 2007). It may be determined by numerous factors including feelings of inadequacy about one's ability to utilize the technology effectively, and concerns about job insecurity (threat of job loss due to the introduction of labour-saving technology). Vieitez et al. (2001) observed a significant relationship between workers' beliefs that technological change would lead to job insecurity and their psychological well-being, including both anxiety and depression. Workers in lower-status jobs and with less education were most fearful of the possibility of job loss due to new technology. Such anxiety can have a paralysing effect on a person's ability to continue working with the technology, given their belief (which may be based in fact) that their job is threatened by the introduction of such technology. In addition technological anxiety can generate both psychological trauma and physical ill health in the longer term (Beckers and Schmidt, 2003).

As well as considering issues such as feelings of job insecurity, researchers have also examined general anxiety about ICT usage. Beckers and Schmidt (2001) developed a six-factor model of computer anxiety which incorporated computer literacy, self-efficacy, physical arousal, affective reactions, and beliefs about both the benefits and dehumanizing effects of ICT. They found that computer literacy was positively related to physical arousal and emotional responses, and computer self-efficacy contributed to increased computer literacy. An important contribution of this study was its differentiation of various components of ICT anxiety, which enabled an assessment of specific relationships between computer usage and anxiety. More recently Beckers et al. (2007) investigated whether computer anxiety is a relatively stable trait or a mutable temporary 'state'. Their research illustrated that both elements can exist in computer anxiety but that trait-like elements are prominent, suggesting that worry and concern about using ICT may be manifestations of underlying anxiety. Further research is needed to tease out the ways in which ICT anxiety develops and is maintained, as well as mechanisms for alleviating such anxiety. Beckers et al. concluded that simply providing training for people in the use of such technology may not be sufficient in itself to reduce anxiety levels significantly.

Like Beckers and his associates, Smith and Caputi (2007) have proposed a model of computer anxiety that positions trait anxiety as a precursor to state anxiety (that is, anxiety specifically about ICT usage). Smith and Caputi referred to their approach as a *cognitive interference model* of computer anxiety, as it focused on the mediating role of negative cognitions which interfered with the person's ability to perform tasks and engage successfully with the technology. The key element of this model is that 'computer anxiety is characterised by an individual's disposition to react with extensive worry, intrusive thoughts, tension, physiological arousal and avoidance behaviour when using, or when thinking about using, computers' (p. 1484). Negative cognitions and the consequent anxiety can have a severe impact on the person's self-concept and their overall well-being, as well as leading to resistance to using and avoidance of computer technology.

Thorpe and Brosnan (2007) reported two studies that compared this form of anxiety to other types of anxiety. These authors noted that 'computer anxiety may reach clinical levels, that some cognitions held by the computer anxious are held in common with the cognitions of those suffering from spider phobia . . . and that a case may be made for computer anxiety to enter into the framework of problematic fears' (p. 1258). However, all anxieties are not identical in their manifestations, and Thorpe and Brosnan observed that typical reactions to ICT usage were mostly associated with social anxiety (making a fool of oneself) and performance anxiety (not being able to utilize the technology effectively). They further suggested that 'the perception of ability to stay calm, feel at ease and be able to cope with a situation' (p. 1270) appears to be inherent in effective coping with ICT, hence the individual's coping strategies may be critical to their adaptation to new technology. Finally Thorpe and Brosnan commented that while it is commonly believed that levels of ICT anxiety will diminish over time as younger generations become more familiar with and adjusted to this technology, research evidence indicates that the prevalence of and problems associated with computer anxiety are not necessarily declining.

As part of a larger project on information networks in Norwegian production companies. Mikkelsen et al. (2002) investigated the relationship between job characteristics. social support. active coping and levels of computer anxiety. These researchers found that decision authority rather than work demands was the single most important job characteristic contributing to anxiety. Workers who had lower levels of decision authority, that is less control and autonomy concerning decisions affecting their work, were more likely to report computer anxiety than their higher decision authority counterparts. This finding illustrates that factors beyond the immediate realm of the technology itself can have a significant impact on reactions to ICT. Coincidentally in this study there were no significant relationships between an 'active' (problem-solving) coping style or social support and levels of anxiety.

Several studies have been conducted to explore other correlates of ICT anxiety, including beliefs about self-efficacy (discussed later), expectations and general emotional states (affect). For instance Compeau et al. (1999) utilized social-cognitive theory to develop predictions about the antecedents of computer anxiety. Their longitudinal research conducted with a diverse Canadian sample. examined relationships between efficacy beliefs. outcome expectations, affect and anxiety. As anticipated, self-efficacy was a strong predictor of (reduced) anxiety while unrealistic expectations were associated with higher anxiety, although not linked with actual usage of the technology. In concert with other evidence their results underscore the importance of examining relationships between specific predictors and anxiety, as well as between anxiety and general well-being.

One form of ICT that has mushroomed in the past few years is the Internet, which is used both for communication with other people (as well as systems and organizations) and for gathering information about a range of diverse topics. Internet usage has become very prevalent in many (if not most) work settings as well as in 'non-work' contexts. Joiner et al. (2007) conducted research in the UK and Australia which demonstrated that most students were not overly anxious about using the Internet, although approximately 8 per cent of their sample did exhibit some level of anxiety and this was (predictably) associated with a lower usage rate. Joiner et al.'s findings appear to reflect those obtained in other studies of Internet usage. For example in a Romanian study Durndell and Haag (2002) also examined student attitudes and experiences with the Internet and found that more positive attitudes toward, and usage of, the Internet were negatively related to anxiety levels. Computer self-efficacy also followed this trend as it demonstrated a negative relationship with anxiety and a positive association with favourable Internet attitudes. Interestingly these authors also observed some gender differences in experiences with the Internet – although males and females reported similar usage rates, the types of usage varied somewhat and males reported spending more time than females on the Internet. Gender differences have not, however, been universally reported and where they have been observed they appear to be relatively minor.

The above research illustrates that anxiety about the use of technology can have severe consequences for workers in terms of their work perform-ance as well as their psychological health and well-being. In addition prolonged anxiety can ultimately induce a state of depression, which is also debilitating for the person. As with other forms and types of anxiety, concerns about one's ability to operate the technology effectively can result in the development of acute phobia toward ICT and ultimately withdrawal from usage. Given that technological advancement is inevitable and that most jobs will become increasingly dependent on effective utilization of ICT, chronic technological anxiety will inevitably have negative conse-quences for an individual worker. It is imperative, therefore, that appropri-ate and effective strategies are developed to assist individuals to overcome their anxieties and to function in the technological environment.

**Frustration with Technology**

Another psychosocial variable that has been explored in connection with ICT implementation and utilization is frustration. Early behavioural defi-nitions of frustration tended to focus simply on the non-achievement of expected goals, but more recent cognitive approaches have taken a some-what broader view of this construct, although lack of goal achievement remains a core element. Whichever approach is adopted it is generally recognized that frustration with technology arises when people's task-completion is interrupted, when errors or faults arise in the technology, or more generally when unexpected and inexplicable events occur such as programming failures and error messages that are difficult to interpret and act upon. Most (perhaps all) ICT users experience these kinds of frustration from time to time and to some extent these experiences may be anticipated. However, ongoing frustration over either the failure of the technology itself or one's inability to understand and utilize it efficiently and effectively can have a significant impact on the person's cognitive and emotional states.

Bessière et al. (2006) proposed a model that incorporates both disposi-tional and situational determinants of computer frustration. According to this model, a key element in the development of frustration is the notion of arousal; too much or too little arousal can impede performance as well as influencing the person's emotional state. Among the dispositional determinants of frustration are the individual's mood, their experience (of ICT) and their feelings of self-efficacy, while dispositional factors include the nature and importance of the task being performed, the time required to deal with and (hopefully) resolve difficulties or problems, the amount of time lost due to malfunctioning and the severity of the interruption of completion. This model, formulated from an information processing perspective, provides a valuable framework for understanding the ways in which ICT-related frustration can arise, the factors which contribute to frustration, and the outcomes (both cognitive and emotional) of these experiences. In their research Bessière et al. found that situational factors contributed about twice as much variance to the experience of frustration as did dispositional factors, but the latter nevertheless made a significant contribution. The researchers noted that frustration is not only debilitating in terms of immediate task completion but also generated more general maladaptive reactions (such as anxiety and anger) and in some circumstances the latter can translate into aggression (either toward the technology or toward other people). This is the well-known 'frustration–aggression' hypothesis articulated by Dollard et al. (1939). We also discussed the recent adaptations to this theory in Chapter 8.

Some of the major contributors to frustration and the amount of time lost due to ICT problems were explored by Lazar et al. (2006). They noted that responses to frustration can be either adaptive (for example solving the problem) or maladaptive (such as 'giving up', becoming aggressive, or resignation to the inevitability of the situation). Using time diaries Lazar and his colleagues obtained data from 50 workers who used computers as part of their job. The data included the nature of incidents that led to frustration, the level of frustration experienced, and the amount of time lost trying to resolve the problem that had occurred. Word processing and email web browsing problems created the highest number of frustrating experiences for people in this sample, and they reported that most of these experiences inhibited, but did not completely block, their task performance. One finding of significant interest in this study was that workers reported wasting around 42 per cent of their time endeavouring to sort out the problem that had caused frustration. Lazar and colleagues concluded that technological frustration is widespread among ICT users and can have a substantial effect on both their emotional well-being and their work performance. Several implications of their findings were presented for users, managers, computer support personnel and ICT designers.

Ceaparu and colleagues (Ceaparu et al., 2004) have also identified some of the major contributors to ICT frustration. They noted that frustration is a relatively common experience among ICT users, and the most cited causes of frustration are 'error messages, dropped network connections,

long download times, and hard-to-find features' (p. 333). They observed
that frustration occurs for most users on a fairly regular basis, mostly
due to the person not knowing what the problem was or how to solve a
problem even when they were able to identify it. The average percentage
of reported time lost due to these occurrences was 38 per cent, which is
very similar to the 42 per cent observed by Lazar et al. (2006) and reflects
a relatively high level of lost time.

Of course frustration is not an inevitable experience when using technology and there are factors which can mitigate the person's reactions
including anticipation of delays, errors or long download times (Ceaparu
et al., 2004). Time pressure may also affect the person's reactions; having
to perform tasks within a limited time period or under deadlines will place
additional demands on the individual worker, and is likely to exacerbate
negative emotional reactions which emerge when technological problems
occur. Increasing users' knowledge of how to resolve problems and deal
with error messages can also alleviate some of the frustration arising from
malfunctions.

It is clear from the above discussion that frustration with ICT is a
relatively common and pervasive experience and that it can impact significantly on the individual's well-being, especially if the sources of frustration
are not modified or removed and the person's experiences are repeated.
Although some of these experiences can be attributed to personal factors
(such as lack of knowledge and capability with ICT) it is evident that
design flaws and system problems, along with lack of information on
how to resolve problems when they do occur, contribute significantly to
frustration among many workers. Ultimately ongoing frustration can lead
the person to psychologically and physically withdraw from usage of the
technology, hence it is critical to develop mechanisms that will effectively
address the causes of frustrating experiences, reduce negative psychological outcomes, and ultimately enhance rather than detract from individual
well-being.

**Feelings of Incompetence versus Mastery**

Allied to frustration with technology is the feeling of incompetence that
an individual can experience when he or she perceives that they are not
able to utilize ICT effectively or to resolve problems that occur. Over time
this feeling can lead to increased anxiety and even depression, along with
a sense of lack of goal achievement. Earlier we referred to the six-factor
model of computer anxiety formulated by Beckers and his colleagues
which incorporates self-efficacy, defined as 'beliefs about one's capabilities to organize and execute the courses of action required to produce goal

attainments' (Bandura, 1997, p. 3). In their model Beckers and Schmidt (2001) described computer (or ICT) self-efficacy as the feeling of compe- tence and assurance that one can master a technology. Such cognitions are important in determining a person's reactions to ICT and their ability to withstand the strain that can emerge when things go wrong. Self-efficacy or perceived competence also reduces anxiety about further ICT usage.

A programme of research on the effects of ICT self-efficacy has been conducted by Salanova and her colleagues based on Bandura's (1997) model of self-efficacy. Their research has examined both direct and mod- erating (buffering) effects of this variable. For instance, Salanova et al. (2000) noted that even when a person is skilled and proficient in ICT usage they can still make mistakes and even perform poorly, but this does not necessarily create anxiety and concern for that person if they gener- ally believe in their ability to master the technology. On the other hand a feeling of incompetence (inability to manage the technology effectively and/or resolve problems associated with its usage) can be very debilitating, leading to low performance and withdrawal as well as reduced psycho- logical health due to the stress of perceived failure. Salanova et al. (2000) found that computer self-efficacy moderated the relationship between training in technology usage and burnout. Specifically while overall a high level of training was associated with reduced cynicism, for workers who were low on computer self-efficacy the opposite effect was obtained – more training was linked with higher cynicism! In other words ICT self-efficacy can have a substantial influence on a person's reactions to technology, and training may not be fully effective if the initial self-efficacy is low.

In a follow-up study Beas and Salanova (2006) differentiated between three kinds of self-efficacy which they labelled 'professional', 'computer' and 'generalized' self-efficacy. They tested the relationship between these three forms of self-efficacy and psychological well-being among ICT workers. As in the above study Beas and Salanova concluded that train- ing per se is not the most important determinant of computer attitudes, but rather the combination of training and underlying self-efficacy con- tributes to reduced anxiety, depression and burnout. Based on the job demands–control model of stress formulated by Karasek (1979), Salanova et al. (2002) examined the moderating effects of both generalized and computer self-efficacy on the relationship between work overload, job control and burnout in a sample of information technology workers in Spanish companies. Salanova and her colleagues argued that self-efficacy can play a very significant role in people's responses to situations where there are high demands and relatively low levels of control over the work environment. This expectation was confirmed, with computer self-efficacy (but not generalized self-efficacy) displaying a significant moderating effect. When computer-based self-efficacy was high, having control over work demands weakened the positive relationship between overload and exhaustion, but this attenuation was not evident when workers possessed low self-efficacy.

Other research has also illustrated the positive effects of self-efficacy. Based on a model of technology acceptance Compeau et al. (1999) conducted a longitudinal study that obtained significant associations between computer self-efficacy and positive affect, reduced anxiety and increased computer usage 12 months later. In fact in this study self-efficacy was a stronger predictor of anxiety than were users' expectations concerning the outcomes of computer use, which on the surface would appear to be a more salient predictor of usage. In an assessment of their computer frustration model Bessière and her colleagues (2006) observed that feelings of competency were associated with reduced frustration when problems occurred in addition to more positive moods. They noted that 'the user's sense of being able to cope with computing technology appears to be a pervasive factor in how frustrated he or she becomes' (p. 958).

In summary there is consistent evidence that feeling competent to use ICT, and to correct problems and difficulties that emerge during use, are very strong contributors to user affect and other responses. Consequently as suggested by Salanova et al. (2000) perhaps more effort needs to be directed toward enhancing feelings of competence and self-efficacy generally, prior to providing training related to specific functions and programmes. Such approaches will assist in the reduction of anxiety and negative mood states as well as enhancing user satisfaction and intention to continue ICT usage.

**Personal Control**

Closely related to the above issue is the extent to which individuals feel they can exert personal control over their environment including the technology they need to utilize in performing work tasks. Chapter 4 discussed the considerable body of research based on Karasek's (1979) job demands–control model and similar theoretical formulations, which suggest that feelings of control over the environment generate mostly positive outcomes for both individuals and their organizations. With respect to ICT experiences specifically, when confronted by excessive technological demands which may create symptoms of psychological strain (such as anxiety, frustration and withdrawal), believing that one has some degree of control over the situation will help to alleviate negative reactions. Alternatively, feeling a lack of control will exacerbate levels of anxiety, frustration and depression, leading ultimately to psychological and behavioural withdrawal from ICT usage. Coovert and Thompson (2003) noted that perceptions of control play a particularly salient role when new technology is being introduced, and that 'lack of control experienced by workers who are required to deal with technological failures, inadequacies, and changes, generate psychological stress' (p. 229).

Several studies have demonstrated the positive benefits (for well-being, as well as other relevant variables) of perceived control over ICT. For instance in a qualitative study of how bank managers coped with technological challenges, Beaudry and Pinsonneault (2005) observed that perceived control over technology can to a large extent determine how a person copes and their level of technostress. Similarly Salanova et al. (2002) found that people reporting greater perceived control experienced fewer symptoms of burnout when they were exposed to high technological demands than did their counterparts who felt less control over these demands, supporting Karasek's (1979) job demands–control model of strain. Although their research focused on university students rather than workers, Beckers and Schmidt (2003) linked perceptions of control to self-efficacy, suggesting that feeling in control of the technology helps to reduce computer anxiety and leads to increased satisfaction in working with computers and intentions to utilize them further. Control can therefore exert an ameliorating effect on anxiety and other negative reactions toward ICT.

A variable which is related to, albeit not synonymous with, perceived control is locus of control (LOC), which is a dispositional (personality) variable rather than a perception of the immediate environment. The effects of LOC appear to be virtually identical to those of perceived control. Specifically individuals with a high internal LOC (who perceive they can exert personal control over outcomes) are likely to experience less psychological strain than those with low internal LOC. High internal LOC has been associated with greater job satisfaction and reduced job-related strain (Korunka and Vitouch, 1999). In a study of email utilization, Hair and his colleagues (2007) also focused on LOC. Interestingly, however, although Hair et al. did record some benefits associated with internal LOC these were not as substantial as those demonstrated by self-esteem. It is likely that LOC and self-esteem are closely interrelated, hence the contribution of LOC may have been somewhat overshadowed by that of self-esteem.

Finally it is also important to consider how much control individuals wish to exert in relation to technology. Having 'too much' control can, in some situations, carry penalties for the person such as assuming uncomfortably high levels of responsibility. Hence desirability of control (that is the person's level of motivation to exert control) may be a relevant variable to consider when investigating the effects of perceived control. This proposition was supported in a study by Dvash and Mannheim (2001) of plant operators in an Israeli manufacturing factory; a greater motivation to have control over the technology moderated the impact of the technology on worker well-being. Although this was an investigation of automated manufacturing technology rather than ICT per se, the implications are also relevant to the latter. As with self-efficacy, research suggests that more attention to the impact of perceived control and locus of control on worker well-being when dealing with ICT would be advantageous.

## CONCLUSION

This chapter has provided a synopsis of research on the relationship between use of technology (specifically, information and communications technology or ICT) and various facets of psychological well-being. Our review of the literature is clearly not exhaustive, but it has highlighted that there are several key psychosocial dimensions that require consideration when this kind of technology is being implemented in work settings. The *technological imperative* (Katz, 1997) suggests that technological innovation and development is inevitable and necessary for the continued effective functioning of organizations, and hence individuals need to be able to respond adaptively to technological change. We have outlined some of the psychological variables that are pertinent to this adaptation. The research described above illustrates that psychosocial factors such as anxiety, frustration and feelings of incompetence can have a very substantial bearing on individual well-being as well as on their usage (or withdrawal from usage) of ICT. Although there has been much discussion of 'user-friendly' ICT (Coovert and Thompson, 2003), frequently there is less than optimal consideration given to human capabilities and modes of operating when ICT is designed and introduced. That such technology can have a substantial impact on individual psychological health as well as physical well-being is indisputable; the challenge is to ensure that the knowledge and information we have obtained on these linkages is utilized to enhance the interface between technology and people.

# 10. Executive coaching

**Co-authored with Olena Stepanova, IESE Business School and Universitat Autònoma de Barcelona**

## OVERVIEW

Coaching has recently emerged as a discipline, a profession, a leadership style, and a new area of empirical research. The practice of coaching has been around for millennia in the form of individualized, professional advice and training, but has only recently been formally recognized as a psychological construct within the corporate and academic arenas. This recognition of coaching has arisen due to recent changes in organizational management practices. A recent study conducted by the Boston Consulting Group in collaboration with the European Association of Personnel Management (EAPM) surveyed 1355 executives from 27 countries in Europe. This study identified the current trends in human resource management as consisting of: managing talent, managing demographics, becoming a learning organization, managing work–life balance, and managing change and cultural transformation. Coaching is expected to play a major role within these trends by offering four distinct advantages to both the individual and organization. First, coaching is an important tool for diagnosing and developing competencies, and for developing individual learning and change. Second, coaching is an important leadership style for managers to practise situational leadership. Third, coaching is needed as a means of supporting and retaining the increasingly scarce numbers of high-performing expert managers by guiding them through tough decisions, helping them to maintain healthy and efficient work patterns and helping them to deal with increasingly demanding clients and employees. Finally, coaching assists in the customization of human resource management to engage talented employees. For instance coaching is employed to customize and monitor individual employee work–life solutions.

Coaching therefore extends beyond a process or technique for developing competencies and reaching ambitious goals. Coaching represents a new paradigm in management, based on individualization, maximization, learning and support. The very fact that the Center of Creative Leadership, a non-profit institution dedicated to leadership and coaching, rivals with the top business schools in customized and executive programmes is a clear sign that leadership and coaching is positioned prominently on the corporate agenda. Sherman and Freas (2004) estimated that approximately one billion US dollars is spent annually on coaching within US organizations. Organizations such as GlaxoSmithKline, Rohm and Haas Company, Pfizer and Colgate-Palmolive position coaching as an executive perk (Wasylyshyn, 2003), while other organizations (for example American Red Cross) offer it as part of a development and productivity programme to non-executive employees (Natale and Diamante, 2005).

A major concern in this field is that academic research in coaching is significantly lagging behind practice. According to the European Coaching Survey 2007/8, there are approximately 18 000 business coaches in the European Union, with an estimated 50 000 coaches operating worldwide (Hyatt, 2003). In addition, several coaching-focused organizations have been founded, including the Association for Coaching (AC), the European Mentoring and Coaching Council (EMCC), and the International Coach Federation (ICF). While professional associations, training and consulting institutions are producing and certifying professional coaches to meet the increasing demand for coaching, knowledge about what actually constitutes efficient and effective coaching is scarce, and is generally published in a handful of non-mainstream academic journals.

Most academic research on coaching occurs within the psychological training and development literature (Kampa-Kokesch and Anderson, 2001; Passmore and Gibbes, 2007). Coaching research originally focused on the role of the *internal* manager acting as coach to the subordinate; more recently the focus has switched to the role of the professional *external* coach (Grant and Zackon, 2004). Research also indicates that organizations use coaching for different needs. *Strategic coaching*, for example, aims to align personal development with organizational needs (Sherman and Freas, 2004). It can help employees adapt to new positions, improve interpersonal interactions and teamwork, and reduce turnover. *Systematic coaching* is designed to intensify relationships with the key employees within a general framework and increase their effectiveness. In this chapter we discuss the common definitions of coaching and provide an overview of coaching research. Figure 10.1 illustrates the coaching process and represents an integrated, theoretical framework of coaching which we suggest can guide coaching research. Specifically this chapter defines coaching as a process and identifies the different stages in the coaching process; we review the antecedents and consequences of the coaching process, describe the role of the organization and formulate recommendations for future research.

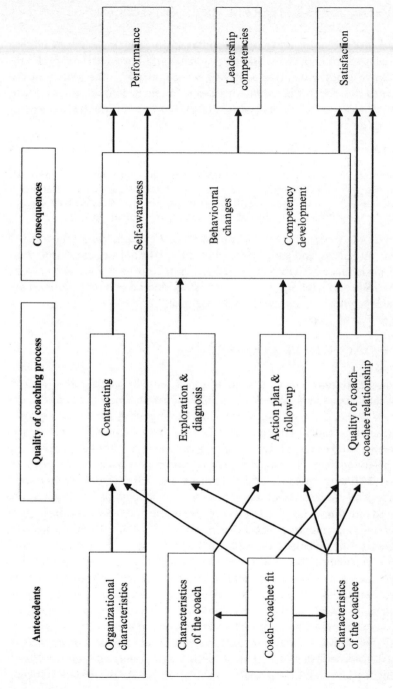

*Figure 10.1   The coaching model*

# DEFINING COACHING

Research describes coaching as a popular approach to training delivery which aims to enhance the worker's potential and improve their performance (Gray, 2006). Executive coaching is recognized by the ability of the coachee to develop his/her own strategies to reach defined goals and to have ownership of the results (Gray, 2006). Kilburg (2000) defined executive coaching as:

> a helping relationship formed between a client who has managerial authority and responsibility in an organization and a consultant who uses a wide variety of behavioural techniques and methods to help the client achieve a mutually identified set of goals to improve his or her professional performance and personal satisfaction and consequently, to improve the effectiveness of the client's organization within a formally defined coaching agreement. (p. 67)

We propose to expand this definition to include a helping relationship between managers and employees, not just external coaches and their clients. Coaching can therefore be defined as an approach focused on work effectiveness, performance, personal satisfaction and enhancement, where the coach provides the coachee with guidance.

# THE COACHING PROCESS

Coaching represents a learning and action-oriented *process*, since it offers the coachee objective feedback about their current behavioural and competency drawbacks, and concentrates on finding ways for their improvement (Larburu and Poelmans, 2007; Ting, 2006). Kampa-Kokesch and Anderson (2001) reported that coaching can serve as a tool for enhancing good behaviour rather than addressing under-performance. By experimenting with new ways of acting, thinking and reflecting on daily issues, coaching leads to greater competencies in the specific areas that require improvement, which may ultimately increase the person's self-confidence, capabilities and sense of control (Sheppard et al., 2006). Possible areas of competency improvement typically include: business, interpersonal and personal efficiency. The goal-setting approach is often used to develop competencies and to keep the coachee motivated throughout the coaching process. Goal-setting consists of selecting specific targets that lead to improvement in desired areas (such as to increase communications with collaborators). The goal-setting approach empowers the coachee by guiding them towards clearly set and measurable objectives. Once reached, the results motivate them to set more challenging goals and therefore reach even higher levels of competence (Johnston, 2005). Besides developing and consolidating the sought competencies, through goal attainment the coachee develops their own self-efficacy, that is the perception of their abilities in dealing with specific situations (Simons, 2006; Gray, 2006).

**Stages of the Coaching Process**

The coaching process typically consists of five phases; contracting, exploration, diagnosis, action plan and follow-up. We briefly review these five phases here.

**1. Contracting**
The aim of the contracting phase is to ensure that the coachee has realistic expectations of the process, understands its theoretical basis and methods to be used. According to Natale and Diamante (2005) there are two ethical issues involved in the contracting phase: confidentiality and conflict of interest. Confidentiality refers to the responsibility of the organization to preserve the confidentiality of the received information, while the latter refers to the possible conflict of interest between the coachees' interest and that of a third-party (usually the organization). An important task of the coach is to create a safe and trusting atmosphere and demonstrate the qualities valued by the coachee (ICF, 2008). Throughout the coaching process the issues of trust and effectiveness are continually revisited (Natale and Diamante, 2005).

**2. Exploration**
Coaching aims to create self-awareness which serves as a foundation for active learning and personal growth, empowering a worker to reach beyond their current level of development (Sherman and Freas, 2004). The understanding of one's own internal processes helps the person to behave and interact effectively with others. Wales (2003) suggested that self-awareness consists of four elements: 'the ability to understand one's past and learn from it; openness to one's own and other's feelings; the ability to reflect on a situation before moving to action; and the ability to make appropriate choices' (p. 278). The *past–present awareness* gives the individual the chance to understand how past experience has influenced the creation of their current attitudes, behaviours and feelings. The *openness to one's feelings* facilitates an individual's congruence in their behaviours and actions, as incongruence may cause miscommunication and misunderstanding with other people. *Reflection* allows the individual to consider the situations and to view it from different angles, and finally, self-awareness supports the individual in generating different *choices* and in decision-making. Wales, for example, reported that increasing managers' self-awareness increased their self-confidence and self-esteem.

### 3. Diagnosis

Feedback is an important constituent of the coaching process as it facilitates the basis for the coachee's learning process, personal development and talent enhancement (Kampa-Kokesch and Anderson, 2001). Feedback based on objective facts serves as the foundation for this growth. Therefore coaches use a variety of assessment tools including feedback questionnaires, qualitative interviews and psychological instruments (Kampa-Kokesch and Anderson, 2001; Passmore, 2008). A popular tool is 360 degree feedback; this provides detailed information about the coachee's behaviours and identifies the gap between a worker's behaviours and the organization's goals and objectives (London and Beatty, 1993; Luthans and Peterson, 2003). This feedback is used to gather anonymous information about the coachee from three different levels: their immediate boss, their colleagues or peers, and their subordinates.

### 4. Action plan

Based on the information obtained from the previous phases, the coach and coachee collaborate in designing an action plan. The action plan incorporates the identified goals and sets targets that are assessable and realistic (Sherman and Freas, 2004). The action plan objectives should be specific, measurable, attainable, relevant and traceable (SMART).

### 5. Follow-up

The follow-up assessment of the coaching process is essential to realize the level of change and to identify areas that require improvement. Follow-up can occur at the beginning and end of the session to identify areas in need of improvement, and to evaluate any performance changes and goal achievement (Sherman and Freas, 2004).

The coaching process is therefore aimed at the acquisition of knowledge, skills and competencies and subsequently behavioural changes by the coachee. These changes are expected to enhance the coachee's performance and lead to increased personal satisfaction. We next review the main antecedents of the coaching process which we specified in Figure 10.1.

## ANTECEDENTS OF THE COACHING PROCESS

### Internal Coach or External Coach

The coach may be internal to the organization or completely external. The main advantages of employing an internal coach are that they possess more diverse information about the coachee's personality, performance and quality of interactions with others. Such knowledge can assist the coach in creating a development plan. Internal coaches, however, may be accused of having a conflict of interest with regard to the communication of results to management and therefore can raise issues of trust and confidentiality (Hall et al., 1999). Wasylyshyn (2003) reported that managers who participated in a coaching process expressed both positive and negative attitudes to working with an external coach. The main advantages of an external coach include: objectivity, experience of working with different companies, higher expertise, no political agenda, and increased trust and confidentiality.

**Personal Characteristics of the Coach**

Van Fleet (1999) described the psychological skills that constitute an effective coach as including interpersonal effectiveness, listening, empathy, patience, adaptability, analytical problem solving, creativity and humour. Whitworth et al. (2007) identified three key coach characteristics: trustworthiness, compatible chemistry and solid reputation. In addition, respect, congruence, collaborative work and discursive communicational approach are also recognized as being important coach characteristics.

**Competencies of the Coach**

The International Coach Federation (ICF) developed eleven core coaching competencies grouped in four clusters that define a coach's skills and practices. The first is setting the foundation, which encompasses meeting ethical guidelines and professional standards and establishing a coaching agreement. The second cluster of competencies consists of co-creating the relationship, the third is communication and the fourth focuses on facilitating learning and results. Research supports the importance of these competencies, in that during the coaching process coachees highly value the coaches' listening and questioning skills, integrity and the ability to challenge the coachee constructively (Hall et al., 1999; Jones and Spooner, 2006).

**Fit between Coach and Coachee**

In addition to the initial contractual agreement that frames the coaching process, a good fit between the coach and coachee is required in order to achieve a successful outcome. Toegel and Nicholson (2005), with a study of 172 senior managers, demonstrated that demographic similarity in the working dyad positively affects leadership development. A good fit also requires the coach to be flexible in adapting to the coachee's preferences and may for example involve a mix of different approaches: face-to-face meetings, audio-video conferencing, email, online assessments, telephone and web-enabled follow-up processes. A good fit between the coach and coachee, whether based on demographic, professional or technological characteristics, contributes to the success of the coaching process.

The coach's ability to create a connection with the client is obviously vital for building a successful relationship. One of the most challenging issues in the coaching relationship is achieving the correct balance between challenge and support (Bluckert, 2005). Bluckert identified four factors that influence the coaching relationship: *unconditional positive regard and acceptance*, which refers to a non-judgemental caring attitude towards the coachee; *accurate empathy*, which involves trying to understand the reality from the coachee's perspective; *congruence/genuineness*, whereby the coach acts in accordance with his/her own values and beliefs; and *non-possessive warmth*, which refers to finding the right amount of expressed friendliness that does not seem effusive for the client, but conveys respect. One of the important coach's competencies is the ability to create a trusting and positive relationship with the coachee, followed by the ability to achieve set goals and improve performance (Boyatzis et al., 2006; Gyllensten and Palmer, 2007).

**The Role of the Organization**

The organization plays an important role in the coaching process primarily in terms of the provision of an environment that will reinforce the coachee's acquired skills. Coaching then consists of a collaborative process between the coachee, the client and the organizational stakeholders (Bluckert, 2005; Orenstein, 2002). Before initiating a coaching process an organization should clearly establish the goals to be achieved, and how these goals can be integrated into the established organizational processes.

In 2005 the Coaching Research Project, involving 144 coaches and managers from over 20 countries, identified ten key success factors for implementing coaching (Bresser, 2005). These factors acknowledge that coaching implementation has to be supported by the organization in three main ways: first by communicating an organization-specific understanding of coaching which is aligned with the business strategy; second by having a systemic approach to its implementation which is secured by top-management support; and finally by marketing coaching implementation as a developmental tool. To assure participation in the coaching process, an organization needs to provide comprehensive information on its content and evaluation and to ensure confidentiality for its users (Bresser, 2005). For example Pfleiderer, a European manufacturing organization, guaranteed confidentiality via the provision of budget stamps to its employees, with which they can purchase coaching services without having to inform HR management (Bresser, 2005).

When implementing coaching, an organization has to ensure that positive and broad information about the coaching process is provided and to communicate its support, hence the coachee's collaborators play an important role in this process (Liao et al., 2004). The organization's role therefore is to support the coachee with feedback on their areas of improvement. Chrysler, for example, promoted its support for organization coaching by introducing the concept of round tables (Bresser, 2005). Thus the coachee's line manager was involved in the evaluation part of the coaching process, to assure that the established goals were appropriate to the organizational aims.

# CONSEQUENCES OF THE COACHING PROCESS

## Individual Outcomes

Research conducted with groups of employees who have been involved in a coaching programme, demonstrated that the coaching process leads to increased self-awareness and more effective leadership (Wasylyshyn, 2003), behaviour change (Hall et al., 1999), self-confidence, increased management skills, assertiveness, better stress management, work–life balance and communication skills (Wales, 2003), and enhances abilities in building teams and developing staff (Parker-Wilkins, 2006). Wales argued that these benefits can be grouped into internal processes (self-awareness and confidence) which fuel the development of external processes (management, assertiveness, understanding difference, stress management and work–life balance). Communication skills serve as a mediator between the two processes, as they facilitate the interchange of ideas, receipt of knowledge and creation of new behaviours, leadership and management competencies.

## Group/team Outcomes

Research has also identified that managers reported different outcomes of the coaching processes at the individual and team levels (Wales, 2003). Individual-level outcomes included a wider organization overview, improved leadership skills, higher level of assertiveness, tolerance and serenity. Individuals were also better able to identify their own vision, producing clarity and inspiration in their jobs. Team outcomes included a better understanding of the team dynamics and team development, more effective meetings, increased openness to others' opinions, and more helpfulness to others. Additionally the managers became more proactive in role management, more skilled in building trusting relationships and dealt with change more successfully (Judge and Cowell, 1997). Olivero et al. (1997) investigated the effects of executive coaching and reported that the process was beneficial for both the coachees and the organization. The participants reported improved skills, increased learning and behavioural changes. Smither et al. (2003) also demonstrated that coaching resulted in improved productivity.

**Organizational Outcomes**

Besides individual and team outcomes, it is important to identify the contribution of coaching on business results. Drawing on the leader member-exchange theory Agarwal et al. (2006) studied the effects of managers' coaching intensity on the performance of their coachees. Agarwal et al. found that managers' coaching intensity influenced the performance of their subordinates after controlling for job satisfaction. The authors concluded that supportive and development oriented leader–member exchange has a positive effect on subordinate performance. The 'Manchester study' also demonstrated that the return on investment (ROI) of coaching was approximately 5.7 times the initial coaching investment (McGovern et al., 2001). More recently, Parker-Wilkins (2006) reported a ROI of 689 per cent and found that coaching produced tangible and financial benefits for seven out of eight key business areas.

# COACHING RESEARCH METHODS

Coaching research is certainly in an embryonic stage, although as we have observed, the practice of coaching is rapidly increasing. In this section we discuss the directions scholars can take in developing the coaching field and formulate some recommendations for both coaching researchers and practitioners.

As discussed above, coaching is by definition a process that develops over time, an interaction between parties who continuously influence each other as time progresses. This process therefore clearly calls for research designs that capture data at several points in time: before, during and after the coaching process. Research also needs to assess baseline measures of performance and competencies before the coaching process begins. Data is required to assess the expectations, credentials, background information and curricula of both coaches and coachees, as well as a range of organizational characteristics that may influence the impact of coaching. Data should be collected at multiple intervals to assess progress in the development of coachees within the five stages of the coaching process and to track evolving relationships with coaches and other stakeholders over time. It is also vital that data is collected after completing the coaching process, in order to assess the real impact of coaching against the baseline measures. Whereas most organizations limit themselves to measures of overall satisfaction, measures of performance and leadership effectiveness are also required in order to assess the impact of coaching on productivity. These processes cannot be appraised using self-report measures only. Research designs should be adopted that enable data to be collected from multiple sources. The use of 360 degree feedback, which requests evaluations from multiple stakeholders, is strongly recommended not only to contrast perceptions but to confirm patterns of *actual* change in the individual, in the interaction between coachees and their colleagues, and in the organization.

Collecting multi-time, multi-source, multi-level data requires close collaboration between researchers and organizations. Interdisciplinary, multi-member research teams are one answer to this challenge. Collaborative international research is also required to identify cross-cultural differences in the definition of coaching, coaching styles and desired outcomes. The concept of meta-cognition research on cultural intelligence (Thomas et al., in press), for example, suggests promising developments for coaching research. Lowman (2005) discussed the lack of scientific research for executive coaching and suggested employing case studies. Lowman argued that case studies can provide insights into this new organizational process and generate empirically testable hypotheses. Verbal protocols may be the only way of capturing reasoning and meta-cognition in coaches, essential in the stages of exploration and diagnosis. One of the major challenges of coaching research, though, is controlling for the numerous factors that can influence the process. Hence there is a need for laboratory research employing experimental designs to study the effect of different types of coaches, coaching styles, coaching competencies and interaction patterns. Feldman and Lankau (2005) for example suggested:

> Rather than putting more energy into delineating the conceptual distinctions of coaching and other types of developmental relationships, it might be more critical at this point to focus on the constellations and patterns of coaching behaviours that typically co-occur and/or are typically most helpful to clients. In other words, some of the research discourse on coaching needs to shift to the relative effectiveness of various *kinds* of coaching relationships. (p. 841)

## CONCLUSION

This chapter has reviewed the emerging practice of organizational coaching. While coaching research is currently scarce, the increasing popularity of this practice reinforces the need for coaching to be brought to the attention of organizational researchers. This chapter reviewed some of the common antecedents and consequences of coaching and discussed the methodologies which will develop this research field further. Given the socio-demographic and business trends we described in the introduction of this chapter, the prevalence of organizational coaching is expected to increase significantly over the coming years in order to meet the increasing demand for employee learning and development.

# 11. Organizational counselling and fitness programmes

## INTRODUCTION

This book has discussed how within the last few decades, workplaces have undergone major transformations due to rapid advances in information technology, globalization, increased female participation, and growing numbers of dual-earner couples and older workers. These changes have had far-reaching consequences for employee health and well-being (O'Driscoll et al., 2008). According to the National Institute for Occupational Safety and Health (NIOSH), occupational stress was one of the ten leading causes of workplace death in the US in 1990 (cited in Sauter et al., 1990). More recent data from the same source indicates an alarming trend for increasing levels of occupational stress: 40 per cent of US employees believe their jobs are 'very' or 'extremely' stressful and at least 26 per cent of employees feel 'burned out' at work (NIOSH, 2006). The American Psychological Association (APA) estimates the cost of job stress incurred by US companies at $300 billion per year due to increased absenteeism, productivity loss, turnover and healthcare costs (APA, 2008). The Business and Economic Roundtable of Canada estimated that the cost in lost productivity, turnover, disability payouts and absenteeism for Canadian organizations is about CA$30 billion a year (Corbett, 2004). In the light of this evidence there is increasing interest among organizations in instituting workplace practices that promote better individual and organizational well-being.

Some organizations have taken a leadership role in promoting the concept of a healthy workplace. The American Association of Critical-Care Nurses, for example, recently established six standards for establishing and sustaining healthy work environments (Viejo, 2005). Similarly the National Quality Council in Canada established healthy workplace awards based on six criteria which form the core of 'Excellence Framework for Healthy Workplace' (Corbett, 2004). The APA has recently instituted a programme that recognizes and honours organizations that demonstrate a high level of commitment to implementing policies that foster employee health and well-being while enhancing organizational performance (APA,

2008). We therefore review in this final chapter four key research areas that inform the concept of a 'psychologically healthy workplace': (a) what is a psychologically healthy workplace; (b) some common psychologically healthy workplace practices and their link to individual and organizational outcomes; (c) some *un*healthy workplace practices and their influence on negative individual and organizational outcomes; and (d) remedial measures organizations have employed to address negative outcomes. We first examine three common terms scholars have used to refer to the 'psychologically healthy workplace', namely *organizational fit, organizational health* and *organizational wellness*.

## ORGANIZATIONAL FITNESS, HEALTH AND WELLNESS

Scholars have utilized different terminologies to describe the state and dynamics of organizations relevant to organizational fitness, health and wellness. Beer (2002) defines the term *organizational fitness* as the capacity of an organization to adapt its organizational design, culture and behaviour, that is its work system (structure), management processes, human resource systems, principles, values and leadership behaviour, in order to accommodate to the changing business environment. Miles (1969) first used the term *organizational health* when he delineated ten properties of healthy organizations (such as goal focus and adaptation). Miles defined organizational health as the ability of an organization's system to function effectively over time. *Organizational wellness* has been defined as a satisfactory state of organizational affairs undertaken by organizations to improve the physical and psychological health of employees in relation to the organizations' objectives to improve organizational effectiveness and productivity (North, 1988). Organizational wellness also includes other aspects of employees' well-being, such as the *welfare* of individuals in the organizational context (Vickers, 2006). Although these three constructs differ somewhat in their emphasis, the common thread running across them is the notion of a 'psychologically healthy workplace'.

We turn our attention next to the research underpinning the concept of a 'psychologically healthy workplace' which is sourced in four interrelated literature areas: (a) the definition of a psychologically healthy workplace; (b) the relationships between employee well-being and organizational improvements; (c) the relationships between healthy workplace practices and organizational improvements; and (d) the associations between healthy workplace practices, employee well-being and organizational improvements (Grawitch et al., 2006). This review is not intended to be exhaustive of all healthy and unhealthy workplace practices that impact on organizational and individual outcomes. Our choice of workplace variables to include under each category is informed by both research and the potential of each workplace variable to impact individual and organizational outcomes.

## CONCEPTUALIZATION OF A 'PSYCHOLOGICALLY HEALTHY WORKPLACE'

In the past three decades a considerable amount of research has focused on furthering our understanding of what constitutes a psychologically healthy workplace. Sauter et al. (1996) defined a psychologically healthy workplace as one that 'maximises the integration of worker goals for well-being and company objectives for profitability and productivity' (p. 250). Corbett (2004) defined a psychologically healthy workplace in terms of holistic workplace health, which includes physical, social, personal and developmental organizational support to improve employees' overall quality of life, both within and outside the workplace. Hence a psychologically healthy workplace is one that sponsors health promotion activities; offers employee assistance programmes, flexible benefits and working conditions; treats employees fairly; and offers programmes of employee development, health, safety and the prevention of work stress (APA, 2008). In all three definitions there is an equal emphasis on achieving high organizational outcomes (such as improved employee performance) and healthy individual outcomes (such as job satisfaction and good health). Browne (2000) argued that human resource practices are progressive only if the concern for organizational outcomes is matched by a concern for the well-being of employees who are directly affected by these practices.

## UNHEALTHY WORKPLACE PRACTICES

Accumulating research in occupational health psychology and related disciplines confirms that certain workplace policies and practices contribute to the development of unhealthy workplaces. The intent of this review is not to delve into the mechanisms through which these policies and practices create unhealthy workplaces, but to examine empirical evidence that links certain workplace practices to reduced individual and organizational outcomes. In this section we discuss a set of five *unhealthy* workplace practices: (a) high job demands, low job control and autonomy; (b) excessive workload; (c) role stressors; (d) reduced supervisory support; and (e) reduced co-worker support.

### High Job Demands, Low Job Control and Autonomy

As we discussed in Chapter 4, Karasek (1979) proposed that two aspects of the work environment determine the effects of work conditions on the health and well-being of employees, namely *job demands* and *job control*. The most stressful jobs are those that fall in the high demands–low control category, which has come to be called 'high strain jobs'. In an extensive review of 20 years of empirical research covering 63 samples between 1977 and 1997, van der Doef and Maes (1999) found that high strain jobs were associated with lower psychological well-being, lower job satisfaction, more burnout, and more job-related psychological distress. These findings have been widely replicated. For example in a study involving 2796 teachers from 13 European countries, Verhoeven et al. (2003) stated that the teachers reporting the most negative outcomes were those who fell under the high demands, low control, low support group. In a prospective cohort study (known as the Whitehall II study) involving 6895 male and 3413 female civil servants, Kuper and Marmot (2003) found that individuals with concurrent low decision latitude and high demands were at the highest risk of coronary heart disease.

A similar conclusion was drawn by Theorell et al. (1998) in a Swedish study of causes of myocardial infarction involving 1047 cases of men 45 to 65 years old who had been working full-time during the previous five years. Theorell et al. reported that low decision latitude was associated with increased risk of a first myocardial infarction, although this association was weakened after adjustment for social class. A decrease in decision latitude during the ten years preceding the myocardial infarction was also associated with increased risk. The combination of high self-reported demands and low self-reported decision latitude was an independent predictor of risk. There is growing evidence that a combination of high demands, low control and low support are risk factors for anxiety and depression among workers. Recent evidence for this assertion comes from a large Norwegian population-based study (the Hordaland Health Study; involving over 5500 men and women) which found that increased job demands and low levels of job control were positively correlated with anxiety and depression (Biringer et al., 2005). Similarly in a US study, Mausner-Dorsch and Eaton (2000) found that high job strain was associated with greater prevalence of all three forms of depression: major depressive episode, depressive syndrome and dysphoria.

**Excessive Workload**

A recent report indicates that the average work year for working couples has increased by nearly 700 hours in the past two decades; consequently 40 per cent of employees believe their jobs are 'very' or 'extremely' stressful and 26 per cent of employees feel 'burned out' at work (NIOSH, 2006). Over-work and time management have each been negatively associated with behavioural, psychological and physiological outcomes (Jex and Elacqua, 1999). In a major review of the literature on psychological ill health manifested in depression, psychological distress, anxiety and mental strain, Michie and Williams (2003) found that key work factors associated with psychological illness were long hours worked, excessive work-load, lack of control over work, lack of participation in decision-making, poor social support, and unclear management and work role.

**Role Stressors**

Role conflict exists when individuals face two or more demands that are incompatible. Newton and Jimmieson (2008) found that high perceptions of role stressors (role conflict, role ambiguity and role overload) were significantly related to lower job satisfaction among Australian Local Government Council members. Similarly Kirk-Brown and Wallace (2004) found that role conflict was a significant predictor of burnout among workplace counsellors. In a cross-national study involving nurses from Hungary, Italy, the US and the UK, Glazer and Beehr (2005) reported that role stressors predicted anxiety across sites. Furthermore, they noted that while there was some variation in the strength of the results, the direction of the relationships was consistent across countries. This finding suggested that effects of role stressors on anxiety were generalizable across cultures. The research evidence therefore confirms that role stressors have a negative impact on employee job satisfaction and are associated with increased anxiety and job burnout.

**Reduced Supervisory Support**

Research has demonstrated that supervisory support is a critical antecedent variable directly contributing to burnout experiences. Bordin et al. (2007), in an investigation of Singaporean IT employees, found that supervisory support is an important determinant of the effects of empowerment on job satisfaction. Muhammad and Hamdy (2005) investigated supervisory support provided by Kuwaiti companies in three industries and found that supervisory support tends to lessen the effect of experienced burnout on employees' job satisfaction, organizational commitment and propensity to leave the job. Tourigny et al. (2005) investigated the cultural meaning and effectiveness of coping strategies on the process of burnout among Japanese employees in the airline industry. Tourigny et al. found that supervisory support had a reverse buffering effect on the relationship between emotional exhaustion and diminished sense of personal accomplishment. In other words supervisory support moderated the negative consequences of emotional exhaustion by preventing an increase in depersonalization. These authors recommended that supervisory support should be used in the early phase of job burnout to prevent depersonalization. Finally Kalliath and Beck (2001) found that in a stressful hospital environment, a lack of supervisory support had negative consequences for nurses and increased their levels of burnout and intentions to quit. Reduced co-worker support has been shown to negatively impact job satisfaction and increase job strain, which in turn have been shown to have an adverse impact on individual and organizational outcomes.

**Reduced Co-worker Support**

Poor interpersonal relations in the workplace have been shown to be a source of stress. For example in several studies relations with co-workers is one of the key variables engendering both direct and indirect effects on outcomes. Beehr et al. (2000) found that support from co-workers had a direct effect on psychological strain. Ndiwane (2000) examined the effects of community, co-worker and organizational support upon levels of job satisfaction of nurses in Cameroon. Results showed significant positive effects of perceived community support, co-worker support and organizational support on job satisfaction. AbuAlRub (2004) investigated the relationship between job stress, job performance and perceived social support from co-workers. The results indicated that perceived support from co-workers enhanced the level of reported job performance and decreased the level of reported job stress. Similarly Park and Wilson (2003) demonstrated that the high strain group of Korean factory workers was more likely to have low levels of satisfaction with their work environment, poor relationships with co-workers and supervisors, a high workload and low global job satisfaction.

In this section we reviewed five key antecedent variables that research has found to be predictors of unhealthy workplace practices resulting in low job satisfaction, high job stress and burnout, high turnover, and low productivity. The evidence surrounding the negative impact of these five workplace variables is consistent over many studies spanning more than two decades of research in occupational health psychology and related disciplines. The review showed that these unhealthy workplace practices can seriously compromise both organizational performance and employee health. Next we turn our attention to a review of healthy workplace practices and their impact on organizational and individual outcomes.

# HEALTHY WORKPLACE PRACTICES

Research has demonstrated an empirical link between certain healthy workplace practices and individual and organizational outcomes. The vast array of healthy workplace practices, programmes and policies commonly utilized by organizations can be categorized under five categories: work–family balance; employee growth and development; employee recognition and empowerment; employee health and safety; and employee involvement (Grawitch et al., 2006).

## Work–family Balance

Chapter 6 provided a comprehensive review of work–family balance, and its relationship specifically with organizational programmes is discussed here. In a longitudinal study in New Zealand, O'Driscoll et al. (2004) found that perceptions of interference between work and family life were associated with dissatisfaction and reduced feelings of well-being. Similar results have been reported by Lu et al. (2006) in cross-cultural settings. In a heterogeneous sample of employees from Taiwan and the UK, these researchers found work–family conflict predicted reduced well-being among both samples. The link between work–family conflict and organizational-level performance has also been demonstrated empirically. In a survey of 527 US firms, Perry-Smith and Blum (2000) found that work–family policies were positively associated with organizational performance. Specifically organizations with a greater range of work–family policies were found to have higher levels of organizational performance, market performance and profit–sales growth. In a recent cross-cultural survey of 732 medium-sized manufacturing firms (in the US, France, Germany and the UK), Bloom et al. (2006) found that work–family balance outcomes were significantly associated with better management practices.

## Employee Growth and Development

Organizations invest in employee growth and development programmes to provide opportunities for employees to expand their knowledge, skills and abilities (KSAs). Examples of such programmes include on-the-job training, leadership development, continuing education and internal career advancement programmes. In a pioneering study of 3452 US firms representing all major industries, Huselid (1995) showed that high performance work practices that improve employees' KSAs and address employee motivation (such as labour–management participation and incentive-based compensation) had a significant positive association with organizational performance. Huselid also found that a one standard deviation increase in the proportion of employees involved in high performance work practices reduced turnover by 7 per cent and increased sales per employee by more than US$27 000 per year.

Similar findings have also been documented in more recent studies. In a study of 14 390 employees in the UK banking sector, Gelade and Ivery (2003) found that progressive human resource practices such as support for professional development and the presence of a favourable psychological work environment were associated with superior organizational performance. Guthrie (2001) showed that New Zealand businesses that utilized high involvement work practices reported higher productivity and lower turnover rates. Although the evidence about the relationship between investment in human capital and high organizational performance is compelling, a recent study by Murphy and Southey (2003) found that the actual adoption of high performance work practices is scarce within Australia and New Zealand. Part of the reason why HRM functions do not play a larger strategic role in harnessing human capital for improving organizational performance is the lack of power and influence HR directors typically possess among senior decision-makers (Sheehan et al., 2006).

**Employee Recognition and Empowerment**

Reinforcement theory suggests that rewarding high performance behaviour with recognition immediately following the behaviour is likely to encourage its repetition (O'Driscoll et al., 2003). Recognition may involve expressing interest, approval and appreciation for a job well done. Effective managers have used recognition as a tool for motivating employees to high performance. A recent survey of organizations in the US and Canada found that 84 per cent of the organizations had some type of programme to recognize worker achievements (Saunderson, 2004). When employees are empowered they feel an increased sense of control, competence and goal internalization (Spreitzer and Doneson, 2005). Schneider et al. (2007) found evidence for the positive effect of empowerment on organizational effectiveness, most visibly through the growth of sales through information, authority and responsibility sharing. Similarly Spreitzer et al. (1999)

found that supervisors who reported high levels of empowerment were seen by their subordinates as being more innovative and inspirational.

## Employee Health and Safety

Estimates of business costs associated with occupational injuries are placed at close to US$170 billion (Occupational Safety and Health Administration, 2008). There are legal safety requirements that every employer is expected to provide under occupational health and safety legislation in most OECD countries. For instance all employers are legally obliged to provide safe premises; safe machinery and substances; safe systems of work; information, instruction, training and supervision; and a suitable working environment and facilities (Smallman, 2001). Scholars have noted that addressing safety and health issues in the workplace saves the employer money and adds value to the business (Smallman, 2001). In a study of safety practices in 62 hospitals in the US, Vredenburgh (2002) found that most participating hospitals implemented only *reactive* practices while only a few had *proactive* measures such as front-end hiring of safety-conscious personnel and the provision of safety training for new personnel.

## Employee Involvement

There are various approaches organizations have adopted to involve their employees. Brown et al. (2007) described three common kinds of involvement: *participative* (workers voluntarily communicating with managers); *representative* (where a representative communicates on behalf of many workers); or *financial* (either through profit-sharing initiatives or some form of company ownership). Pérotin and Robinson (2002) noted that one-fifth of private sector companies in the four largest European countries participate in financial employee involvement practices. Just as there are tangible benefits to employee involvement, so too are there intangible benefits such as intellectual capital development, higher skill development and greater organizational innovation (Morrell and Wilkinson, 2002).

From the perspective of promoting healthy workplace practice, the five practices reviewed provide evidence of their positive impact on individual and organizational outcomes. Proactive organizations are engaged in adopting these practices for business and employee well-being (Corbett, 2004; Harter et al., 2002). However, institutionalizing healthy workplace practices requires leadership that recognizes and values employee potential and its development for organizational excellence and employee well-being (Poelmans et al., 2008).

# REMEDIAL WORKPLACE PROGRAMMES

In the previous two sections we examined evidence concerning five workplace practices that contribute to creating a psychologically healthy workplace and five workplace practices that lead to a psychologically unhealthy workplace. As we have seen, there is compelling evidence that successful organizations institute human resource policies and practices that enhance employee well-being (and organizational success; Harter et al., 2002). However, most organizations are *reactive* rather than proactive in that they fail to institute progressive human resource practices unless compelled to do so through external (legal compliance) or internal demands (union demands; Lervik et al., 2005). In this section we discuss four organizational programmes that attempt to remedy gaps created by unhealthy workplace practices: employee assistance programmes; employee fitness programmes; stress and burnout management programmes; and workplace violence prevention programmes.

## Employee Assistance Programmes

Employee assistance programmes (EAPs) are counselling programmes offered by organizations aimed directly at employees. They facilitate employees in overcoming obstacles in their professional or personal lives, and are increasingly becoming the norm in business and organizational practice (van den Bergh, 2000). EAPs assist with problems ranging from personal crises to smoking prevention. Originating from the demands of workers' unions for worksite counselling programmes in the nineteenth century, organizations in the 1940s established occupational alcohol programmes (OAPs) to combat the effects of alcoholism on workplace productivity (Attridge et al., 2006). These programmes gradually evolved into EAPs and their role changed from the *prevention* of illness, stress and disease to the *promotion* of health and well-being in both the professional and personal spheres of the employee (DeGroot and Kiker, 2003). As targeting particular employees or habits may be seen as an intrusive measure, EAPs are often integrated into a general health programme as a way to reduce the stigma and confrontation associated with seeking assistance from an EAP. However, the definitive role that an EAP has in improving workplace productivity is difficult to ascertain. In a study involving Australian organizations with and without an EAP provision, Kirk (2006) reported that organizations are generally unaware of the benefits of EAPs and that decisions made in favour of EAP implementation often lack a strategic focus.

## Employee Fitness and Exercise Programmes

Employee fitness and exercise programmes (EFPs, sometimes known as health promotion programmes) are derived from EAPs and are an approach to improving general health in the workplace, rather than as a targeted approach to a specific problem. Organizations may be interested in EFPs for the purposes of improving their image, as well as reducing direct and indirect health costs associated with poor productivity, absenteeism and insurance. Research of EFPs suggests that companies that engage in EFPs to improve workplace health have reduced health costs over the longer term. The prevalence of EFPs is certainly increasing. OSHA (2008), for example, noted that approximately 95 per cent of US workplaces employing 50 or more staff implemented some kind of health promotion programme.

Adoption of appropriate health promotion activities can reduce occupational illness and injury and reduce productivity loss through absenteeism. Musich et al. (2000) reported that participation in health promotion programmes did indeed moderate health costs amongst workers. Research by Thøgersen-Ntoumani et al. (2005) suggested that workplace health promotion that included exercise successfully reduced workplace injuries and absenteeism and improved workers' levels of self-esteem and job satisfaction. Childress and Lindsay (2006) estimated that for every dollar spent on a health promotion programme, there was an average of $3.50 saved in healthcare and absenteeism costs.

## Stress and Burnout Management Programmes

Burnout is largely a psychological response to a stressful working environment which we discussed in detail in Chapter 5. Burnout can occur due to a sustained mismatch between employee and task (Maslach and Leiter, 1997) or long periods of exposure to work (Halbesleben et al., 2006). Shirom (2005) noted the similarity of rates of job stress leading to burnout across mainland European countries; 7 per cent in Holland, 7.4 per cent in Finland, and 10 per cent in Denmark. Stress and burnout management initiatives typically include time management and assertion training, stress coping methods and goal alignment training. These programmes, however, have produced mixed results. For instance Salmela-Aro et al. (2004), in their study on employee well-being, note that *psychotherapeutic* interventions (role-play, music and physical expression) have little effect on the emotional component of stress and burnout. In a systematic review of job stress intervention evaluation literature from 2000 to 2005, Lamontagne et al. (2007) rated 90 studies in terms of the systems approach

used. A systems approach emphasizes primary prevention and incorporates a meaningful participation of intervention groups. Lamontagne et
al. found that individual-focused stress interventions (such as employee
counselling) were effective at the individual level but tended to have little
impact at the organizational level of performance. Organizationally-
focused stress interventions (such as job redesign) were beneficial at *both*
the individual and organizational levels. These authors recommended that
further measures are needed to foster the implementation of a systems
approach for job stress interventions.

**Workplace Violence and Bullying Prevention Programmes**

A distinction is made between violence and bullying in the workplace, and
we discussed this in detail in Chapter 8. Hauge et al. (2007), for example,
found strong evidence for a positive correlation between bad, destructive or
passive leadership and workplace bullying. Branch et al. (2007) noted the
characteristics of the perpetrators and the targets themselves, the former
often having high self-esteem and a threatened ego, and the latter triggering
responses in an environment of high stress or tension. Mechanisms in place
to respond to or prevent workplace bullying and harassment are often
viewed as inadequate, despite most countries having legislation requiring
workplaces to mitigate bullying. Vickers (2006) discussed the difficulties associated with bringing workplace bullies to justice with the current
(Australian) laws, while Ferris (2004) argued that seeking assistance from
the organization may actually be detrimental to the victim, as there are
barriers within organizations that disallow action to be taken, such as the
inability of managers to take seriously the complaints of victims.

In this section we reviewed four workplace remedial programmes and their
impact on employee well-being. Many of these programmes are put in place
by organizations to comply with legal requirements. However, relativity
few organizations have gone beyond meeting these legal requirements to
think strategically and to embrace a philosophy of management that strives
to establish and sustain healthy work environments (Corbett, 2004).

# CONCLUSION

Although knowledge about creating healthy workplaces is widely available, few organizations have consciously ventured to undertake this journey
towards excellence, even though evidence shows that healthy organizations perform substantially better (Corbett, 2004; Harter et al., 2002).

Clearly there is a need for organizational leadership that takes a strategic approach to establishing psychologically healthy workplaces (Corbett, 2004). Some scholars have argued that what is needed is a paradigm shift in the top management conception of human resource management as human *potential* management (Poelmans and Masuda, in press; Poelmans et al., 2008). Human *potential* management holds people as the greatest asset of the organization and the development of the potential of people at the heart of its management philosophy (Kalliath et al., in press). Such an approach to the management of organizational behaviour recognizes, for example, that the way an organization treats its employees is the way that employees in turn will treat the customers (Corbett, 2004).

## ACKNOWLEDGEMENTS

We thank Jerry Marmen Simanjuntak for assistance with the literature review for this chapter.

# References

AbuAlRub, R.F. (2004), 'Job stress, job performance, and social support among hospital nurses', *Journal of Nursing Scholarship*, **36**(1), 73–8.

Adams, J.S. (1965), 'Inequity in social exchange', in L. Berkowitz (ed.), *Advances in Experimental Social Psychology*, Vol. 2, New York: Academic Press, pp. 267–99.

Agarwal, R., C.M. Angst and M. Magni (2006), 'The performance effects of coaching: A multilevel analysis using hierarchical linear modeling', Robert H. Smith School Research Paper No. RHS 06-031, retrieved 1 June, 2008, from http://papers.ssrn.com/sol3/papers.cfm?abstract_id=918810.

Agerbo, E., D. Gunnell, J.P. Bonde, P.B. Mortensen and M. Nordentoft (2007), 'Suicide and occupation: the impact of socioeconomic, demographic and psychiatric differences', *Psychological Medicine*, **37**(8), 1131–40.

Allen, R.S., M. Takeda and C.S. White (2005), 'Cross-cultural equity sensitivity: A test of differences between the United States and Japan', *Journal of Managerial Psychology*, **20**(8), 641–62.

Allen, T.D. (2001), 'Family-supportive work environments: The role of organizational perceptions', *Journal of Vocational Behavior*, **58**(3), 414–35.

Allen, T.D. and J.E.A. Russell (1999), 'Parental leave of absence: Some not so family-friendly implications', *Journal of Applied Social Psychology*, **29**(1), 166–91.

Allen, T.D., D.E.L. Herst, C.S. Bruck and M. Sutton (2000), 'Consequences associated with work-to-family conflict: A review and agenda for future research', *Journal of Occupational Health Psychology*, **5**(2), 278–308.

American Psychological Association (APA) (2008), 'Creating a psychologically healthy workplace', retrieved 17 July, 2008, from http://www.phwa.org/resources/creating_a_healthy_workplace.php.

Amick, B.C., P. McDonough, H. Chang, W.H. Rogers, C.F. Pieper and G. Duncan (2002), 'Relationship between all-cause mortality and cumulative working life course psychosocial and physical exposures in the United States labor market from 1968 to 1992', *Psychosomatic Medicine*, **64**(3), 370–81.

Andreassen, C.S., H. Ursin and H.R. Eriksen (2007), 'The relationship between strong motivation to work, "workaholism", and health', *Psychology and Health*, **22**(5), 615–29.

Aquino, K., S.L. Grover, M. Bradfield and D.G. Allen (1999), 'The effects of negative affectivity, heirarchical status, and self-determination on workplace victimization', *Academy of Management Journal*, **42**(3), 260–72.

Arnetz, J.E., and B.B. Arnetz (2000), 'Implementation and evaluation of a practical intervention programme for dealing with violence towards health care workers', *Journal of Advanced Nursing*, **31**(3), 668–80.

Aryee, S., V. Luk, A. Leung and S. Lo (1999), 'Role stressors, inter role conflict and wellbeing: The moderating influence of spousal support and coping behaviors among employed parents in Hong Kong', *Journal of Vocational Behavior*, **54**(2), 259–78.

Aspinwall, L.G. (2004), 'Proactive coping, wellbeing, and health', in N.J. Smelser and P.B. Baltes (eds), *International Encyclopedia of the Social and Behavioral Sciences*, Oxford, UK: Elsevier, pp. 16447–51.

Attridge, M., P.A. Herlihy and R.P. Maiden (2006), *The Integration of Employee Assistance, Work/life, and Wellness Services*, Binghamton, NY: The Haworth Press.

Australian Safety and Compensation Council (2007), 'Trends over time, 1996–97 to 2003–4. Compendium of workers' compensation statistics Australia, 2004–05', Canberra, Australian Capital Territory: Australian Safety and Compensation Council.

Aziz, S. and M.J. Zickar (2006), 'A cluster analysis investigation of workaholism as a syndrome', *Journal of Occupational Health Psychology*, **11**(1), 52–62.

Babbar, S. and D.J. Aspelin (1998), 'The overtime rebellion: Symptom of a bigger problem?', *Academy of Management Executive*, **12**(1), 68–76.

Bacharach, S.B., P. Bamberger and S. Conley (1991), 'Work–home conflict among nurses and engineers: Mediating the impact of role stress on burnout and satisfaction at work', *Journal of Organizational Behavior*, **12**, 39–53.

Bakker, A.B. and E. Demerouti (2007), 'The job demands–resources model: State of the art', *Journal of Managerial Psychology*, **22**(3), 309–28.

Bakker, A.B., E. Demerouti and W.B. Schaufeli (2003), 'Dual processes at work in a call centre: An application of the job demands–resources model', *European Journal of Work and Organizational Psychology*, **12**(4), 393–417.

Bakker, A.B., J.J. Hakanen, E. Demerouti and D. Xanthopoulou (2007), 'Job resources boost work engagement, particularly when job demands are high', *Journal of Educational Psychology*, **99**(2), 274–84.

Bandura, A. (1997), *Self-efficacy: The Exercise of Control*, New York: Freeman.

Barnett, R. and J. Hyde (2001), 'Women, men, work and family: An expansionist theory', *American Psychologist*, **56**(10), 781–96.

Baron, R.A. (2004), 'Workplace aggression and violence: Insights from basic research', in R.W. Griffin and A.M. O'Learly-Kelly (eds), *The Dark Side of Organizational Behavior*, San Francisco: Jossey-Bass, pp. 23–61.

Beas, M.I. and M. Salanova (2006), 'Self-efficacy beliefs, computer training and psychological well-being among information and communication technology workers', *Computers in Human Behavior*, **22**(6), 1043–58.

Beaton, R.D., S.A. Murphy, K.C. Pike and W. Corneil (1997), 'Social support and network conflict in firefighters and paramedics', *Western Journal of Nursing Research*, **19**(3), 297–313.

Beatty, C.A. (1996), 'The stress of managerial and professional women: Is the price too high?', *Journal of Organizational Behavior*, **17**, 233–51.

Beaudry, A. and A. Pinsonneault (2005), 'Understanding user responses to information technology: A coping model of user adaptation', *MIS Quarterly*, **29**(3), 493–524.

Beckers, J.J. and H.G. Schmidt (2001), 'The structure of computer anxiety: A six-factor model', *Computers in Human Behavior*, **17**(1), 35–49.

Beckers, J.J. and H.G. Schmidt (2003), 'Computer experience and computer anxiety', *Computers in Human Behavior*, **19**(6), 785–97.

Beckers, J.J., J.M. Wicherts and H.G. Schmidt (2007), 'Computer anxiety: "Trait" or "state"'? *Computers in Human Behavior*, **23**(6), 2851–62.

Beech, B. and P. Leather (2006), 'Workplace violence in the health care sector: A review of staff training and integration of training evaluation models', *Aggression and Violent Behavior*, **11**(1), 27–43.

Beehr, T.A., S.M. Jex, B.A. Stacy and M.A. Murray (2000), 'Work stressors and coworker support as predictors of individual strain and job performance', *Journal of Organizational Behavior*, **21**(4), 391–405.

Beer, M. (2002), 'Building organizational fitness in the 21st Century', Harvard Business School Working Paper Series, No. 02-044.

Behson, S.J. (2002), 'Coping with work-to-family conflict: The role of informal work accommodations to family', *Journal of Occupational Health Psychology*, **7**(4), 324–41.

Belkic, K.L., P. Landsbergis, P.L. Schnall and D. Baker (2004), 'Is job strain a major source of cardiovascular disease risk?', *Scandinavian Journal of Work, Environment and Health*, **30**(2), 85–128.

Bellotti, V., N. Ducheneaut, M. Howard, I. Smith and R.E. Grinter (2005), 'Quality versus quantity: E-mail-centric task management and its relation with overload', *Human–Computer Interaction*, **20**(1/2), 89–138.

Bender, K.A., S.M. Donohue and J.S. Heywood (2005), 'Job satisfaction and gender segregation', *Oxford Economic Papers*, **57**(3), 479–96.

Bennett, J. and D. O'Donovan (2001), 'Substance misuse by doctors, nurses and other healthcare workers', *Current Opinion in Psychiatry*, **14**(3), 195–9.

Berg, A. (2004), 'Commission to examine parental leave', retrieved 22 November, 2005, from http://www.eiro.eurofound.eu.int/2004/06/inbrief/se0406102n.html.

Bessière, K., J.E. Newhagen, J.P. Robinson and B. Shneiderman (2006), 'A model for computer frustration: The role of instrumental and dispositional factors on incident, session, and post-session frustration and mood', *Computers in Human Behavior*, **22**(6), 941–61.

Biringer, E., A. Mykletun, A.A. Dahl, A.D. Smith, K. Engedal, H.A. Nygaard, et al. (2005), 'The association between depression, anxiety, and cognitive function in the elderly general population–the Hordaland health study', *International Journal of Geriatric Psychiatry*, **20**(10), 989–97.

Bishop, G.D., H.C. Enkelmann, E.M.W. Tong, Y.P. Why, S.M. Diong, J. Ang, et al. (2003), 'Job demands, decisional control, and cardiovascular responses', *Journal of Occupational Health Psychology*, **8**(2), 146–56.

Bloom, N., T. Kretschmer and J.M. Van Reenen (2006), 'Work–life balance, management practices and productivity', retrieved 26 August, 2006, from http://cep.lse.ac.uk/pubs/download/special/wlbmanagementpractices.pdf.

Bluckert, P. (2005), 'Critical factors in executive coaching – the coaching relationship', *Industrial and Commercial Training*, **37**(7), 336–40.

Böckerman, P. and P. Ilmakunnas (2006), 'Interaction of job disamenities, job satisfaction, and sickness absences: Evidence from a representative sample of Finnish workers', MPRA Paper 1800, University Library of Munich, Germany, retrieved 1 June, 2008, from http://mpra.ub.uni-muenchen.de/1800/.

Boden, L.I., E.A. Biddle and E.A. Spieler (2001), 'Social and economic impacts of workplace illness and injury: Current and future directions for research', *American Journal of Industrial Medicine*, **40**(4), 398–402.

Boehm, J.K. and S. Lyubomirsky (2008), 'Does happiness promote career success?', *Journal of Career Assessment*, **16**(1), 101–16.

Boggild, H. and A. Knutsson (1999), Shift work, risk factors and cardiovascular disease', *Scandinavian Journal of Work, Environment and Health*, **25**(2), 85–99.

Bonebright, C.A., D.L. Clay and R.D. Ankenmann (2000), 'The relationship of workaholism with work–life conflict, life satisfaction, and purpose in life', *Journal of Counseling Psychology*, **47**(4), 469–77.

Bordin, C., T. Bartram and G. Casimir (2007), 'The antecedents and consequences of psychological empowerment among Singaporean IT employees', *Management Research News*, **30**(1), 34–46.

Boswell, W.R., J.B. Olson-Buchanan and M.A. LePine (2004), 'Relations between stress and work outcomes: The role of felt challenge, job control, and psychological strain', *Journal of Vocational Behavior*, **64**(1), 165–81.

Bowling, N.A. (2007), 'Is the job satisfaction–job performance relationship spurious? A meta-analytic examination', *Journal of Vocational Behavior*, **71**(2), 167–85.

Bowling, N.A. and T.A. Beehr (2006), 'Workplace harassment from the victim's perspective: A theoretical model and meta-analysis', *Journal of Applied Psychology*, **91**(5), 998–1012.

Bowling, N.A., T.A. Beehr and L.R. Lepisto (2006), 'Beyond job satisfaction: A five-year prospective analysis of the dispositional approach to work attitudes', *Journal of Vocational Behavior*, **69**(2), 315–30.

Boyar, S.L., C.P. Maertz, A.W. Pearson and S. Keough (2003), 'Work–family conflict: A model of linkages between work and family domain variables and turnover intentions', *Journal of Managerial Issues*, **15**, 175–90.

Boyatzis, R.E., M.L. Smith and N. Blaize (2006), 'Developing sustainable leaders through coaching and compassion', *Academy of Management Learning and Education*, **5**(1), 8–24.

Branch, S., S. Ramsay and M. Barker (2007), 'The bullied boss: A conceptual exploration of upwards bullying', in I.A. Glendon, B.M. Thompson and B. Myors (eds), *Advances in Organisational Psychology* Sydney: Australian Academic Press, pp. 93–112.

Brandt, L.P.A. and C.V. Nielsen (1992), 'Job stress and adverse outcome of pregnancy: A causal link or recall bias?', *American Journal of Epidemiology*, **135**(3), 302–11.

Brandth, B. and E. Kvande (2002), 'Reflexive fathers: Negotiating parental leave and working life', *Gender, Work and Organization*, **9**(2), 186–203.

Brayfield, A.H. and W.H. Crockett (1955), 'Employee attitudes and employee performance', *Psychological Bulletin*, **52**(5), 396–424.

Bresser, F. (2005), 'Best implementation of coaching in business', *Coaching Today*, pp. 20–21.

Brett, K.M., D.S. Strogatz and D.A. Savitz (1997), 'Employment, job strain, and preterm delivery among women in North Carolina', *American Journal of Public Health*, **87**(2), 199–204.

Brief, A.P. (1998), *Attitudes in and around Organizations*, Thousand Oaks, CA: Sage Publications.

Brief, A.P. and L. Roberson (1989), 'Job attitude organization: An exploratory study', *Journal of Applied Social Psychology*, **19**(9), 717–27.

Brief, A.P. and H.M. Weiss (2002), 'Organizational behaviour: Affect in the workplace', *Annual Review of Psychology*, **53**, 279–307.

Brinker, P.A. (1985), 'Violence by US labor unions', *Journal of Labor Research*, **6**(4), 417–27.

Broadbent, K. (2007), 'Sisters organising in Japan and Korea: The development of women-only unions', *Industrial Relations Journal*, **38**(3), 229–51.

Brod, C. (1984), *Technostress: The Human Cost of the Computer Revolution*, Reading, MA: Addison-Wesley.

Brough, P. (2005a), 'A comparative investigation of the predictors of work-related psychological well-being within police, fire and ambulance workers', *New Zealand Journal of Psychology*, **34**(2), 126–34.

Brough, P. (2005b), 'Workplace violence experienced by paramedics: Relationships with social support, job satisfaction, and psychological strain', *Australasian Journal of Disaster and Trauma Studies*, **2**, retrieved 5 December, 2005, from http://www.massey.ac.nz/~trauma/issues/2005-2/brough.htm.

Brough, P. and A. Biggs (2009), 'Occupational stress in police and prison staff', in J. Brown and E. Campbell (eds), *The Cambridge Handbook of Forensic Psychology*, Cambridge: Cambridge University Press.

Brough, P. and R. Frame (2004), 'Predicting police job satisfaction and turnover intentions: The role of social support and police organisational variables', *New Zealand Journal of Psychology*, **33**(1), 8–16.

Brough, P. and A. Kelling (2002), 'Women, work and well-being: The influence of work–family and family–work conflict', *New Zealand Journal of Psychology*, **31**(1), 29–38.

Brough, P. and M. O'Driscoll (2005), 'Work–family conflict and stress', in A. Antoniou and C. Cooper (eds), *A Research Companion to Organizational Health Psychology*, Cheltenham, UK and Northampton, MA, USA: Edward Elgar, pp. 346–65.

Brough, P., M. O'Driscoll and T. Kalliath (2005), 'The ability of "family friendly" organisational resources to predict work–family conflict and job and family satisfaction', *Stress and Health*, **21**, 223–34.

Brough, P., M. O'Driscoll and T. Kalliath (2007), 'Work–family conflict and facilitation: Achieving work–family balance', in A.I. Glendon, B.M. Thompson and B. Myors (eds), *Advances in Organisational Psychology: An Asia-Pacific Perspective*, Brisbane: Australian Academic Press, pp. 73–92.

Brough, P., J. Holt, R. Bauld, A. Biggs and C. Ryan (2008), 'The ability of work–life balance policies to influence key social/organisational issues', *Asian-Pacific Journal of Human Resources*, **46**, 261–74.

Brown, M., L.A. Geddes and J.S. Heywood (2007), 'The determinants of employee-involvement schemes: Private sector Australian evidence', *Economic and Industrial Democracy*, **28**(2), 259–91.

Browne, J.H. (2000), 'Benchmarking HRM practices in healthy work organizations', *American Business Review*, **18**(2), 54–61.

Bruck, C.S., T.D. Allen and P.E. Spector (2002), 'The relation between work–family conflict and job satisfaction: A finer-grained analysis', *Journal of Vocational Behavior*, **60**(3), 336–53.

Brunner, E.J., M. Kivimäki, J. Siegrist, T. Theorell, R. Luukkonen, H. Riihimäki et al. (2004), 'Is the effect of work stress on cardiovascular mortality confounded by socioeconomic factors in the Valmet study?', *Journal of Epidemiology and Community Health*, **58**(12), 1019–20.

Budd, T. (1999), 'Violence at work: Findings from the British crime survey', retrieved 14 July, 2008, from www.homeoffice.gov.uk/rds/pdfs/occ-violencework.pdf.

Buelens, M. and S.A.Y. Poelmans (2004), 'Enriching the Spence and Robbins' typology of workaholism: Demographic, motivational, and organizational correlates', *Journal of Organizational Change Management*, **17**(5), 440–58.

Burke, R.J. (1999), 'Workaholism in organizations: Gender differences', *Sex Roles*, **41**(5/6), 333–45.

Burke, R.J. (2001a), 'Workaholism components, job satisfaction, and career progress', *Journal of Applied Social Psychology*, **31**(11), 2339–56.

Burke, R.J. (2001b), 'Predictors of workaholism components and behaviours', *International Journal of Stress Management*, **8**(2), 113–27.

Burke, R.J. (2004), 'Workaholism, self-esteem, and motives for money', *Psychological Reports*, **94**(2), 457–63.

Burke, R.J. (2006), *Research Companion to Working Time and Work Addiction*, Cheltenham, UK and Northampton, MA, USA: Edward Elgar Publishing.

Burke, R.J., S.B. Matthiesen and S. Pallesen (2006), 'Workaholism, organizational life, and well-being of Norwegian nursing staff', *Career Development International*, **11**, 463–77.

Carlson, D.S. and M.R. Frone (2003), 'Relation of behavioral and psychological involvement to a new four-factor conceptualization of work–family interference', *Journal of Business and Psychology*, **17**, 515–35.

Carlson, D.S. and P.L. Perrewe (1999), 'The role of social support in the stressor–strain relationship: An examination of work–family conflict', *Journal of Management*, **25**(4), 513–40.

Carlson, D.S., K. Kacmar and L. Williams (2000), 'Construction and initial validation of a multidemensional measure of work/family conflict', *Journal of Vocational Behavior*, **56**(2), 249–76.

Carlson, J.R., R.H. Anson and G. Thomas (2003), 'Correctional officer burnout and stress: Does gender matter?', *The Prison Journal*, **83**(3), 277–88.

Carr, D. (2002), 'The psychological consequences of work–family trade-offs for three cohorts of men and women', *Social Psychology Quarterly*, **65**(3), 103–24.

Cartwright, S. and C.L. Cooper (1997), *Managing Workplace Stress*, Thousand Oaks, CA: Sage Publications.

Castillo, D.N. and E.L. Jenkins (1994), 'Industries and occupations at high risk for work-related homicide', *Journal of Occupational Medicine*, **36**(2), 125–32.

Catalano, R., D. Dooley, G. Wilson and R. Hough (1993), 'Job loss and alcohol abuse: A test using data from the Epidemiologic Catchment Area Project', *Journal of Health and Social Behavior*, **34**(3), 215–25.

Caulfield, N., D. Chang, M.F. Dollard and C. Elshaug (2004), 'A review of occupational stress interventions in Australia', *International Journal of Stress Management*, **11**(2), 149–66.

Cavanaugh, M.A., W.R. Boswell, M.V. Roehling and J.W. Boudreau (2000), 'An empirical examination of self-reported work stress among US managers', *Journal of Applied Psychology*, **85**(1), 65–74.

Ceaparu, I., J. Lazar, K. Bessière, J. Robinson and B. Shneiderman (2004), Determining causes and severity of end-user frustration', *International Journal of Human–Computer Interaction*, **17**(3), 333–56.

Cheng, Y., I. Kawachi, E.H. Coakley, J. Schwartz and G. Colditz (2000), 'Association between psychosocial work characteristics and health functioning in American women: Prospective study', *British Medical Journal*, **320**(7247), 1432–6.

Childress, J.M. and G.M. Lindsay (2006), 'National indications of increasing investment in workplace health promotion programs by large and medium-size companies', *North Carolina Medical Journal*, **67**(6), 449–52.

Chinchilla, N., S. Poelmans, C. León and J. Tarrés (2004), 'Guía de Buenas Prácticas de la Empresa Flexible. Hacia la Conciliación de la Vida Laboral, Familiar Personal', www.iese.edu/icwf.

Christie, A., P.J. Jordan, A. Troth and S.A. Lawrence (2007), 'Testing the links between emotional intelligence and motivation', *Journal of Management and Organization*, **13**(3), 212–26.

Chu, C., G. Breucker, N. Harris, A. Stitzel, X. Gan, X. Gu, et al. (2000), 'Health-promoting workplaces – international settings development', *Health Promotion International*, **15**(2), 155–67.

Church, S., M. Henderson, M. Barnard and G. Hart (2001), 'Violence by clients towards female prostitutes in different work settings: question-naire survey', *British Medical Journal*, **322**(7285), 524–5.

Clark, A.E. (1997), 'Job satisfaction and gender: Why are women so happy at work?', *Labour Economics*, **4**(4), 341–72.

Clark, A.E. (2005), 'What makes a good job? Evidence from OECD countries', in S. Bazen, C. Luciflora and W. Salverda (eds), *Job Quality and Employer Behaviour*, Basingstoke: Palgrave Macmillan, pp. 11–30.

Clark, A.E. and A.J. Oswald (1994), 'Unhappiness and unemployment', *Economic Journal*, **104**(424), 648–59.

Cleary, S.D. (2000), 'Adolescent victimization and associated suicidal and violent behaviors', *Adolescence*, **35**(140), 671–82.

Clugston, M. (2000), 'The mediating effects of multidimensional commitment on job satisfaction and intent to leave', *Journal of Organizational Behavior*, **21**(4), 477–86.

Compeau, D., C.A. Higgins and S. Huff (1999), 'Social cognitive theory and individual reactions to computing technology: A longitudinal study', *MIS Quarterly*, **23**(2), 145–58.

Connolly, J.J. and C. Viswesvaran (2000), 'The role of affectivity in job satisfaction: A meta-analysis', *Personality and Individual Differences*, **29**(2), 265–81.

Cooper, C.L. (1996), 'Working hours and health (Editorial)', *Work and Stress*, **10**(1), 1–4.

Cooper, C.L. (2005), *Handbook of Stress Medicine and Health*, Boca Raton, FL: CRC Press.

Cooper, C.L. (2006), 'The challenges of managing the changing nature of workplace stress', *Journal of Public Mental Health*, **5**(4), 6–9.

Cooper, C.L. and J. Marshall (1976), 'Occupational sources of stress: A review of the literature relating to coronary heart disease and mental ill-health', *Journal of Occupational Psychology*, **49**(1), 11–28.

Cooper, C.L., P.J. Dewe and M.P. O'Driscoll (2001), *Organizational Stress: A Review and Critique of Theory, Research and Applications*, Thousand Oaks, CA: Sage Publications.

Coovert, M.D. and L.F. Thompson (2003), 'Technology and workplace health', in J.C. Quick and L.E. Tetrick (eds), *Handbook of Occupational Health Psychology*, Washington, DC: American Psychological Association, pp. 221–41.

Coovert, M.D., L.F. Thompson and J.P. Craiger (2005), 'Technology', in J. Barling, E.K. Kelloway and M.R. Frone (eds), *Handbook of Work Stress*, Thousand Oaks, CA: Sage Publications, pp. 299–324.

Corbett, D. (2004), 'Excellence in Canada: Healthy organizations – Achieve results by acting responsibly', *Journal of Business Ethics*, **55**(2), 125–33.

Cox, S., T. Cox and J. Pryce (2000a), 'Work-related reproductive health: A review', *Work and Stress*, **14**(2), 171–80.

Cox, T., A. Griffiths, C. Barlowe, R. Randall, L. Thomson and E. Rial González (2000b), *Organizational Interventions for Work Stress: A Risk Management Approach*, Nottingham: Institute of Work, Health and Organisations; University of Nottingham Business School.

Cropanzano, R., and T.A. Wright (2001), 'When a "happy" worker is really a "productive" worker: A review and further refinement of the happy-productive worker thesis', *Consulting Psychology Journal: Practice and Research*, **53**(3), 182–99.

Daniels, K., P. Brough, A. Guppy, K.M. Peters-Bean and L. Weatherstone (1997), 'A note on a modification to Warr's measures of affective well-being at work', *Journal of Occupational and Organizational Psychology*, **70**(2), 129–38.

Danna, K. and R.W. Griffin (1999), 'Health and well-being in the workplace: A review and synthesis of the literature', *Journal of Management*, **25**(3), 357–84.

Deelstra, J.T., M.C.W. Peeters, W.B. Schaufeli, W. Stroebe, F.R.H. Zijlstra and L.P. van Doornen (2003), 'Receiving instrumental support at work: When help is not welcome', *Journal of Applied Psychology*, **88**(2), 324–31.

DeGroot, T. and D.S. Kiker (2003), 'A meta-analysis of the non-monetary effects of employee health management programs', *Human Resource Management*, **42**(1), 53–69.

de Lange, A.H., T.W. Taris, M.A.J. Kompier, I.L.D. Houtman and P.M. Bongers (2003), '"The *very* best of the millennium": Longitudinal research and the demand–control–(support) model', *Journal of Occupational Health Psychology*, **8**(4), 282–305.

Dembe, A.E., J.B. Erickson, R.G. Delbos and S.M. Banks (2005), 'The impact of overtime and long work hours on occupational injuries and illnesses: New evidence from the United States', *Occupational and Environmental Medicine*, **62**(9), 588–97.

Demerouti, E., A.B. Bakker, F. Nachreiner and W.B. Schaufeli (2001), 'The job demands–resources model of burnout', *Journal of Applied Psychology*, **86**(3), 499–512.

Department of Trade and Industry (2003), 'Balancing work and family life: enhancing choice and support for parents', retrieved 28 November, 2005, from http://www.dti.gov.uk/er/individual/balancing.pdf.

De Witte, H., E. Verhofstadt and E. Omey (2007), 'Testing Karasek's learning and strain hypotheses on young workers in their first job', *Work and Stress*, **21**(2), 131–41.

Diener, E. (1984), 'Subjective well-being'. *Psychological Bulletin*, **95**(3), 542–75.

Diener, E. and R.E. Lucas (1999), 'Personality and subjective well-being', in D. Kahneman, E. Diener, and N. Schwarz (eds), *Well-being: The Foundations of Hedonic Psychology*, New York: Russell Sage Foundation, pp. 213–29.

Diener, E. and M.E.P. Seligman (2002), 'Very happy people', *Psychological Science*, **13**(1), 81–4.

Diener, E. and M.E.P. Seligman (2004), 'Beyond money. Towards an economy of well-being', *Psychological Science in the Public Interest*, **5**(1), 1–31.

Diener, E., C. Nickerson, R.E. Lucas and E. Sandvik (2002), 'Dispositional affect and job outcomes', *Social Indicators Research*, **59**(3), 229–59.

Diener, E., E. Sandvik, L. Seidlitz and M. Diener (1993), 'The relationship between income and subjective well-being: Relative or absolute?', *Social Indicators Research*, **28**(3), 195–223.

Diener, E., E.M. Suh, R.E. Lucas and H.L. Smith (1999), 'Subjective well-being: Three decades of progress', *Psychological Bulletin*, **125**(2), 276–302.

Dollard, J., L.W. Doob, N.E. Miller, O.H. Mowrer and R.R. Sears (1939), *Frustration and Aggression*, New Haven, CT: Yale University Press.

Douglas, S.C., C. Kiewitz, M.J. Martinko, P. Harvey, Y. Kim and J.U. Chun (2008), 'Cognitions, emotions, and evaluations: An elaboration likelihood model for workplace aggression', *Academy of Management Review*, **33**(2), 425–51.

Dupré, K.E., M. Inness, C.E. Connelly, J. Barling and C. Hoption (2006), 'Workplace aggression in teenage part-time employees', *Journal of Applied Psychology*, **9**(5), 987–97.

Durndell, A. and Z. Haag (2002), 'Computer self efficacy, computer anxiety, attitudes towards the internet and reported experience with the internet, by gender, in an East European sample', *Computers in Human Behavior*, **18**(5), 521–35.

Dvash, A. and B. Mannheim (2001), 'Technological coupling, job characteristics and operators' well-being as moderated by desirability of control', *Behaviour and Information Technology*, **20**(3), 225–36.

Eden, D. (2001), 'Vacations and other respites: Studying stress on and off the job', in C.L. Cooper and I.T. Robertson (eds), *International Review of Industrial and Organizational Psychology*, Chichester: Wiley, pp. 121–46.

Edwards, J.R. (1988), 'The determinants and consequences of coping with stress', in C.L. Cooper and R. Payne (eds), *Causes, Coping and Consequences of Stress and Work*, Chichester and New York: John Wiley, pp. 233–63.

Edwards, J.R. and M.E. Parry (1993), 'On the use of polynomial regression equations as an alternative to difference scores in organizational research', *Academy of Management Journal*, **36**(6), 1577–613.

Einarsen, S., H. Hoel, D. Zapf and C.L. Cooper (2003), 'The concept of bullying at work: The European tradition', in S. Einarsen, H. Hoel, D. Zapf and D.L. Cooper (eds), *Bullying and Emotional Abuse in the Workplace: International Perspectives in Research and Practice*, London: Taylor and Francis, pp. 3–30.

Enzmann, D. (2005), 'Burnout and emotions: An underresearched issue in search of theory', in A.S. Antoniou and C.L. Cooper (eds), *Research Companion to Organizational Health Psychology*, Cheltenham, UK and Northampton, MA, USA: Edward Elgar, pp. 495–502.

Ersoy-Kart, M. (2005), 'Reliability and validity of the workaholism battery (work-BAT): Turkish form', *Social Behavior and Personality*, **33**(6), 609–18.

Escriba-Aguir, V. and S. Pèrez-Hoyos (2007), 'Psychological well-being and psychosocial work environment characteristics among emergency medical and nursing staff', *Stress and Health*, **23**(3), 153–60.

European Foundation for the Improvement of Living and Working Conditions (2004), 'Working conditions: violence, bullying and harassment in the workplace', retrieved 8 July, 2008, from http://www.eurofound.europa.eu/ewco/reports/TN0406TR01/TN0406TR01.htm.

Eyer, J. (1977), 'Prosperity as a cause of death', *International Journal of Health Service*, **7**(1), 125–50.

Eysenck, H.J. (1997), 'Addiction, personality, and motivation', *Human Psychopharmacology*, **12**(S2), 79–87.

Faragher, E.B., M. Cass and C.L. Cooper (2005), 'Relationship between job satisfaction and health: A meta-analysis', *Occupational and Environmental Medicine*, **62**(2), 105–12.

Fassel, D. (1990), *Working Ourselves to Death: The High Costs of Workaholism, the Rewards of Recovery*, San Francisco: HarperCollins.

Feldman, D.C. and M.J. Lankau (2005), 'Executive coaching: A review and agenda for future research', *Journal of Management*, **31**(6), 829–48.

Ferrer-i-Carbonell, A. and P. Frijters (2004), 'How important is methodology for the estimates of the determinants of happiness?', *Economic Journal*, **114**(497), 641–59.

Ferris, P. (2004), 'A preliminary typology of organisational response to allegations of workplace bullying: See no evil, hear no evil, speak no evil', *British Journal of Guidance and Counselling*, **32**(3), 389–95.

Feskanich, D., J.L. Hastrup, J.R. Marshall, G.A. Colditz, M.J. Stampfer, W.C. Willett, et al. (2002), 'Stress and suicide in the nurses' health study', *Journal of Epidemiology and Community Health*, **56**(2), 95–8.

Figà-Talamanca, I. (2006), 'Occupational risk factors and reproductive health of women', *Occupational Medicine*, **56**(8), 521–31.

Finkelstein, S. (2003), *Why Smart Executives Fail*, London: Penguin Putnam.

Fischer, J.A.V. and A. Sousa-Poza (2006), 'Does job satisfaction improve health? New evidence using panel data and objective measures of health', FAA Discussion Paper No. DP-110. University of St. Gallen, retrieved 1 June, 2008, from http://papers.ssrn.com/sol3/papers.cfm?abstract_id=955734.

Fischer, J.A.V. and A. Sousa-Poza (2008), 'Does job satisfaction improve the health of workers? New evidence using panel data and objective measures of health', *Health Economics*, retrieved 1 June, 2008, from http://ideas.repec.org/p/iza/izadps/dp3256.html.

Fleetwood, S. (2007), 'Why work–life balance now?', *International Journal of Human Resource Management*, **18**(3), 387–400.

Folkman, S. (2008), 'The case for positive emotions in the stress process', *Anxiety, Stress and Coping: An International Journal*, **21**(1), 3–14.

Folkman, S. and J.T. Moskowitz (2003), 'Positive psychology from a coping perspective', *Psychological Inquiry*, **14**(2), 121–5.

Folkman, S. and J.T. Moskowitz (2004), 'Coping: Pitfalls and promise', *Annual Review of Psychology*, **55**, 745–74.

Fox, M.L., D.J. Dwyer and D.C. Ganster (1993), 'Effects of stressful job demands and control on physiological and attitudinal outcomes in a hospital setting', *Academy of Management Journal*, **36**(2), 289–318.

Frankenhaeuser, M., U. Lundberg, M. Fredikson, B. Melin, M. Tuomisto, A. Myrstern et al. (1989), 'Stress on and off the job as related to sex and occupational status in white-collar workers', *Journal of Organizational Behavior*, **10**(4), 321–46.

Fredrickson, B.L., M.M. Tugade, C.E. Waugh and G.R. Larkin (2003), 'What good are positive emotions in crises? A prospective study of resilience and emotions following the terrorist attacks on the United States on September 11th, 2001', *Journal of Personality and Social Psychology*, **84**(2), 365–76.

French, J.R.P., R.D. Caplan and R.V. Harrison (1982), *The Mechanisms of Job Stress and Strain*, Chichester: John Wiley.

Frone, M.R. (1999), 'Work stress and alcohol use', *Alcohol Research and Health*, **23**(4), 284–91.

Frone, M.R. (2003), 'Work–family balance', in J.C. Quick and L.E. Tetrick (eds), *Handbook of Occupational Health Psychology*, Washington, DC: American Psychological Association, pp. 143–62.

Frone, M.R. and J.K. Yardley (1996), 'Workplace family-supportive programmes: Predictors of employed parents' importance ratings', *Journal of Occupational and Organizational Psychology*, **69**(4), 351–66.

Frone, M.R., M. Russell and G.M. Barnes (1996), 'Work–family conflict to substance use among employed mothers: The role of negative affect', *Journal of Marriage and the Family*, 56, 1019–30.

Frone, M.R., J.K. Yardley and K.S. Markel (1997), 'Developing and testing an integrative model of the work–family interface', *Journal of Vocational Behavior*, 50, 145–67.

Gallo, W.T., E.H. Bradley, M. Siegel and S.V. Kasl (2001), 'The impact of involuntary job loss on subsequent alcohol consumption by older workers: Findings from the Health and Retirement Survey', *The Journals of Gerontology: Series B: Psychological Sciences and Social Sciences*, 56(1), 3–9.

Gates, D.M., C.S. Ross and L. McQueen (2006), 'Violence against emergency department workers', *Journal of Emergency Medicine*, 31(3), 331–7.

Gazioglu, S. and A. Tansel (2002), 'Job satisfaction in Britain: Individual and job-related factors', Economic Research Centre Working Papers in Economics 03/03, Ankara, retrieved 1 June, 2008, from http://ideas.repec.org/p/met/wpaper/0303.html.

Gelade, G.A. and M. Ivery (2003), 'The impact of human resource management and work climate on organizational performance', *Personnel Psychology*, 56(2), 383–404.

Gignac, M.A.M., E.K. Kelloway and B.H. Gottlieb (1996), 'The impact of caregiving on employment: A mediational model of work–family conflict', *Canadian Journal on Aging*, 15, 525–42.

Glaser, R., J.K. Kiecolt-Glaser, C.E. Speicher and J.E. Holliday (1985), 'Stress, loneliness, and changes in herpesvirus latency', *Journal of Behavioral Medicine*, 8(3), 249–60.

Glazer, S. and T.A. Beehr (2005), 'Consistency of implications of three role stressors across four countries', *Journal of Organizational Behavior*, 26(5), 467–87.

Goetzel, R.Z., D. Shechter, R.J. Ozminkowski, P.F. Marmet, M.J. Tabrizi and E.C. Roemer (2007), 'Promising practices in employer health and productivity management efforts: Findings from a benchmarking study', *Journal of Occupational and Environmental Medicine*, 49(2), 111–30.

Goldberg, C.B. and D.A. Waldman (2000), 'Modeling employee absenteeism: Testing alternative measures and mediated effects based on job satisfaction', *Journal of Organizational Behavior*, 21(6), 665–76.

Grandey, A.A. and R. Cropanzano (1999), 'The conservation of resources model applied to work–family conflict and strain', *Journal of Vocational Behavior*, 54(2), 350–70.

Grandey, A.A., D.N. Dickter and H.-P. Sin (2004), 'The customer is *not* always right: Customer aggression and emotion regulation of service employees', *Journal of Organizational Behavior*, **25**(3), 397–418.

Grant, A.M. and R. Zackon (2004), 'Executive, workplace and life coaching: Findings from a large-scale survey of International Coach Federation members', *International Journal of Evidence-Based Coaching and Mentoring*, **2**(2), 1–15.

Grawitch, M.J., M. Gottschalk and D.C. Munz (2006), 'The path to a healthy workplace: A critical review linking healthy workplace practices, employee well-being, and organizational improvements', *Consulting Psychology Journal*, **58**(3), 129–47.

Gray, D.E. (2006), 'Executive coaching: Towards a dynamic alliance of psychotherapy and transformative learning processes', *Management Learning*, **37**(4), 475–97.

Greenberg, J. (1990), 'Organizational justice: Yesterday, today, and tomorrow', *Journal of Management*, **16**(2), 399–432.

Greenglass, E.R. (2005), 'Proactive coping, resources and burnout: Implications for occupational stress', in A.S. Antoniou and C.L. Cooper (eds), *Research Companion to Organizational Health Psychology*, Cheltenham, UK and Northampton, MA, USA: Edward Elgar, pp. 503–15.

Greenhaus, G.H. and D. Allen (in press), 'Work–family balance: Exploration of a concept', in *Handbook of Families and Work*.

Greenhaus, J.H. and N.J. Beutell (1985), 'Sources of conflict between work and family roles', *Academy of Management Review*, **10**(1), 76–88.

Greenhaus, J.H., K.M. Collins and J.D. Shaw (2003), 'The relation between work–family balance and quality of life', *Journal of Vocational Behavior*, **63**(3), 510–31.

Greenhaus, J.H., S. Parasuraman and K.M. Collins (2001), 'Career involvement and family involvement as moderators of relationships between work and family conflict and withdrawal from a profession', *Journal of Occupational Health Psychology*, **6**(2), 91–100.

Griffeth, R.W., P.W. Hom and S. Gaertner (2000), 'A meta-analysis of the antecedents and correlates of employee turnover: Update, moderator tests, and research implications for the next millennium', *Journal of Management*, **26**(3), 463–88.

Griffin, R.W. and A.M. O'Learly-Kelly (eds) (2004), *The Dark Side of Organizational Behavior*, San Francisco: Jossey-Bass.

Grzywacz, J. and N. Marks (2000), 'Family, work, family–work spillover, and problem drinking during mid-life', *Journal of Marriage and Family*, **62**(2), 336–48.

Gustafsson, E., L. Dellve, M. Edlund and M. Hagberg (2003), 'The use of information technology among young adults: Experience, attitudes and health beliefs', *Applied Ergonomics*, **34**(6), 565–70.

Guthrie, J.P. (2001), 'High-involvement work practices, turnover, and productivity: Evidence from New Zealand', *Academy of Management Journal*, **44**(1) 180–90.

Gyllensten, K. and S. Palmer (2007), 'The coaching relationship: An interpretative phenomenological analysis', *International Coaching Psychology Review*, **2**(2), 168–77.

Hackett, R.D., L.M. Lapierre and P.A. Hausdorf (2001), 'Understanding the links between work commitment constructs', *Journal of Vocational Behavior*, **58**(3), 392–413.

Hackman, J.R. and G.R. Oldham (1975), 'Development of the job diagnostic survey', *Journal of Applied Psychology*, **60**(2), 159–70.

Hair, M., K.V. Renaud and J. Ramsay (2007), 'The influence of self-esteem and locus of control on perceived email-related stress', *Computers in Human Behavior*, **23**(6), 2791–803.

Hakanen, J.J., A.B. Bakker and E. Demerouti (2005), 'How dentists cope with their job demands and stay engaged: The moderating role of job resources', *European Journal of Oral Sciences*, **113**(6), 479–87.

Halberg, F., M. Engeli and C. Hamburger (1965), 'The 17-ketosteroid excretion of a healthy man on weekdays and weekends', *Experimental Medicine and Surgery*, **23**(1), 61–9.

Halbesleben, J.R.B., H.K. Osburn and M.D. Mumford (2006), 'Action research as a burnout intervention: Reducing burnout in the federal fire service', *Journal of Applied Behavioural Science*, **42**(2), 244–66.

Hall, D.T., K.L. Otazo and G.P. Hollenbeck (1999), 'Behind closed doors: What really happens in executive coaching', *Organizational Dynamics*, **27**(3), 39–53.

Hallman, T., H. Thomsson, G. Burell, J. Lisspers and S. Setterlind (2003), 'Stress, burnout and coping: Differences between women with coronary heart disease and healthy matched women', *Journal of Health Psychology*, **8**(4), 433–45.

Hanson, M.A. and W.C. Borman (2006), 'Citizenship performance: An integrative review and motivational analysis', in W. Bennett, Jr., C.E. Lance and D.J. Woehr (eds), *Performance Measurement: Current Perspectives and Future Challenges*, Mahwah, NJ: Lawrence Erlbaum Associates Publishers, pp. 141–73.

Harpaz, I. and R. Snir (2003), 'Workaholism: Its definition and nature', *Human Relations*, **56**(3), 291–319.

Harris, M.M. and L.L. Heft (1992), 'Alcohol and drug use in the workplace: Issues, controversies, and directions for future research', *Journal of Management*, **18**(2), 239–66.

Harter, J.K., F.L. Schmidt and T.L. Hayes (2002), 'Business-unit-level relationship between employee satisfaction, employee engagement, and business outcomes: A meta-analysis', *Journal of Applied Psychology*, **87**(2), 268–79.

Hauge, L.J., A. Skogstad and S. Einarsen (2007), 'Relationships between stressful work environments and bullying: Results of a large representative study', *Work and Stress*, **21**(3), 220–42.

Haworth, C.L. and P.E. Levy (2001), 'The importance of instrumentality beliefs in the prediction of organizational citizenship behaviors', *Journal of Vocational Behavior*, **59**(1), 64–75.

Haynes, S.G., E.D. Eaker and M. Feinleib (1984), 'The effects of unemployment, family, and job stress on coronary heart disease patterns in women', in E.B. Gold (ed.), *The Changing Risk of Disease in Women: An Epidemiological Approach*, Lexington, MA: Heath, pp. 37–48.

Heiskanen, M. (2007), 'Violence at work in Finland: Trends, contents and prevention', *Journal of Scandinavian Studies in Criminology and Crime Prevention*, **8**, 22–40.

Hershcovis, M.S., N. Turner, J. Barling, K.A. Arnold, K.E. Dupré, M. Inness et al. (2007), 'Predicting workplace aggression: A meta-analysis', *Journal of Applied Psychology*, **92**(1), 228–38.

Heslop, P., G. Davey Smith, D. Carroll, J. Macleod, F. Hyland and C. Hart (2001), 'Perceived stress and coronary heart disease risk factors: The contribution of socio-economic position', *British Journal of Health Psychology*, **6**(2), 167–78.

Hewitt, J.B. and P.F. Levin (1997), 'Violence in the workplace', *Annual Review of Nursing Research*, **15**, 81–99.

Hobfoll, S.E. (1989), 'Conservation of resources: A new attempt at conceptualizing stress', *American Psychologist*, **44**(3), 513–24.

Hoel, H., C.L. Cooper and B. Faragher (2001), 'The experience of bullying in Great Britain: The impact of organizational status', *European Journal of Work and Organizational Psychology*, **10**(4), 443–65.

Hoel, H., C. Rayner and C.L. Cooper (1999), 'Workplace bullying', in C.L. Cooper and I.T. Robertson (eds), *International Review of Industrial and Organizational Psychology* (Vol. 14), Chichester: Wiley.

Hogh, A., V. Borg and K.L. Mikkelsen (2003), 'Work-related violence as a predictor of fatigue: A 5-year follow-up of the Danish work environment cohort study', *Work and Stress*, **17**(2), 182–94.

Holmes, T.H. and R.H. Rahe (1967), 'The social readjustment rating scale', *Journal of Psychosomatic Research*, **11**(2), 213–18.

Hom, P.W. and A.J. Kinicki (2001), 'Toward a greater understanding of how dissatisfaction drives employee turnover', *Academy of Management Journal*, **44**(5), 975–87.

House, J.S. (1981), *Work Stress and Social Support*, Reading, MA: Addison-Wesley.

Houtman, I.L.D., P.M. Bongers, P.G.W. Smulders and M.A.J. Kompier (1994), 'Psychosocial stressors at work and musculoskeletal problems', *Scandinavian Journal of Work, Environment and Health*, **20**(2), 139–45.

Howard, J. (1996), 'State and local regulatory approaches to preventing workplace violence', *Occupational Medicine*, **11**(2), 293–301.

Howard, W.G., H.H. Donofrio and J.S. Boles (2004), 'Inter-domain work–family, family–work conflict and police work satisfaction', *Policing: An International Journal of Police Strategies and Management*, **27**(3), 380–95.

Hunter, J.E. and F.L. Schmidt (1990), *Methods of Meta-analysis: Correcting Error and Bias in Research Findings*, Newbury Park, CA: Sage Publications.

Hurrell, J.J. (2005), 'Organizational stress intervention', in J. Barling, E.K. Kelloway and M.R. Frone (eds), *Handbook of Work Stress*, London: Sage, pp. 623–45.

Huselid, M.A. (1995), 'The impact of human resource management practices on turnover, productivity, and corporate financial performance', *Academy of Management Journal*, **38**(3), 635–72.

Hyatt, J. (2003), 'The inner game of business: Thomas Leonard built an industry out of the contradictions in himself', *Fortune Small Business*, retrieved 1 January, 2004 from http://www.fortune.com/fortune/small business/articles/2000,15114,449263,449200.html.

Hyde, J., M.J. Essex, R. Clark, M.H. Klein and J.E. Byrd (1996), 'Parental leave: Policy and research', *Journal of Social Issues*, **52**(3), 91–109.

Iaffaldano, M.T. and P.M. Muchinsky (1985), 'Job satisfaction and job performance: A meta-analysis', *Psychological Bulletin*, **97**(2), 251–73.

Ilies, R., J.D. Nahrgang and F.P. Morgeson (2007), 'Leader–member exchange and citizenship behaviors: A meta-analysis', *Journal of Applied Psychology*, **92**(1), 269–77.

International Coach Federation (2008), www.coachfederation.org.

International Labour Organization (2007), 'Safe and healthy workplaces. Making decent work a reality', The ILO Report for World Day for Safety and Health at Work Geneva, 2007, Geneva: International Labour Office.

Ironson, G.H., P.C. Smith, M.T. Brannick, W.M. Gibson and K.B. Paul (1989), 'Construction of a job in general scale: A comparison of global, composite, and specific measures', *Journal of Applied Psychology*, **74**(2), 193–200.

Jackson, C.J. and P.J. Corr (2002), 'Global job satisfaction and facet description: The moderating role of facet importance', *European Journal of Psychological Assessment*, **18**(1), 1–8.

Jackson, D., J. Clare and J. Mannix (2002), 'Who would want to be a nurse? Violence in the workplace – a factor in recruitment and retention', *Journal of Nursing Management*, **10**(1), 13–20.

Jacobs, J.A., and K. Gerson (2004), *The Time Divide: Balancing Work and Family in Contemporary Society*, Cambridge, MA: Harvard University Press.

James, W. (1884), 'What is an emotion?', *Mind*, **9**(34), 188–205.

Janicak, C.A. (1999), 'An analysis of occupational homicides involving workers 19 years old and younger', *Journal of Occupational and Environmental Medicine*, **41**(12), 1140–45.

Jennifer, D., H. Cowie and K. Ananiadou (2003), 'Perceptions and experience of workplace bullying in five different working populations', *Aggressive Behavior*, **29**(6), 489–96.

Jex, S.M. and T.C. Elacqua (1999), 'Time management as a moderator of relations between stressors and employee strain', *Work and Stress*, **13**(2), 182–91.

Johnson, J.V. and E.M. Hall (1988), 'Job strain, work place social support, and cardiovascular disease: A cross-sectional study of a random sample of the Swedish working population', *American Journal of Public Health*, **78**(10), 1336–42.

Johnson, J.V. and J. Lipscomb (2006), 'Long working hours, occupational health and the changing nature of work organization', *American Journal of Industrial Medicine*, **49**(11), 921–9.

Johnston, S. (2005), 'Applying goal setting theory to coaching', *The Coaching Psychologist*, **2**(2), 10–12.

Joiner, R., M. Brosnan, J. Duffield, J. Gavin and P. Maras (2007), 'The relationship between Internet identification, Internet anxiety and Internet use', *Computers in Human Behavior*, **23**(3), 1408–20.

Jones, F., D.B. O'Connor, M. Conner, B. McMillan and E. Ferguson (2007), 'Impact of daily mood, work hours, and iso-strain variables on self-reported health behaviors', *Journal of Applied Psychology*, **92**(6), 1731–40.

Jones, G. and K. Spooner (2006), 'Coaching high achievers', *Consulting Psychology Journal: Practice and Research*, **58**(1), 40–50.

Judge, T.A. and J.E. Bono (2001), 'Relationship of core self-evaluations traits – self-esteem, generalized self-efficacy, locus of control, and emotional stability – with job satisfaction and job performance: A meta-analysis', *Journal of Applied Psychology*, **86**(1), 80–92.

Judge, T.A. and R.J. Larsen (2001), 'Dispositional affect and job satisfaction: A review and theoretical extension', *Organizational Behavior and Human Decision Processes*, **86**(1), 67–98.

Judge, T.A., J.E. Bono and E.A. Locke (2000), 'Personality and job satisfaction: The mediating role of job characteristics', *Journal of Applied Psychology*, **85**(2), 237–49.

Judge, T.A., J.E. Bono, A. Erez and E.A. Locke (2005), 'Core self evaluations and job and life satisfaction: The role of self-concordance and goal attainment', *Journal of Applied Psychology*, **90**(2), 257–68.

Judge, T.A., D. Heller and M.K. Mount (2002), 'Five-factor model of personality and job satisfaction: A meta-analysis', *Journal of Applied Psychology*, **87**(3), 530–41.

Judge, T.A., C.J. Thoresen, J.E. Bono and G.K. Patton (2001), 'The job satisfaction–job performance relationship: A qualitative and quantitative review', *Psychological Bulletin*, **127**(3), 376–407.

Judge, W.Q. and J. Cowell (1997), 'The brave new world of executive coaching', *Business Horizons*, **40**(4), 71–7.

Jung, K., M.J. Moon and S.D. Hahm (2007), 'Do age, gender, and sector affect job satisfaction? Results from the Korean labor and income panel data', *Review of Public Personnel Administration*, **27**(2), 125–46.

Kahn, H. and C.V.J. Nutter (2005), 'Stress in veterinary surgeons: A review and pilot study', in A.S.G. Antoniou and C.L. Cooper (eds), *Research Companion to Organizational Health Psychology*, Cheltenham, UK and Northampton, MA, USA: Edward Elgar, pp. 293–303.

Kahn, R., D. Wolfe, R. Quinn and J. Snoek (1964), *Organizational Stress: Studies in Role Conflict and Ambiguity*, New York: Wiley.

Kahneman, D., E. Diener and N. Schwarz (eds) (1999), *Well-being: The Foundations of Hedonic Psychology*, New York: Russell Sage Foundation.

Kahneman, D., A.B. Krueger, D. Schkade, N. Schwarz and A. Stone (2004), 'Toward national well-being accounts', *American Economic Review*, **94**(2), 429–34.

Kaiser, L.C. (2005), 'Gender–job satisfaction differences across Europe: An indicator for labor market modernization', DIW Berlin, German Institute for Economic Research.

Kalliath, T. and A. Beck (2001), 'Is the path to burnout and turnover paved by a lack of supervisory support? A structural equations test', *New Zealand Journal of Psychology*, **30**(2), 72–8.

Kalliath, T. and P. Brough (2008), 'Work–life balance: A review of the meaning of the balance construct', *Journal of Management and Organization*, **14**(3), 323–7.

Kalliath, T., P. Brough, M. O'Driscoll, M. Manimala and O.L. Siu (2009), *Organisational Behaviour: An Organisational Psychology Perspective*, Sydney, Australia: McGraw-Hill.

Kampa-Kokesch, S. and M.Z. Anderson (2001), 'Executive coaching: A comprehensive review of the literature', *Consulting Psychology Journal: Practice and Research*, **53**(4), 205–28.

Kanai, A. (2006), 'Economic and employment conditions, karoshi (work to death) and the trend of studies on workaholism in Japan', in R.J. Burke (ed.), *Research Companion to Working Time and Work Addiction*, Cheltenham, UK and Northampton, MA, USA: Edward Elgar, pp. 158–72.

Kanai, A. and M. Wakabayashi (2001), 'Workaholism among Japanese blue collar employees', *International Journal of Stress Management*, **8**(2), 129–45.

Karasek, R.A. (1979), 'Job demands, job decision latitude, and mental strain: Implications for job redesign', *Administrative Science Quarterly*, **24**(2), 285–308.

Katz, R. (1997), *The Human Side of Managing Technological Innovation: a Collection of Readings*, New York: Oxford University Press.

Kaufmann, G.M. and T.A. Beehr (1986), 'Interactions between job stressors and social support: Some counterintuitive results', *Journal of Applied Psychology*, **71**(3), 522–6.

Kelloway, E.K., B.H. Gottlieb and L. Barham (1999), 'The source, nature, and direction of work and family conflict: A longitudinal investigation', *Journal of Occupational Health Psychology*, **4**, 337–46.

Kessler, R.C., K.D. Mickelson and D.R. Williams (1999), 'The prevalence, distribution, and mental health correlates of perceived discrimination in the United States', *Journal of Health and Social Behavior*, **40**(3), 208–30.

Kilburg, R.R. (2000), *Executive Coaching: Developing Managerial Wisdom in a World of Chaos*, Washington, DC: American Psychological Association.

Kinicki, A.J., F.M. McKee and K.J. Wade (1996), 'Annual Review, 1991–1995: Occupational Health', *Journal of Vocational Behavior*, **49**(2), 190–220.

Kirchmeyer, C. (2000), 'Work-life initiatives: Greed or benevolence regarding workers' time', in C.L. Cooper and D.M. Rousseau (eds), *Trends in Organizational Behavior*, Vol. 7, Chichester: Wiley, pp. 79–93.

Kirk, A. (2006), 'Employee assistance program adoption in Australia: Strategic human resource management or knee-jerk solutions', *Journal of Workplace Behavioral Health*, **21**(1), 78–95.

Kirk-Brown, A. and D. Wallace (2004), 'Predicting burnout and job satisfaction in workplace counselors: The influence of role stressors, job challenge, and organizational knowledge', *Journal of Employment Counseling*, **41**(1), 29–37.

Kivimäki, M., M. Virtanen, M. Vartia, J. Elovainio, J. Vahtera and L.

Keltikangas-Jarvinen (2003), 'Workplace bullying and the risk of cardiovascular disease and depression', *Occupational and Environmental Medicine*, **60**(10), 779–83.

Kivimäki, M., J. Head, J.E. Ferrie, E. Brunner, M.G. Marmot, J. Vahtera et al. (2006), 'Why is evidence on job strain and coronary heart disease mixed? An illustration of measurement challenges in the Whitehall II study', *Psychosomatic Medicine*, **68**(3), 398–401.

Knutsson, A. (2003), 'Health disorders of shift workers', *Occupational Medicine*, **53**(2), 103–108.

Korn, E.R., G.J. Pratt and P.T. Lambrou (1987), *Hyper-performance: The A.I.M. Strategy for Releasing your Business Potential*, New York: Wiley.

Korunka, C. and O. Vitouch (1999), 'Effects of the implementation of information technology on employees' strain and job satisfaction: a context-dependent approach', *Work and Stress*, **13**(4), 341–63.

Kossek, E., B. Lautsch and S. Eaton (2006), 'Telecommuting, control, and boundary management: Correlates of policy use and practice, job control, and work–family effectiveness', *Journal of Vocational Behavior*, **68**(2), 347–67.

Kraus, J.F. (1987), 'Homicide while at work: persons, industries, and occupations at high risk', *American Journal of Public Health*, **77**(10), 1285–9.

Kristensen, N. and N. Westergård-Nielsen (2004), 'Does low job satisfaction lead to job mobility?', IZA Discussion Paper No. 1026, retrieved 1 June, 2008, from http://papers.ssrn.com/sol3/papers.cfm?abstract_id=511722.

Kristensen, T.S. (1996), 'Job stress and cardiovascular disease: A theoretic critical review', *Journal of Occupational Health Psychology*, **1**(3), 246–60.

Kristensen, T.S., M. Borritz, E. Villadsen and K.B. Christensen (2005), 'The Copenhagen Burnout Inventory: A new tool for the assessment of burnout', *Work and Stress*, **19**(3), 192–207.

Kropf, M.B. (2002), 'Reduced work arrangements for managers and professionals: A potential solution to conflicting demands', in D.L. Nelson and R.J. Burke (eds), *Gender, Work Stress and Health*, Washington, DC: American Psychological Association, pp. 155–67.

Kuper, H. and M. Marmot (2003), 'Job strain, job demands, decision latitude, and risk of coronary heart disease within the Whitehall II study', *Journal of Epidemiology and Community Health*, **57**(2), 147–53.

Kushnir, T. and S. Melamed (1991), 'Work-load, perceived control and psychological distress in Type A/B industrial workers', *Journal of Organizational Behavior*, **12**(2), 155–68.

Laaksonen, M., O. Rahkonen, P. Martikainen and E. Lahelma (2006),

'Associations of psychosocial working conditions with self-rated general health and mental health among municipal employees', *International Archives of Occupational and Environmental Health*, **79**(3), 205–12.

Lambert, S.J. (2000), 'Added benefits: The link between work–life benefits and organizational citizenship behavior', *Academy of Management Journal*, **43**(5), 801–15.

Lamontagne, A.D., T. Keegel, A.M. Louie, A. Ostry and P.A. Landsbergis (2007), 'A systematic review of the job-stress intervention evaluation literature, 1990–2005', *International Journal of Occupational and Environmental Health*, **13**(3), 268–80.

Landsbergis, P.A. (2003), 'The changing organization of work and the safety and health of working people: A commentary', *Journal of Occupational and Environmental Medicine*, **45**(1), 61–72.

Landsbergis, P.A. and M.C. Hatch (1996), 'Epidemiology of reproductive hazards in the workplace', *Epidemiology*, **7**(4), 346–51.

Langan-Fox, J. and M. Sankey (2007), 'Tyrants and workplace bullying', in J. Langan-Fox, C.L. Cooper and R.J. Klimoski (eds), *Research Companion to the Dysfunctional Workplace: Management Challenges and Symptoms*, Cheltenham, UK and Northampton, MA, USA: Edward Elgar, pp. 58–74.

Lapierre, L.M., P.E. Spector, T.D. Allen, S. Poelmans, C.L. Cooper, M. O'Driscoll, et al. (2008), 'Family-supportive organization perceptions, multiple dimensions of work–family conflict, and employee satisfaction: A test of model across five samples', *Journal of Vocational Behavior*, **73**, 92–106.

LaRocco, J.M., J.S. House and J.R.P. French, Jr. (1980), 'Social support, occupational stress, and health', *Journal of Health and Social Behavior*, **21**(3), 202–18.

Larburu, A. and S. Poelmans (2005), *Foundations of Coaching*, Barcelona: IESE Publishing.

Larburu, A. and S. Poelmans (2007), *The Action Orientation of a Coach*, Barcelona: IESE.

Larsen, R.J. and T. Ketelaar (1991), 'Personality and susceptibility to positive and negative emotional states', *Journal of Personality and Social Psychology*, **61**(1), 132–40.

Lawrence, S.A., J. Gardner and V.J. Callan (2007), 'The support appraisal for work stressors inventory: Construction and initial validation', *Journal of Vocational Behavior*, **70**(1), 172–204.

Lazar, J., A. Jones and B. Shneiderman (2006), 'Workplace user frustration with computers: an exploratory investigation of the causes and severity', *Behaviour & Information Technology*, **25**(3), 239–51.

Lazarus, R.S. (1966), *Psychological Stress and the Coping Process*, New York: McGraw-Hill.

Lazarus, R.S. and S. Folkman (1984), *Stress, Appraisal and Coping*, New York: Springer Publications.

Lazarus, R.S., A. Kanner and S. Folkman (1980), 'Emotions: A cognitive-phenomenological analysis', in R.P.H. Kellerman (ed.), *Theories of Emotion*, New York: Academic Press, pp. 189–217.

LeBlanc, M.M. and E.K. Kelloway (2002), 'Predictors and outcomes of workplace violence and aggression', *Journal of Applied Psychology*, **87**(3), 444–53.

LeDoux, J. and J. Armony (1999), 'Can neurobiology tell us anything about human feelings?', in D. Kahneman, E. Diener and N. Schwarz (eds), *Well-being: The Foundations of Hedonic Psychology*, New York: Russell Sage Foundation, pp. 489–99.

Lee, J.A. (1997), 'Balancing elder care responsibilities and work: Two empirical studies', *Journal of Occupational Health Psychology*, **2**, 220–28.

Lee, R.T. and B.E. Ashforth (1996), 'A meta-analytic examination of the correlates of three dimensions of job burnout', *Journal of Applied Psychology*, **81**(2), 123–33.

Leigh, J.P. and J.A. Robbins (2004), 'Occupational disease and workers' compensation: Coverage, costs, and consequences', *The Milbank Quarterly*, **82**(4), 689–721.

Leigh, J.P., S.B. Markowitz, M. Fahs, C. Shin and P.J. Landrigan (1997), 'Occupational injury and illness in the United States. Estimates of costs, morbidity, and mortality', *Archives of Internal Medicine*, **157**(14), 1557–68.

Lent, R.W. and S.D. Brown (2006), 'On conceptualizing and assessing social cognitive constructs in career research: A measurement guide', *Journal of Career Assessment*, **14**(1), 12–35.

Leroux, I., C. Brisson and S. Montreuil (2006), 'Job strain and neck–shoulder symptoms: A prevalence study of women and men white-collar workers', *Occupational Medicine*, **56**(2), 102–09.

Lervik, J.E., B.W. Hennestad, R.P. Amdam, R. Lunnan and S.M. Nilsen (2005), 'Implementing human resource development best practices: Replication or re-creation?', *Human Resource Development International*, **8**(3), 345–60.

Lewig, K.A. and M.F. Dollard (2003), 'Emotional dissonance, emotional exhaustion and job satisfaction in call centre workers', *European Journal of Work and Organizational Psychology*, **12**(4), 366–92.

Liao, H., A. Joshi and A. Chuang (2004), 'Sticking out like a sore thumb: Employee dissimilarity and deviance at work', *Personnel Psychology*, **57**, 969–1000.

Liu, Y. and H. Tanaka (2002), 'Overtime work, insufficient sleep, and risk of non-fatal acute myocardial infarction in Japanese men', *Occupational and Environmental Medicine*, **59**(7), 447–51.

Llorens, S., A.B. Bakker, W.B. Schaufeli and M. Salanova (2006), 'Testing the robustness of the job demands–resources model', *International Journal of Stress Management*, **13**(3), 378–91.

Lo, S. (2003), 'Perceptions of work–family conflict among married female professionals in Hong Kong', *Personnel Review*, **32**(3), 376–90.

Locke, E.A. (1976), 'The nature and causes of job satisfaction', in M.D. Dunnette (ed.), *Handbook of Industrial and Organizational Psychology*, New York: Wiley, pp. 1297–351.

London, M. and R.W. Beatty (1993), '360-degree feedback as a competitive advantage', *Human Resource Management*, **32**(2/3), 353–72.

Loomis, D., S.W. Marshall, S.H. Wolf, C.W. Runyan and J.D. Butts (2002), 'Effectiveness of safety measures recommended for prevention of workplace homicide', *Journal of the American Medical Association*, **287**(8), 1011–17.

Loomis, D., S.H. Wolf, C.W. Runyan, S.W. Marshall and J.D. Butts (2001), 'Homicide on the job: Workplace and community determinants', *American Journal of Epidemiology*, **154**(10), 410–17.

Lowman, R.L. (2005), 'Executive coaching: The road to dodoville needs paving with more than good assumptions', *Consulting Psychology Journal: Practice and Research*, **57**(1), 90–96.

Lu, L., R. Gilmour, S.-F. Kao and M.-T. Huang (2006), 'A cross-cultural study of work/family demands, work/family conflict and well-being: The Taiwanese vs British', *Career Development International*, **11**(1), 9–27.

Lucas, R.E., A.E. Clark, Y. Georgellis and E. Diener (2004), 'Unemployment alters the set point for life satisfaction', *Psychological Science*, **15**(1), 8–13.

Lum, L., J. Kervin, K. Clark, F. Reid and W. Sirola (1998), 'Explaining nursing turnover intent: Job satisfaction, pay satisfaction, or organizational commitment?', *Journal of Organizational Behavior*, **19**(3), 305–20.

Luszczynska, A. and R. Cieslak (2005), 'Protective, promotive, and buffering effects of perceived social support in managerial stress: The moderating role of personality', *Anxiety, Stress, and Coping*, **18**(3), 227–44.

Luthans, F. and S.J. Peterson (2003), '360-degree feedback with systematic coaching: Empirical analysis suggests a winning combination', *Human Resource Management*, **42**(3), 243–56.

MacEwen, K.E. and J. Barling (1994), 'Daily consequences of work interference with family and family interference with work', *Work and Stress*, **8**, 244–54.

Major, B. (1993), 'Gender, entitlement, and the distinction of family labor', *Journal of Social Issues*, **49**, 141–59.

Major, V., K. Klein and M. Ehrhart (2002), 'Work time, work interference with family and psychological distress', *Journal of Applied Psychology*, **87**(3), 427–36.

Mäkikangas, A., T. Feldt and U. Kinnunen (2007), 'Warr's scale of job-related affective well-being: A longitudinal examination of its structure and relationships with work characteristics', *Work and Stress*, **21**(3), 197–219.

Mamaghani, F. (2006), 'Impact of information technology on the workforce of the future: An analysis', *International Journal of Management*, **23**(4), 845–50.

Marmot, M.G. (1984), 'Alcohol and coronary heart disease', *International Journal of Epidemiology*, **13**(2), 160–67.

Marshall, G.W., C.E. Michaels and J.P. Mulki (2007), 'Workplace isolation: Exploring the construct and its measurement', *Psychology and Marketing*, **24**(3), 195–223.

Martin, J.K. and P.M. Roman (1996), 'Job satisfaction, job reward characteristics, and employees' problem drinking behaviours', *Work and Occupations*, **23**(1), 4–25.

Maslach, C. and M.P. Leiter (1997), *The Truth about Burnout: How Organizations Cause Personal Stress and What to Do About it*, San Francisco, CA: Jossey-Bass.

Maslach, C., S.E. Jackson and M.P. Leiter (1996), *Maslach Burnout Inventory Manual*, (3rd edn), Palo Alto, CA: Consulting Psychologists Press.

Maslach, C., W.B. Schaufeli and M.P. Leiter (2001), 'Job burnout', *Annual Review of Psychology*, **52**, 397–422.

Matsui, T., T. Ohsawa and M.-L. Onglatco (1995), 'Work–family conflict and the stress-buffering effects of husband support and coping behaviour among Japanese married working women', *Journal of Vocational Behavior*, **47**, 178–92.

Mausner-Dorsch, H. and W.W. Eaton (2000), 'Psychosocial work environment and depression: Epidemiologic assessment of the demand–control model', *American Journal of Public Health*, **90**(11), 1765–70.

Mayhew, C. and M. Quinlan (2002), 'Fordism in the fast food industry: Pervasive management control and occupational health and safety risks for young temporary workers', *Sociology of Health and Illness*, **24**(3), 261–84.

McCarthy, P. and C. Mayhew (2004), *Safeguarding the Organization against Violence and Bullying*, Basingstoke: Palgrave MacMillan.

McCarthy, P., C. Mayhew, M. Barker and M. Sheehan (2003), 'Bullying and occupational violence in tertiary education: Risk factors, perpetrators and prevention', *Journal of Occupational Health and Safety, Australia and New Zealand*, **19**(4), 319–26.

McClenahan, C.A., M.L. Giles and J. Mallett (2007), 'The importance of context specificity in work stress research: A test of the demand–control–support model in academics', *Work and Stress*, **21**(1), 85–95.

McCrae, R.R. and P.T. Costa Jr. (1996), 'Toward a new generation of personality theories: Theoretical contexts for the five-factor model', in J.S. Wiggins (ed.), *The Five-factor Model of Personality: Theoretical Perspectives*, New York: Guilford Press, pp. 51–87.

McFarlin, D.B. and R.W. Rice (1992), 'The role of facet importance as a moderator in job satisfaction processes', *Journal of Organizational Behavior*, **13**(1), 41–54.

McGovern, J., M. Lindemann, M. Vergara, S. Murphy, L. Barker and R. Warrenfeltz (2001), 'Maximizing the impact of executive coaching: Behavioral change, organizational outcomes, and return on investment', *The Manchester Review*, **6**(1), 1–9.

McMillan, L.H.W., E.C. Brady, M.P. O'Driscoll and N.V. Marsh (2002), 'A multifaceted validation study of Spence and Robbins' (1992) workaholism battery', *Journal of Occupational and Organizational Psychology*, **75**(3), 357–68.

McMillan, L.H.W., M.P. O'Driscoll and E.C. Brady (2004), 'The impact of workaholism on personal relationships', *British Journal of Guidance and Counseling*, **32**(2), 171–86.

Messenger, J.C. (2006), 'Decent working time: Balancing the needs of workers and employers', in R.J. Burke (ed.), *Research Companion to Working Time and Work Addiction*, Cheltenham, UK and Northampton, MA: Edward Elgar, pp. 221–41.

Michie, S. and S. Williams (2003), 'Reducing work related psychological ill health and sickness absence: A systematic literature review', *Occupational and Environmental Medicine*, **60**(1), 3–9.

Mikkelsen, A., T. Øgaard and P. Landsbergis (2005), 'The effects of new dimensions of psychological job demands and job control on active learning and occupational health', *Work and Stress*, **19**(2), 153–75.

Mikkelsen, A., T. Øgaard, P.H. Lindøe and O.E. Olsen (2002), 'Job characteristics and computer anxiety in the production industry', *Computers in Human Behavior*, **18**(3), 223–39.

Miles, M.B. (1969), 'Planned change and organizational health: Figure and ground', in F.D. Carver and T.J. Sergiovanni (eds), *Organizations and Human Behavior*, New York: McGraw-Hill, pp. 375–91.

Mobley, W.H. (1977), 'Intermediate linkages in the relationship between job satisfaction and employee turnover', *Journal of Applied Psychology*, **62**(2), 237–40.

Morgan, C. and S.R. Cotten (2003), 'The relationship between Internet activities and depressive symptoms in a sample of college freshmen', *CyberPsychology and Behavior*, **6**(2), 133–42.

Morgan, R.D., R.A. van Haveren and C.A. Pearson (2002), 'Correctional officer burnout: Further analyses', *Criminal Justice and Behavior*, **29**(2), 144–60.

Morrell, K. and A. Wilkinson (2002), 'Empowerment: through the smoke and past the mirrors?', *Human Resource Development International*, **5**(1), 119–30.

Morrison, D. and R.L. Payne (2001), 'Test of the demands, supports-constraints framework in predicting psychological distress amongst Australian public sector employees', *Work and Stress*, **15**(4), 314–27.

Morschhäuser, M. and R. Sochert (2006), *Healthy Work in an Ageing Europe: Strategies and Instruments for Prolonging Work Life*, Essen, Germany: European Network for Workplace Health Promotion.

Muhammad, A.H. and H.I. Hamdy (2005), 'Burnout, supervisory support, and work outcomes: A study from an Arabic cultural perspective', *International Journal of Commerce and Management*, **15**(3/4) 230–42.

Murphy, G.D. and G. Southey (2003), 'High performance work practices: Perceived determinants of adoption and the role of the HR practitioner', *Personnel Review*, **32**(1/2), 73–92.

Murphy, L.R. (1988), 'Workplace interventions for stress reduction and prevention', in C.L. Cooper and R. Payne (eds), *Causes, Coping, and Consequences of Stress at Work*, New York: Wiley, pp. 301–39.

Musich, S.A., L. Adams and D.W. Edington (2000), 'Effectiveness of health promotion programs in moderating medical costs in the USA', *Health Promotion International*, **15**(1), 5–15.

Nagy, M. (2002), 'Using a single-item approach to measure facet job satisfaction', *Journal of Occupational and Organizational Psychology*, **75**(1), 77–86.

Natale, S.M. and T. Diamante (2005), 'The five stages of executive coaching: Better process makes better practice', *Journal of Business Ethics*, **59**(4), 361–74.

National Institute for Occupational Safety and Health (NIOSH) (2002), *The Changing Organization of Work and the Safety and Health of Working People*, Cincinnati, OH: National Institute for Occupational Safety and Health.

National Institute for Occupational Safety and Health (NIOSH) (2006), 'Stress. . .At work', retrieved 15 March, 2008, from http://www.cdc.gov/niosh/stresswk.html.

Ndiwane, A. (2000), 'The effects of community, coworker and

organizational support to job satisfaction of nurses in Cameroon', *The ABNF Journal*, **11**(6), 145–9.

Nelson, S., Y. Brunetto, R. Farr-Wharton and S. Ramsay (2007), 'Organisational effectiveness of Australian fast growing small to medium-sized enterprises (SMEs)', *Management Decision*, **45**(7),1143–62.

Netemeyer, R., J. Boles and R. McMurrian (1996), 'Development and validation of work–family conflict and family–work conflict scales', *Journal of Applied Psychology*, **81**(4), 400–410.

Neuman, J.H. and R.A. Baron (1998), 'Workplace violence and workplace aggression: Evidence concerning specific forms, potential causes, and preferred targets', *Journal of Management*, **24**(3), 391–419.

Neveu, J.-P. (2007), 'Jailed resources: Conservation of resources theory as applied to burnout among prison guards', *Journal of Organizational Behavior*, **28**(1), 21–42.

Newton, C.J. and N.L. Jimmieson (2008), 'Role stressors, participative control, and subjective fit with organisational values: Main and moderating effects on employee outcomes', *Journal of Management and Organization*, **14**(1), 20–39.

New Zealand Department of Labour (2004), 'Parental leave', retrieved 5 December, 2005, from http://www.ers.dol.govt.nz/parentalleave/.

Ng, D.M. and R.W. Jeffery (2003), 'Relationships between perceived stress and health behaviors in a sample of working adults', *Health Psychology*, **22**(6), 638–42.

Ng, T.W.H., L.T. Eby, K.L. Sorensen and D.C. Feldman (2005), 'Predictors of objective and subjective career success: A meta-analysis', *Personnel Psychology*, **58**(2), 367–408.

Ng, T.W.H., K.L. Sorensen and D.C. Feldman (2007), 'Dimensions, antecedents, and consequences of workaholism: a conceptual integration and extension', *Journal of Organizational Behavior*, **28**(1), 111–36.

Niedhammer, I., S. David and S. Degioanni (2007), 'Economic activities and occupations at high risk for workplace bullying: results from a large-scale cross-sectional survey in the general working population in France', *International Archives of Occupational and Environmental Health*, **80**(4), 346–53.

Noor, N.M. (2002a), 'Work–family conflict, locus of control and woman's well-being: Test of alternative pathways', *Journal of Social Psychology*, **142**(5), 645–62.

Noor, N.M. (2002b), 'The moderating effect of spouse support on the relationship between work variables and women's work–family conflict', *Psychologia: An International Journal of Psychology in the Orient*, **45**(1), 12–23.

Nordenmark, M. (2002), 'Multiple social roles – a resource or a burden:

Is it possible for men and women to combine paid work with family life in a satisfactory way?', *Gender, Work and Organization*, **9**, 125–45.

North, S. (1988), 'Feeling good: The bottom line on wellness programs', *Chief Financial Officer*, **4**(6), 53–5.

Oates, W. (1971), *Confessions of a Workaholic: The Facts about Work Addiction*, Nashville, TN: Abingdon Press.

Occupational Safety and Health Administration (OSHA) (2008), 'Safety and health add value', retrieved 14 March, 2008, from http://www.osha.gov/dcsp/smallbusiness/index.html.

Occupational Safety and Health Service (2004), 'Preventing violence to employees in health and social services: Discussion paper', retrieved 17 July, 2008, from www.osh.govt.nz/order/catalogue/drafts/ViolenceDiscussionPaper15Oct04.pdf.

O'Driscoll, M. and P. Brough (2003), 'Job stress and burnout', in M. O'Driscoll, P. Taylor and T. Kalliath (eds), *Organisational Psychology in Australia and New Zealand*, Melbourne: Oxford University Press, pp. 188–211.

O'Driscoll, M., P. Brough and A. Biggs (2007), 'Work–family balance: Concepts, implications and interventions', in J. Houdmont and S. McIntyre (eds), *Occupational Health Psychology: European Perspectives on Research, Education and Practice*, Lisbon, Portugal: ISMAI Publishers, pp. 193–217.

O'Driscoll, M., P. Brough and T. Kalliath (2004), 'Work–family conflict, psychological well-being, satisfaction and social support: A longitudinal study in New Zealand', *Equal Opportunities International*, **23**(1/2), 36–56.

O'Driscoll, M., P. Brough and T. Kalliath (2008), 'Stress and coping', in C. Cartwright and C.L. Cooper (eds), *The Oxford Handbook of Organizational Well being*, Oxford: Oxford University Press, pp. 237–66.

O'Driscoll, M., P. Taylor and T. Kalliath (2003), 'Introduction to organisational psychology', in M. O'Driscoll, P. Taylor and T. Kalliath (eds), *Organisational Psychology in Australia and New Zealand*, Melbourne, Victoria: Oxford University Press, pp. 1–7.

Olivero, G., K.D. Bane and R.E. Kopelman (1997), 'Executive coaching as a transfer of training tool: Effects on productivity in a public agency', *Public Personnel Management*, **26**(4), 461–9.

Orenstein, R.L. (2002), 'Executive coaching: It's not just about the executive', *Journal of Applied Behavioral Science*, **38**(3), 355–74.

Organ, D.W. and J.P. Near (1985), 'Cognition vs affect in measures of job satisfaction', *International Journal of Psychology*, **20**(1), 241–53.

Overgaard, D., F. Gyntelberg and B.L. Heitmann (2004), 'Psychological workload and body weight: Is there as association? A review of the literature', *Occupational Medicine*, **54**(1), 35–41.

Paetzold, R.L., A. O'Learly-Kelly and R.W. Griffin (2007), 'Workplace violence, employer liability, and implications for organizational research', *Journal of Management Inquiry*, **16**(4), 362–70.

Palmer, S., C.L. Cooper and K. Thomas (2004), 'A model of work stress', retrieved 8 July, 2008, from www.counsellingatwork.org.uk/journal_pdf/acw_winter04_a.pdf.

Parasuraman, S. and C. Simmers (2001), 'Type of employment, work–family conflict and well-being', *Journal of Organizational Behavior*, **22**(5), 551–68.

Park, K.-O. and M.G. Wilson (2003), 'Psychosocial work environments and psychological strain among Korean factory workers', *Stress and Health*, **19**(3), 173–9.

Parker, S.K. (2007), '"That *is* my job": How employees' role orientation affects their job performance', *Human Relations*, **60**(3), 403–34.

Parker-Wilkins, V. (2006), 'Business impact of executive coaching: Demonstrating monetary value', *Industrial and Commercial Training*, **38**(3), 122–7.

Passmore, J. (2008), *Psychometrics in Coaching: Using Psychological and Psychometric Tools for Development*, London: Kogan Page.

Passmore, J. and C. Gibbes (2007), 'The state of executive coaching research: What does the current literature tell us and what's next for coaching research?', *International Coaching Psychology Review*, **2**(2), 116–28.

Payne, N., F. Jones and P. Harris (2002), 'The impact of working life on health behavior: The effect of job strain on the cognitive predictors of exercise', *Journal of Occupational Health Psychology*, **7**(4), 342–53.

Peek-Asa, C., C.W. Runyan and C. Zwerling (2001), 'The role of surveillance and evaluation research in the reduction of violence against workers', *American Journal of Preventive Medicine*, **20**(2), 141–8.

Peek-Asa, C., C. Casteel, J.F. Kraus and P. Whitten (2006), 'Employee and customer injury during violent crimes in retail and service businesses', *American Journal of Public Health*, **96**(10), 1867–72.

Peiperl, M. and B. Jones (2001), 'Workaholics and overworkers: Productivity or pathology?', *Group and Organization Management*, **26**(3), 369–93.

Pérotin, V. and A. Robinson (2002), 'Employee participation in profit and ownership: a review of the issues and evidence', retrieved 3 February, 2008, from European Federation of Employee Share Ownership, European Parliament website: http://www.efesonline.org/EUROINST%20EN.htm.

Perry-Smith, J.E., and T.C. Blum (2000), 'Work–family human resource bundles and perceived organizational performance', *Academy of Management Journal*, **43**(6), 1107–17.

Petty, M.M., G.W. McGee and J.W. Cavender (1984), 'A meta-analysis of the relationships between individual job satisfaction and individual performance', *Academy of Management Review*, **9**(4), 712–21.

Poelmans, S.A.Y. and A. Masuda (in press), 'Flexibility and diversity in the twenty-first century – the responsibility of human potential managers', in S.A.Y. Poelmans and P. Caligiuri (eds), *Harmonizing Work, Family and Personal Life: From Policy to Practice*, Cambridge: Cambridge University Press.

Poelmans, S.A.Y., T. Kalliath and P. Brough (2008), 'Achieving work–life balance: Current theoretical and practical issues', *Journal of Management and Organization*, **14**(3), 227–38.

Potterat, J.J., D.D. Brewer, S.Q. Muth, R.B. Rothenberg, D.E. Woodhouse J.B. Muth, et al. (2004), 'Mortality in a long-term open cohort of prostitute women', *American Journal of Epidemiology*, **159**(8), 778–85.

Pozzi, C. (1998), 'Exposure of pre-hospital providers to violence and abuse', *Journal of Emergency Nursing*, **24**, 320–23.

Quarstein, V.A., R.B. McAfee and M. Glassman (1992), 'The situational occurrences theory of job satisfaction', *Human Relations*, **45**(8), 859–73.

Quinlan, M., C. Mayhew and P. Bohle (2001), 'The global expansion of precarious employment, work disorganization, and consequences for occupational health: A review of recent research', *International Journal of Health Services*, **31**(2), 335–414.

Rains, S. (2001), 'Don't suffer in silence: Building an effective response to bullying at work', in N. Tehrani (ed.), *Building a Culture of Respect: Managing Bullying at Work*, London: Taylor and Francis, pp. 155–64.

Raver, J.L. and M.J. Gelfand (2005), 'Beyond the individual victim: Linking sexual harassment, team processes, and team performance', *Academy of Management Journal*, **48**(3), 387–400.

Rhoades, L. and R. Eisenberger (2002), 'Perceived organizational support: A review of the literature', *Journal of Applied Psychology*, **87**(4), 698–714.

Richardson, K.M. and H.R. Rothstein (2008), 'Effects of occupational stress management intervention programs: A meta-analysis', *Journal of Occupational Health Psychology*, **13**(1), 69–93.

Robertson, A., A. Gilloran, T. McGlew, K. McKee, A. McKinley and D. Wight (1995), 'Nurses' job satisfaction and the quality of care received by patients in psychogeriatric wards', *International Journal of Geriatric Psychiatry*, **10**(7), 575–84.

Robinson, B.E. (1999), 'The work addiction risk test: Development of a tentative measure of workaholism', *Perceptual and Motor Skills*, **88**(1), 199–210.

Robinson, B.E. (2007), *Chained to the Desk: A Guidebook for Workaholics, their Partners and Children, and the Clinicians who Treat Them* (2nd edn), New York: New York University Press.

Robinson, B.E. and L. Kelley (1998), 'Adult children of workaholics: Self-concept, anxiety, depression, and locus of control', *The American Journal of Family Therapy*, **26**(2), 223–38.

Robinson, B.E., C. Flowers and J. Carroll (2001), 'Work stress and marriage: A theoretical model examining the relationship between workaholism and marital cohesion', *International Journal of Stress Management*, **8**(2), 165–75.

Roethlisberger, F.J. and W.J. Dickson (1939), *Management and the Worker: An Account of a Research Program conducted by the Western Electric Company, Hawthorne Works, Chicago*, Cambridge, MA: Harvard University Press.

Rosen, J. (2001), 'A labor perspective of workplace violence prevention: Identifying research needs', *American Journal of Preventive Medicine*, **20**(2), 161–8.

Rosengren, A., S. Hawken, S. Ôunpuu, K. Sliwa, M. Zubaid, W.A. Almahmeed et al. (2004), 'Association of psychosocial risk factors with risk of acute myocardial infarction in 11119 cases and 13648 controls from 52 countries (the INTERHEART study): Case-control study', *The Lancet*, **364**(9438), 953–62.

Rospenda, K.M. and J.A. Richman (2005), 'Harassement and discrimination', in J. Barling, E.K. Kelloway and M.R. Frone (eds), *Handbook of Work Stress*, London: Sage.

Rospenda, K.M., J.A. Richman and C.A. Shannon (2006), 'Patterns of workplace harassment, gender, and use of services: An update', *Journal of Occupational Health Psychology*, **11**(4), 379–93.

Rotter, J.B. (1966), 'Generalized expectancies for internal versus external control of reinforcement', *Psychological Monographs*, **80**(1), 1–28.

Runyan, C.W., R.C. Zakocs and C. Zwerling (2000), 'Administrative and behavioral interventions for workplace violence prevention', *American Journal of Preventive Medicine*, **18**(4), 116–27.

Salanova, M., R.M. Grau, E. Cifre and S. Llorens (2000), 'Computer training, frequency of usage and burnout: the moderating role of computer self-efficacy', *Computers in Human Behavior*, **16**(6), 575–90.

Salanova, M., J.M. Peiró and W.B. Schaufeli (2002), 'Self-efficacy specificity and burnout among information technology workers: An extension of the job demand-control model', *European Journal of Work and Organizational Psychology*, **11**(1), 1–25.

Salfati, C.G., A.R. James and L. Ferguson (2008), 'Prostitute homicides: A descriptive study', *Journal of Interpersonal Violence*, **23**(4), 505–43.

Salin, D. (2001), 'Prevalence and forms of bullying among business professionals: A comparison of two different strategies for measuring bullying', *European Journal of Work and Organizational Psychology*, **10**(4), 425–41.

Salmela-Aro, K., P. Näätänen and J.-E. Nurmi (2004), 'The role of work-related personal projects during two burnout interventions: A longitudinal study', *Work and Stress*, **18**(3), 208–30.

Sami, L.K. and N.B. Pangannaiah (2006), '"Technostress": A literature survey on the effect of information technology on library users', *Library Review*, **55**(7), 429–39.

Sargent, L.D. and D.J. Terry (2000), 'The moderating role of social support in Karasek's job strain model', *Work and Stress*, **14**(3), 245–61.

Saunderson, R. (2004), 'Survey findings of the effectiveness of employee recognition in the public sector', *Public Personnel Management*, **33**(3), 255–75.

Sauter, S., S.Y. Lim and L.R. Murphy (1996), 'Organizational health: A new paradigm for occupational stress research at NIOSH', *Japanese Journal of Occupational Mental Health*, **4**, 248–54.

Sauter, S.L., L.R. Murphy and J.J. Hurrell Jr. (1990), 'Prevention of work-related psychological disorders: A national strategy proposed by the National Institute for Occupational Safety and Health (NIOSH)', *American Psychologist*, **45**(10), 1146–58.

Scarpello, V. and J.P. Campbell (1983), 'Job satisfaction: Are all the parts there?', *Personnel Psychology*, **36**(3), 577–600.

Schat, A.C. and E.K. Kelloway (2003), 'Reducing the adverse consequences of workplace aggression and violence: The buffering effects of organizational support', *Journal of Occupational Health Psychology*, **8**(2), 110–22.

Schat, A.C.H. and E.K. Kelloway (2005), 'Workplace aggression', in J. Barling, E.K. Kelloway and M.R. Frone (eds), *Handbook of Work Stress*, London: Sage, pp. 189–218.

Schat, A.C.H., M.R. Frone and E.K. Kelloway (2006), 'Prevalence of workplace aggression in the US workforce. Findings from a national study', in E. Kelloway, J. Barling and J.J. Hurrell (eds), *Handbook of Workplace Violence*, California: Sage Publications, pp. 47–89.

Schaubroeck, J., and D.E. Merritt (1997), 'Divergent effects of job control on coping with work stressors: The key role of self-efficacy', *Academy of Management Journal*, **40**(3), 738–54.

Schaufeli, W.B., M. Salanova, V. González-Romá and A.B. Bakker (2002), 'The measurement of engagement and burnout: A two-sample confirmatory factor analytic approach', *Journal of Happiness Studies*, **3**(1), 71–92.

Schnabel, C. and J. Wagner (2007), 'Union density and determinants of union membership in 18 EU countries: Evidence from micro data, 2002/03', *Industrial Relations Journal*, **38**(1), 5–32.

Schneider, J.K., M. Dowling and S. Raghuram (2007), 'Empowerment as a success factor in start-up companies', *Review of Managerial Science*, **1**(2), 167–84.

Schrijvers, C.T.M., H.D. van de Mheen, K. Stronks and J.P. Mackenbach (1998), 'Socioeconomic inequalities in health in the working population: The contribution of working conditions', *International Journal of Epidemiology*, **27**(6), 1011–18.

Schulte, P.A., G.R. Wagner, A. Ostry, L.A. Blanciforti, R.G. Cutlip, K. Krajnak et al. (2007), 'Work, obesity, and occupational safety and health', *American Journal of Public Health*, **97**(3), 428–36.

Schwab, D.P. (2005), *Research Methods for Organizational Studies* (2nd edn), Mahwah, NJ: Lawrence Erlbaum Associates.

Scott, K.S., K.S. Moore and M.P. Miceli (1997), 'An exploration of the meaning and consequences of workaholism', *Human Relations*, **50**(3), 287–328.

Shallcross, L., M. Sheehan and S. Ramsay (2008), 'Workplace mobbing: Experiences in the public sector', *International Journal of Organizational Behavior*, **13**(2), 56–70.

Sheehan, C., P. Holland and H. De Cieri (2006), 'Current developments in HRM in Australian organisations', *Asia Pacific Journal of Human Resources*, **44**(2), 132–52.

Sheiner, E.K., E. Sheiner, R. Carel, G. Potashnik and I. Shoham-Vardi (2002), 'The potential association between male infertility and occupational psychological stress', *Journal of Occupational and Environmental Medicine*, **44**(12), 1093–9.

Sheppard, B., M. Canning, L. Mellon, P. Anderson, M. Tuchinsky and C. Campbell (2006), *Coaching and Feedback for Performance*, Duke Corporate Education, Chicago, IL: Dearborn Trade, a Kaplan Professional Company.

Sherman, S. and A. Freas (2004), 'The wild west of executive coaching', *Harvard Business Review*, **82**(11), 82–90.

Shields, M.A. and M. Ward (2001), 'Improving nurse retention in the National Health Service in England: The impact of job satisfaction on intentions to quit', *Journal of Health Economics*, **20**(5), 677–701.

Shirom, A. (2005), 'Reflections on the study of burnout', *Work and Stress*, **19**(3), 263–70.

Siegrist, J. (1988), 'Adverse health effects of effort reward imbalance at work', in C.L. Cooper (ed.), *Theories of Organizational Stress*, Oxford: Oxford University Press.

Siegrist, J., B. Falck and L. Joksimovic (2005), 'The effects of reward-imbalance at work on health', in A.S. Antoniou and C.L. Cooper (eds), *Research Companion to Organizational Health Psychology*, Cheltenham, UK and Northampton, MA, USA: Edward Elgar, pp. 430–54.

Siemiatycki, J., L. Richardson, K. Straif, B. Latreille, R. Lakhani, S. Campbell, et al. (2004), 'Listing occupational carcinogens', *Environmental Health Perspectives*, **112**(15), 1447–59.

Simons, C. (2006), 'Should there be a counseling element within coaching?', *The Coaching Psychologist*, **2**(2), 23–5.

Siu, O.L. (2002), 'Predictors of job satisfaction and absenteeism in two samples of Hong Kong nurses', *Journal of Advanced Nursing*, **40**(2), 218–29.

Smallman, C. (2001), 'The reality of "Revitalizing Health and Safety"', *Journal of Safety Research*, **32**(4), 391–439.

Smith, B. and P. Caputi (2007), 'Cognitive interference model of computer anxiety: Implications for computer-based assessment', *Computers in Human Behavior*, **23**(3), 1481–98.

Smith, P.C., L.M. Kendall and C.L. Hulin (1969), *Measurement of Satisfaction in Work and Retirement: A Strategy for the Study of Attitudes*, Chicago: Rand McNally.

Smither, J.W., M. London, R. Flautt, Y. Vargas and I. Kucine (2003), 'Can working with an executive coach improve multisource feedback ratings over time? A quasi-experimental field study', *Personnel Psychology*, **56**(1), 23–44.

Snir, R. and I. Harpaz (2006), 'The workaholism phenomenon: A cross-national perspective', *Career Development International*, **11**(5), 374–93.

Snyder, L.A., P.Y. Chen, P.L. Grubb, R.K. Roberts, S.L. Sauter and N.G. Swanson (2005), 'Workplace aggression and violence against individuals and organizations: Causes, consequences, and interventions', in P.L. Perrewe and D.C. Ganster (eds), *Exploring Interpersonal Dynamics*, Oxford: Elsevier, pp. 1–65.

Sousa-Poza, A. and A.A. Sousa-Poza (2000), 'Well-being at work: A cross-national analysis of the levels and determinants of job satisfaction', *Journal of Socio-Economics*, **29**(6), 517–38.

Sousa-Poza, A. and A.A. Sousa-Poza (2003), 'Gender differences in job satisfaction in Great Britain, 1991–2000: Permanent or transitory?', *Applied Economics Letters*, **10**(11), 691–4.

Sparks, K., C. Cooper, Y. Fried and A. Shirom (1997), 'The effects of hours of work on health: A meta-analytic review', *Journal of Occupational and Organizational Psychology*, **70**(4), 391–408.

Sparks, K., B. Faragher and C.L. Cooper (2001), 'Well-being and occupational health in the 21st century workplace', *Journal of Occupational and Organizational Psychology*, **74**(4), 489–509.

Spector, P.E. (1978), 'Organizational frustration: A model and review of the literature', *Personnel Psychology*, **31**(4), 815–29.

Spector, P.E. (1994), 'Using self-report questionnaires in OB research: A comment on the use of a controversial method', *Journal of Organizational Behavior*, **15**(5), 385–92.

Spector, P.E. (1997), 'The role of frustration in antisocial behavior at work', in R.A. Giacalone and J. Greenberg (eds), *Antisocial Behavior in Organizations*, Thousand Oaks, CA: Sage, pp. 1–17.

Spector, P.E., M.L. Coulter, H.G. Stockwell and M.W. Matz (2007), 'Perceived violent climate: A new construct and its relationship to workplace physical violence and verbal aggression, and their potential consequences', *Work and Stress*, **21**(2), 117–30.

Spence, J.T. and A.S. Robbins (1992), 'Workholism: Definition, measurement, and preliminary results', *Journal of Personality Assessment*, **58**(1), 160–78.

Sprankley, J.K. and H. Ebel (1987), *The Workaholic Syndrome*, New York: Walker Publishing.

Spreitzer, G.M. and D. Doneson (2005), 'Musings on the past and future of employee empowerment', in T. Cummings (ed.), *Handbook of Organizational Development*, Thousand Oaks, CA: Sage.

Spreitzer, G.M., S.C. De Janasz and R.E. Quinn (1999), 'Empowered to lead: The role of psychological empowerment in leadership', *Journal of Organizational Behaviour*, **20**(4), 511–26.

Stack, S. (2001), 'Occupation and suicide', *Social Science Quarterly*, **82**(2), 384–96.

Stark, C., A. Belbin, P. Hopkins, D. Gibbs, A. Hay and D. Gunnell (2006), 'Male suicide and occupation in Scotland', *Health Statistics Quarterly*, **29**(1), 26–9.

Staw, B.M. (2004), 'The dispositional approach to job attitudes: An empirical and conceptual review', in B. Schneider and D.B. Smith (eds), *Personality and Organizations*, Mahwah, NJ: Lawrence Erlbaum Associates, pp. 163–91.

Staw, B.M. and Y. Cohen-Charash (2005), 'The dispositional approach to job satisfaction: More than a mirage, but not yet an oasis', *Journal of Organizational Behavior*, **26**(1), 59–78.

Stephens, M.A.P., A.L. Townsend, L.M. Martire and J.A. Druley (2001), 'Balancing parent care with other roles: Interrole conflict of adult daughter caregivers', *Journal of Gerontology*, **56B**(1), 24–34.

Stevens, J.R. (1972), *Modern Office Procedures*, Industrial Publishing Company.

Stoeva, A.Z., R.K. Chiu and J.H. Greenhaus (2002), 'Negative affectivity, role stress and work–family conflict', *Journal of Vocational Behavior*, **60**, 1–16.

Storr, C.L., A.M. Trinkoff and J.C. Anthony (1999), 'Job strain and non-medical drug use', *Drug and Alcohol Dependence*, **55**(1/2), 45–51.

Tajfel, H. and J.C. Turner (1979), 'An integrative theory of intergroup conflict', in W.G. Austin and S. Worchel (eds), *The Social Psychology of Intergroup Relations*, Monterey, CA: Brooks-Cole, pp. 94–109.

Taris, T.W. (2006), 'Is there a relationship between burnout and objective performance? A critical review of 16 studies', *Work and Stress*, **20**(4), 316–34.

Tausig, M. and R. Fenwick (2001), 'Unbinding time: Alternate work schedules and work–life balance', *Journal of Family and Economic Issues*, **22**(2), 101–19.

Tellegen, A., D.T. Lykken, T.J. Bouchard Jr., K.J. Wilcox, N.L. Segal and S. Rich (1988), 'Personality similarity in twins reared apart and together', *Journal of Personality and Social Psychology*, **54**(6), 1031–9.

Theorell, T., A. Tsutsumi, J. Hallquist, C. Reuterwall, C. Hogstedt, P. Fredlund, et al. (1998), 'Decision latitude, job strain, and myocardial infarction: A study of working men in Stockholm', *American Journal of Public Health*, **88**(3), 382–8.

Thieblot, A.J., T.R. Haggard and H.R. Northrup (1999), *Union Violence: The Record and the Response by the Courts, Legislatures and the NLRB*, (Rev. edn), Fairfax, VA: George Mason University: John M Olin Institute of Employment Practice and Policy.

Thøgersen-Ntoumani, C., K.R. Fox and N. Ntoumanis (2005), 'Relationships between exercise and three components of mental well-being in corporate employees', *Psychology of Sport and Exercise*, **6**(6), 609–27.

Thomas, L. and D. Ganster (1995), 'Impact of family-supportive work variables on work–family conflict and strain', *Journal of Applied Psychology*, **80**(1), 6–15.

Thomas, D.C., G. Sthal, E.C. Ravlin, S. Poelmans, A. Pekerti, M. Maznevski, et al. (in press), 'Cultural intelligence: Domain and assessment', *International Journal of Cross-Cultural Management*.

Thomée, S., M. Elköf, E. Gustafsson, R. Nilsson and M. Hagberg (2007),

'Prevalence of perceived stress, symptoms of depression and sleep disturbances in relation to information and communication technology (ICT) use among young adults – an explorative prospective study', *Computers in Human Behavior*, **23**(3), 1300–21.

Thompson, B., P. Brough and H. Schmidt (2006), 'Supervisor and subordinate work–family values: Does similarity make a difference?', *International Journal of Stress Management*, **13**(1), 45–63.

Thompson, C.A., L.L. Beauvais and K.S. Lyness (1999), 'When work–family benefits are not enough: The influence of work–family culture on benefit utilization, organizational attachment, and work–family conflict', *Journal of Vocational Behavior*, **54**(3), 392–415.

Thorpe, S.J. and M.J. Brosnan (2007), 'Does computer anxiety reach levels which conform to DSM IV criteria for specific phobia?', *Computers in Human Behavior*, **23**(3), 1258–72.

Ting, S. (2006), 'Our view of coaching for leadership development', in S. Ting and P. Scisco (eds), *The CCL Handbook of Coaching. A Guide for the Leader Coach*, San Francisco, CA: Jossey-Bass, pp.15–33.

Toegel, G. and N. Nicholson (2005), 'Multisource feedback, coaching, and leadership development: gender homophily in coaching dyads', *Academy of Management Best Conference Paper 2005* MC: F1-6.

Tourigny, L., V.V. Baba and T.R. Lituchy (2005), 'Job burnout among airline employees in Japan: A study of the buffering effects of absence and supervisory support', *International Journal of Cross Cultural Management*, **5**(1), 67–85.

Turner, S., S. Lines, Y. Chen, L. Hussey and R. Agius (2005), 'Work-related infectious disease reported to the Occupational Disease Intelligence Network and The Health and Occupation Reporting network in the UK (2000–2003)', *Occupational Medicine*, **55**(4), 275–81.

US Census Bureau (2000), 'Married couple family groups, by labor force status of both spouses, and race and Hispanic origin', retrieved 9 September, 2002, from http://www.census.gov/population/socdemo/hh-fam/p20-537/2000/tabFG1.txt.

Vahtera, J., M. Kivimäki and J. Pentti (1997), 'Effect of organisational downsizing on health of employees', *The Lancet*, **350**(9085), 1124–8.

van den Bergh, N. (2000), 'Where have we been?. . . Where are we going?: Employee assistance practice in the 21st century', *Employee Assistance Quarterly*, **16**(1/2), 1–13.

van der Doef, M. and S. Maes (1999), 'The job demand–control(–support) model and psychological well-being: A review of 20 years of empirical research', *Work and Stress*, **13**(2), 87–114.

van Fleet, R. (1999), 'Diversifying psychological practice to industry:

Getting started', *The Pennsylvania Psychologist Quarterly*, May, pp. 15–24.

van Horn, J.E., T.W. Taris, W.B. Schaufeli and P.J.G. Schreurs (2004), 'The structure of occupational well-being: A study among Dutch teachers', *Journal of Occupational and Organizational Psychology*, **77**(3), 365–75.

van Saane, N., J.K. Sluiter, J.H.A.M. Verbeek and M.H.W. Frings-Dresen (2003), 'Reliability and validity of instruments measuring job satisfaction: A systematic review', *Occupational Medicine*, **53**(3), 191–200.

Vartia, M. and J. Hyyti (2002), 'Gender differences in workplace bullying among prison officers', *European Journal of Work and Organizational Psychology*, **11**(1), 113–26.

Verhoeven, C., S. Maes, V. Kraaij and K. Joekes (2003), 'The job demand–control–social support model and wellness/health outcomes: A European study', *Psychology and Health*, **18**(4), 421–40.

Vickers, M.H. (2006), 'Towards employee wellness: Rethinking bullying paradoxes and masks', *Employee Responsibilities and Rights Journal*, **18**(4), 267–81.

Vieitez, J.C., A.D.L.T. Carcia and M.T.V. Rodríguez (2001), 'Perception of job security in a process of technological change: its influence on psychological well-being', *Behaviour and Information Technology*, **20**(3), 213–23.

Viejo, A. (2005), 'AACN standards for establishing and sustaining healthy work environments: A journey to excellence', *American Journal of Critical Care*, **14**(3), 187–97.

Voydanoff, P. (2002), 'Linkages between the work–family interface and work, family, and individual outcomes: An integrative model', *Journal of Family Issues*, **23**(1), 138–64.

Vrendenburgh, A.G. (2002), 'Organizational safety: Which management practices are most effective in reducing employee injury rates?', *Journal of Safety Research*, **33**(2), 259–76.

Vroom, V. (1965), *Motivation in Management*, New York: American Foundation for Management Research.

Vyhmeister, R., P.R. Mondelo and M. Novella (2006), 'Towards a model for assessing workers' risks resulting from the implementation of information and communication systems and technologies', *Human Factors and Ergonomics in Manufacturing*, **16**(1), 39–59.

Wager, N., G. Fieldman and T. Hussey (2003), 'The effect on ambulatory blood pressure of working under favourably and unfavourably perceived supervisors', *Occupational and Environmental Medicine*, **60**(7), 468–74.

Wales, S. (2003), 'Why coaching?', *Journal of Change Management*, **3**(3), 275–82.

Wall, T.D., P.R. Jackson, S. Mullarkey and S.K. Parker (1996), 'The demands–control model of job strain: A more specific test', *Journal of Occupational and Organizational Psychology*, **69**(2), 153–66.

Wanous, J.P., A.E. Reichers and M.J. Hudy (1997), 'Overall job satisfaction: How good are single-item measures?', *Journal of Applied Psychology*, **82**(2), 247–52.

Ward, E.M., P.A. Schulte, S. Bayard, A. Blair, P. Brandt-Rauf, M.A. Butler, et al. (2003), 'Priorities for development of research methods in occupational cancer', *Environmental Health Perspectives*, **111**(1), 1–12.

Warr, P. (1987), *Work, Unemployment, and Mental Health*, New York: Oxford University Press.

Warr, P. (1990), 'The measurement of well-being and other aspects of mental health', *Journal of Occupational Psychology*, **63**(3), 193–210.

Warr, P. (1999), 'Well-being and the workplace', in D. Kahneman, E. Diener and N. Schwarz (eds), *Well-being: The Foundations of Hedonic Psychology*, New York: Russell Sage Foundation, pp. 392–412.

Warr, P. (2005), 'Work, well-being, and mental health', in J.L. Barling, E.K. Kelloway and M.R. Frone (eds), *Handbook of Work Stress* Thousand Oaks, CA: Sage Publications, pp. 547–74.

Warr, P.B. (2007), *Work, Happiness, and Unhappiness*, Mahwah, NJ: Lawrence Erlbaum Associates.

Wasylyshyn, K.M. (2003), 'Executive coaching: An outcome study', *Consulting Psychology Journal: Practice and Research*, **55**(2), 94–106.

Watson, D., L.A. Clark and A. Tellegen (1988), 'Development and validation of brief measures of positive and negative affect: The PANAS scales', *Journal of Personality and Social Psychology*, **54**(6), 1063–70.

Weatherbee, T. and E.K. Kelloway (2006), 'A case of cyberdeviancy', in E.K. Kelloway, J. Barling and J.J. Hurrell (eds), *Handbook of Workplace Violence*, London: Sage Publications, pp. 445–87.

Wegge, J., K.H. Schmidt, C. Parkes and R. van Dick (2007), 'Taking a sickie: Job satisfaction and job involvement as interactive predictors of absenteeism in a public organization', *Journal of Occupational and Organizational Psychology*, **80**(1), 77–89.

Weinberg, A. and C.L. Cooper (2007), *Surviving the Workplace: A Guide to Emotional Well-being*, London: Thomson.

Westman, M. and D. Eden (1997), 'Effects of a respite from work on burnout: Vacation relief and fade-out', *Journal of Applied Psychology*, **82**(4), 516–27.

White, J. and J. Beswick (2003), *Working Long Hours*, Sheffield, UK: Health and Safety Laboratory.

Whiting, S.W., P.M. Podsakoff and J.R. Pierce (2008), 'Effects of task performance, helping, voice, and organizational loyalty on performance appraisal ratings', *Journal of Applied Psychology*, 93(1), 125–39.

Whitworth, L., H. Kimsey-House and P. Sandahl (2007), *Co-active Coaching: New Skills for Coaching People Toward Success in Work and Life*, Palo Alto, CA: Davies-Black Publishing.

Willness, C.R., P. Steel and K. Lee (2007), 'A meta-analysis of the antecedents and consequences of workplace sexual harassment', *Personnel Psychology*, 60(1), 127–62.

Winwood, P.C. and A.H. Winefield (2004), 'Comparing two measures of burnout among dentists in Australia', *International Journal of Stress Management*, 11(3), 282–9.

Wong, S.-S., G. DeSanctis and N. Staudenmayer (2007), 'The relationship between task interdependency and role stress: A revisit of the job demands–control model', *Journal of Management Studies*, 44(2), 284–303.

Wood, G.J. and J. Newton (2006), 'Childlessness and women managers: "Choice", context and discourses', *Gender, Work and Organization*, 13(4), 338–58.

World Health Organization (1948), 'World Health Organization definition of health', retrieved 22 May, 2008, from http://www.who.int/about/definition/en/print.html.

Wright, T.A. (2006), 'The emergence of job satisfaction in organisational behaviour. A historical overview of the dawn of job attitude research', *Journal of Management History*, 12(3), 262–77.

Wright, T.A. and D.G. Bonett (2007), 'Job satisfaction and psychological well-being as nonadditive predictors of workplace turnover', *Journal of Management*, 33(2), 141–60.

Wright, T.A., R. Cropanzano and D.G. Bonett (2007), 'The moderating role of employee positive well being in the relation between job satisfaction and job performance', *Journal of Occupational Health Psychology*, 12(2), 93–104.

Wynne, R., N. Clarkin, T. Cox and A. Griffiths (1997), *Guidance on the Prevention of Violence at Work*, Brussels: European Commission, DG-V, Ref CE/VI-4/97.

Yamada, Y., M. Ishizaki and I. Tsuritani (2002), 'Prevention of weight gain and obesity in occupational populations: A new target of health promotion services at worksites', *Journal of Occupational Health*, 44(6), 373–84.

Yamada, Y., M. Kameda, Y. Noborisaka, H. Suzuki, M. Honda and S.

Yamada (2001), 'Excessive fatigue and weight gain among cleanroom workers after changing from an 8-hour to a 12-hour shift', *Scandinavian Journal of Work, Environment and Health*, **27**(5), 318–26.

Yeh, W.-Y., Y. Cheng, C.-J. Chen, P.-Y. Hu and T.S. Kristensen (2007), 'Psychometric properties of the Chinese version of Copenhagen Burnout Inventory among employees in two companies in Taiwan', *International Journal of Behavioral Medicine*, **14**(3), 126–33.

Yun, S., R. Takeuchi and W. Liu (2007), 'Employee self-enhancement motives and job performance behaviors: Investigating the moderating effects of employee role ambiguity and managerial perceptions of employee commitment', *Journal of Applied Psychology*, **92**(3), 745–56.

Zapf, D., C. Dormann and M. Frese (1996), 'Longitudinal studies in organizational stress research: A review of the literature with reference to methodological issues', *Journal of Occupational Health Psychology*, **1**(2), 145–69.

Zapf, D., S. Einarsen, H. Hoel and M. Vartia (2003), 'Empirical findings on bullying in the workplace', in S. Einarsen, H. Hoel, D. Zapf and C.L. Cooper (eds), *Bullying and Emotional Abuse in the Workplace: International Perspectives in Research and Practice*, London: Taylor and Francis, pp. 103–26.

Zhang, Z. and W.E. Snizek (2003), 'Occupation, job characteristics, and the use of alcohol and other drugs', *Social Behavior and Personality*, **31**(4), 395–412.

# Index

absenteeism 16
  job satisfaction and 37–8
  work–family balance and 79
AbuAlRub, R.F. 148
accidents 19, 24
action plans 136
adaptive coping 59
addiction to work 87–8, 96–7
  antecedents 91–2
    demographic characteristics 92–3
    personality 92
  consequences 95–6
  as shortcoming or merit 88–91
affective well-being model 3
age
  ageing workforce 31
  violence in the workplace and 110
aggression 101–2, 103–4
  cyberaggression 114
alcohol 28–30
Allen, R.S. 35
Allen, T.D. 79
Anderson, M.Z. 134
Andreassen, C.S. 91, 95
anxiety 2, 3
  technological 121–4
appraisal support 54
Aquino, K. 106
Armony, J. 5
arousal 2, 3
Aryee, S. 81
audit, stress 112
autonomy
  cocaine use and 30
  technological anxiety and 123

Bacharach, S.B. 78
Bakker, A.B. 50, 61
Barling, J. 79
Barnett, R. 81
Baron, R.A. 98, 101, 103

Beas, M.I. 127
Beaton, R.D. 114
Beatty, C.A. 77
Beaudry, A. 129
Beck, A. 148
Beckers, J.J. 121–2, 126, 129
Beehr, T.A. 56, 57, 104, 147, 148
Beer, M. 144
Behson, S.J. 82
Belkic, K.L. 25
Bellotti, V. 119
Bessière, K. 124, 125
Beswick, J. 25
Beutell, N.J. 74
biological antecedents of psychological
  well-being 5–6
Bloom, N. 149
Bluckert, P. 138
Blum T.C. 149
Böckerman, P. 38
Boehm, J.K. 15
Boggild, H. 25
Bonett, D.G. 39
Bordin, C. 147
Boswell, W.R. 50
Bowling, N.A. 37, 40, 104
Boyar, S.L. 76, 79
Branch, S. 107
Brief, A.P. 34
Brosnan, M.J. 122
Brough, P. 8, 16, 74, 75, 77, 79, 83,
  105, 109
Brown, M. 151
Brown, S.D. 36
Browne, J.H. 145
Bruck, C.S. 42
Brunner, E.J. 26
Buelens, M. 90, 93
bullying 105–8
  prevention programmes 154
Burke, R.J. 95